William L.L.F. de Ros

Memorials of the Tower of London

William L.L.F. de Ros

Memorials of the Tower of London

ISBN/EAN: 9783337429140

Printed in Europe, USA, Canada, Australia, Japan

Cover: Foto ©ninafisch / pixelio.de

More available books at **www.hansebooks.com**

BY LIEUT.-GEN. LORD DE ROS
LIEUT.-GOVERNOR OF THE TOWER.

WITH ILLUSTRATIONS.

LONDON:
JOHN MURRAY. ALBEMARLE STREET.
1866.

The right of Translation is reserved.

THE TOWER, June, 1866.

MY DEAR SIR JOHN BURGOYNE,

A formal dedication to an officer of your European celebrity would require the enumeration of those long, brilliant, and useful services by which you have attained the well-merited honours and distinctions you enjoy.

However briefly such a list might be drawn out, your military career ranges over so long a period, and is so connected with the triumphs of the British arms in almost every part of the world, that it would occupy a space neither suitable to the humble pretensions of this volume, nor agreeable to the simplicity and absence of ostentation which marks your character.

The latest honour conferred on you by the Queen was your appointment as Constable of the Tower, and it is owing to this circumstance, which has placed me under your command, that I venture to present you these Memorials of The Tower as a tribute of respect and regard.

I am, my dear Sir John,

Very sincerely yours,

DE ROS,
Lieut.-Governor of the Tower.

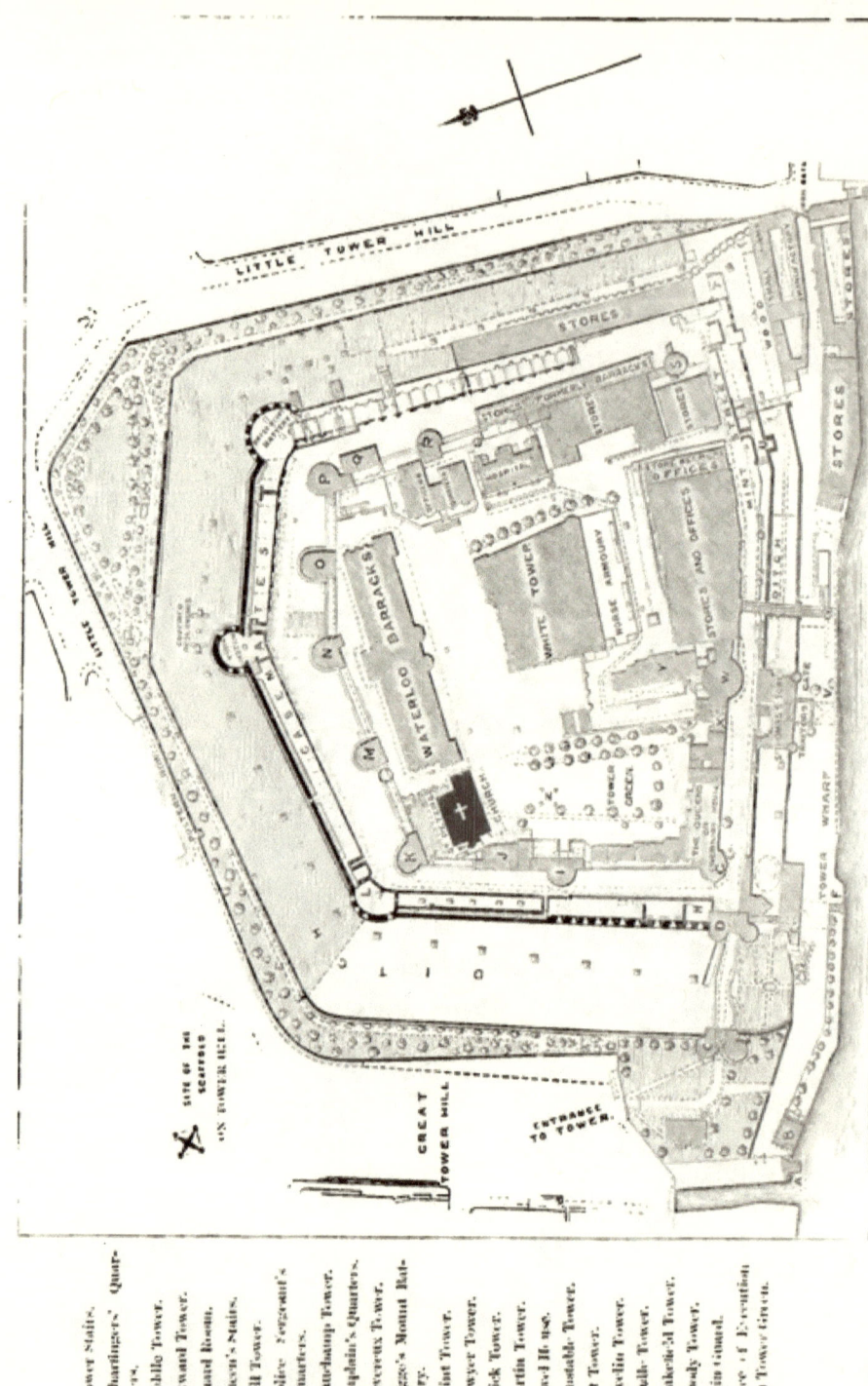

A. Tower Stairs.
B. Warder's Quarters.
C. Middle Tower.
D. Byward Tower.
E. Guard Room.
F. Queen's Stairs.
G. Bell Tower.
H. Police Sergeant's Quarters.
I. Beauchamp Tower.
J. Chaplain's Quarters.
K. Devereux Tower.
L. Legge's Mount Battery.
M. Flint Tower.
N. Bowyer Tower.
O. Brick Tower.
P. Martin Tower.
Q. Jewel House.
R. Constable Tower.
S. Salt Tower.
T. Develin Tower.
U. Cradle Tower.
W. Wakefield Tower.
X. Bloody Tower.
Y. Main Guard.
Z. Place of Execution on Tower Green.

INTRODUCTION.

AMONG the objects of interest which attract the notice of the stranger in London, perhaps there is not one which is more generally popular than the Tower. Unfortunately, its situation renders it less accessible than most of the sights of London, not only from actual distance, but from the prodigious throng of carriages of all kinds, which encumber and block the principal streets leading to Tower Hill from the northern and western parts of the town. In spite of these inconveniences, the Tower of London appears to possess an universal attraction for all ranks and classes, from the antiquary and historian to the labourer and artizan, and from the distinguished foreigner to the schoolboy taken out for a holiday of sight-seeing and amusement.

It seems strange that no popular account of this venerable and celebrated Palace and Fortress should yet have been offered to the public. Mr. Bailey's elaborate work upon the Tower presents, no doubt, the result of a vast quantity of laborious historical and antiquarian research; but it is too bulky in form (two large quarto volumes), and gives too much dry detail, to suit the ordinary reader; nor do the doubts in which he has shown such an inclination to indulge, upon some of the most received historical traditions, by any means add to the interest of his book, though it bears, in many respects, the stamp of diligent and careful inquiry. Mr. Ainsworth has regarded the Tower rather as a suitable scene for an interesting work of fiction, than as a subject of historical illustration.

In attempting a Memoir of this Royal Palace and Fortress, and of the most remarkable and notorious persons who have been inmates of the Tower, it would be unjust not to acknowledge the value of Messrs. Britton and Brayley's book, as the most satisfactory reference for most of the disputed questions of Tower tradition, as well as for the general historical accuracy with which they have treated the whole of the subject.

CONTENTS.

PAGE

INTRODUCTION v

GENERAL DESCRIPTION.

Situation of the Tower, page 1. Capacity for defence, 1. Ditch, pleasure-ground, scarp, 2. Main entrance, 2. Ramparts, 2. Mint-street, abuses, 3. White Tower, 3. Ballium-wall, 3. STATE PRISON — Beauchamp Tower, 4. Memorials of prisoners, 4. Former neglect, 4. Sir George Cathcart's plans for restoration—carried out by Mr. Salvin, 5. Preservation of inscriptions, 5. Continuation of Ballium-wall, 5. Towers on the north face, 6. Scenes in Shakespeare's plays laid in the Tower, 6. Disfigurement by modern erections, 7. The Salt Tower, 8. Site of the Palace, 8. The Palace destroyed by Cromwell, 8. Curtain-wall, 9. Exterior defences, and wharf, 9. Restoration of St. Thomas's Tower and Traitors' Gate, 9. WAKEFIELD TOWER:—Scene of Henry VI.'s murder, 10. The funeral, 10. Reputed miracles wrought at his tomb, 11. Vault under this Tower, place of confinement of Scots prisoners of '45, 12. Abuses in government of the Tower, 12. Misappropriation of its chambers, 13. Barracks, 13. Responsibility of Warders, 13. Effects of the fire of 1841, 14. Sir George Cathcart appointed Lieutenant-Governor by the Duke of Wellington—his improvements, 14. Parliamentary provision for restorations, 15. Stores erected during the Crimean war, 15. Recent repairs and restorations, 16. Difficulty attending them, 16. Authority of Chief Commissioners of Works, 17. Veto of Chancellor of the Exchequer, 17. Modern disfigurement of the river front, 18. Improved practice at present, 18. Control over the architecture of the Tower established by the Prince Consort, 19.

THE WHITE TOWER.

Improper use of St. John's Chapel, 21. Remedied by General Peel, 21. The Chapel restored by Mr. Salvin under auspices of Hon. W. Cowper, 21. Historical recollections, 22. The Chapel gallery, 22. Tradition of the civil wars, 23. Underground dungeons—cells of Guy Fawkes and Bishop Fisher, 24. "Cold Harbour," 25. Arrangement of flooring, 25. Corridor in the wall, 25. Scene of imprisonment and murder of Matilda FitzWalter, 26. Modern disfigurements. 27.

ST. PETER'S CHAPEL.

Situation, and modern disfigurements, 28. Improvements in 1862, 29. Monuments, 29. Royal and illustrious persons buried in the Chapel, 29, 30. Pepys's visit, 30. Coffin-plates of Scotch lords, 31. Tablet to the memory of Talbot Edwards, 31. Proposed further improvements, 31. Increase of public interest in the Tower, 32.

RICHARD II.—1377.

Richard's residence in the Tower—his attempt to pacify the insurgents, 33. Proposal of Walworth, the Mayor, 33. Brutality of the mob, 34. Death of Jack Straw, 34. The King takes refuge from the Duke of Gloucester—the Duke of Ireland's attempt to assist him, 34. Richard besieged in the Tower—murder of Sir Simon Burley, 35. The King's revenge, 35. His compelled resignation by Bolingbroke, and murder, 36. His parting with his Queen pictured by Shakespeare, 37.

PRISONERS OF AGINCOURT.—1415.

Heavy ransoms demanded from prisoners of war—distress caused by, 38. Prisoners of note taken at Agincourt, 39. Ransom demanded from Charles of Orleans, 39. His long captivity, 40.

MURDER OF EDWARD V. AND DUKE OF YORK.—1483.

Question how the Princes were disposed of—the generally received tradition, 41. Imposture of Perkin Warbeck, 42. Probabilities of the case, 42. Was the Duchess of Burgundy deceived by Warbeck? 43. Question of the locality of the murder, 43. Visit of James I., 44. Disposal of the bodies, 44. Discovery in Charles II.'s time, 45. The bodies transferred by Charles to Westminster, 46. The mulberry-tree, 46. Rewards bestowed on the murderers, 47. Confessions of Tyrrell and Dighton, 47.

GERALD, NINTH EARL OF KILDARE.—1534.

Perennial disturbances in Ireland, 48. Rebellion of Gerald, the eighth Earl—his capture, 48. His trial—made Governor of Ireland by Henry VII., 49. Gerald, the ninth Earl, succeeds, 49. His vicissitudes, 50. Rebellion of his son "Silken Thomas," 51. Murder of Archbishop Allen, 52. Siege of Dublin Castle, 52. Storm of Maynooth Castle by Sir W. Skeffington, 53. Death of the Earl in prison, 53. "Silken Thomas" and his five uncles committed to the Tower, and executed at Tyburn, 53. 54.

ANNE BOLEYN.—1536.

Tablet to her memory, 55. Cause of her committal to the Tower, 55. Sir W. Kingston's account of her behaviour, 56. Her trial, 56. The sentence, 57. Execution of Rochford and others, 57. Kingston's letter to Cromwell, 57. Execution of Anne, 58. Her character, 59.

ANNE ASKEW.—1545.

Her marriage to Mr. Kyme; character of her husband: driven from his house, 60. The Six Articles, 61. Mrs. Kyme examined at Guildhall, and by Bishop Bonner, 61. Examined at Greenwich by Wriothesley, and again at Guildhall, 62. Tortured in the Tower; barbarity of Wriothesley, 63. Burnt in Smithfield, 64.

EDWARD COURTENAY, EARL OF DEVONSHIRE.—1553.

His long captivity; cause of his committal, 65. Released by Mary, again committed, and again released; his death, 66.

THE PRINCESS ELIZABETH.—1553.

Arrested at Ashridge, 67. Her journey to London, 68. Charged with being privy to Wyatt's conspiracy, 69. Departure for the Tower, 70. Entrance at Traitors' Gate, 71. The Earl of Sussex's advice to the Council, 72. Elizabeth examined by Gardiner and others, 73. Sir James Croft's speech to her, 74. Severity of her treatment, 74. Suspicions of the Constable; his quarrel with Elizabeth's attendants about her provisions, 75. Elizabeth released; her friendship for Miss Williams, afterwards Lady Norris, 76. Her gift to some City churches, 77. Her accession, 77. Her return to the Tower, 78. Her procession through the City to Westminster, 79-81.

LORD STOURTON'S MURDER OF THE HARTGILLS.

Cause of Lord Stourton's dislike of Mr. Hartgill, 82. Attack on Hartgill's mansion; the assailants repulsed by the younger Hartgill, 83. Lord Stourton bound over to keep the peace; his renewed persecutions; summoned before the Council, 83. Fined by the Star Chamber for a murderous attack on the younger Hartgill, 84. Seizes the Hartgills on a pretended charge of felony, 85. Causes them to be murdered, 85. Conceals the bodies, 86. Inquiry set on foot by Sir Anthony Hungerford; Lord Stourton committed to the Tower; his trial, 86. Lord Stourton executed at Salisbury; a peculiar privilege of the peerage; execution of the servants, 87. Hanging in chains, 87, 88.

LADY JANE GREY.—1554.

Her personal innocence; her learning and acquirements, 89. Lives of the upper classes in the sixteenth century; female education, 90. Causes of Lady Jane's classical knowledge; her freedom from pedantry, 91. Ground of the resolution to put her to death, 91. Wyatt's insurrection, 92. Its failure; his committal, 93. Queen Mary's personal dislike of Jane, 93. Outrage on her religious feelings; Lord Guildford Dudley beheaded, 94. Jane's last moments, 95. Her execution and interment. 96. Her name on her prison-wall, 96. Genuineness of similar inscriptions, 97.

LADY CATHERINE GREY.

Commencement of her acquaintance with Lord Hertford, 98. Lady Catherine in attendance on the Queen; Lady Jane Seymour's commission to her, 99. Lord Hertford's proposal accepted, 99. The marriage; the clergyman unknown, 100. Lord Hertford determines to go abroad, 101. New cause of anxiety, 101. Death of Lady Jane Seymour, 102. Character of Lord Hertford, 102. Lady Catherine confides in Mrs. St. Lo, and is committed to the Tower, notwithstanding the intercession of Lord Robert Dudley; birth of her first child, 103. Return and committal of Lord Hertford, 104. The marriage declared null and void, 104. Birth of a second child; increased severity towards Lady Catherine and her husband, 104. Fruitless appeals to Elizabeth's clemency; death of Lady Catherine, 105. Unnatural harshness of the Queen, 106.

GERALD, ELEVENTH EARL OF KILDARE.
(Murder of the Keatings.)—1574.

Committal of Hickey and Barry for the murder, 107. The Keatings guests of the Earl, 107. The Earl's treachery: murder of Shan Keating, 108. Murder of Meyler Keating;

question of Sir W. Fitzwilliam's complicity; Hickey and Barry executed, 109. Inquiry into the conduct of the Earl, 110.

PHILIP EARL OF ARUNDEL.—1585.

Accused of conspiracy by the Earl of Leicester; imprisoned, and released; resolves to leave England, 111. Thrown into the Tower, and sentenced to death, 112. His petitions to Elizabeth cruelly refused, 112. His death and burial; suspicion of poison, 113.

THE GUNPOWDER PLOT.—1605.

Origin of the plot; Catesby's chief part in it, 114. Thomas Winter, John Wright, Guy Fawkes, Thomas Percy, 115. The Treshams, 116. Mining operations of the conspirators, in a house adjoining the Parliament House; their superstition, 117. Cellar under Parliament House hired and stored with gunpowder, 118. New associates; Fawkes's preparations; apparent inconsistency of his precautions, 119. Programme of the conspirators; question as to warning Catholic peers and members, 120. The letter to Lord Monteagle, 121. Laid before the King by Lord Salisbury, 122. Inspection of the cellars under the Parliament House, 123. Seizure of Fawkes; flight of the conspirators; their muster at Holbeach, 124. Their defence against the Sheriff's force, 125. Results of the conflict; Tresham arrested; tradition concerning the torture of Fawkes, 126. Trial and execution of conspirators, 127. Torture and subsequent escape of Gerard, 128. Search at Hendlip; capture of Owen and Chambers, 128. Garnet and Oldcorn taken, 129. Garnet's trial; speech of Lord Northampton, 130. Execution of Garnet, 131. Torture and execution of Oldcorn, 131, 132. Character of the conspirators, 132. Their general conviction of the righteousness of their attempt, 133. Absence of sympathy for them, 134.

LADY ARABELLA STUART.—1611.

Her parentage and connexion with the Crown, 135. Her suitors; her presence at Lord Cobham's trial, 136. The King's meanness towards her, 136. Her marriage with William Seymour: is placed in charge of Sir T. Parry; Seymour committed to the Tower, 137. Arabella's letter complaining of the severity of her treatment, 138. Her escape, 139. Reaches Blackwall with her attendants, and proceeds down the river, 140. The fugitives received on board a French ship, 141. A Berwick captain's description of the party, 141. Seymour's escape from the Tower, 142. He reaches Ostend, 143. Consternation at Court, 143. The King's Proclamation, 144. The pursuit, 145. Arabella recaptured, and sent to the Tower, 146. List of persons committed to prison, 147. Examination of Arabella and the Countess of Shrewsbury, 148. Conduct of Seymour, 149. Treatment of Lady Shrewsbury: her firmness, 150. Insanity and death of Arabella, 151. Her burial in Henry VII.'s Chapel, 152.

MURDER OF SIR THOMAS OVERBURY.—1613.

Overbury's advice to Carr, who obtains his committal to the Tower, 153. Waad, the Lieutenant, replaced by Elways, 153. Overbury murdered by poison, 154. Inquiry into his death; committal of the Earl and Countess of Somerset, 154. Confessions of Weston the gaoler; his trial, 154. Execution of Weston and Mrs. Turner, 155. Trial and sentence of Elways; his dress on the scaffold, 155. His speech and execution, 156. Trial of the Earl and Countess; their re-committal to the Tower, and subsequent pardon, 157.

SIR WALTER RALEIGH.—1618.

His favour with Elizabeth, 158. His committal to the Tower: his release and marriage; his expedition to Guiana, 159. His statesmanship; James prejudiced against him, 160.

Accused and convicted of treason, 161. Paltry stratagem of the King, 162. Raleigh's letter to his wife, when awaiting his execution, 162, 163. His 'History of the World,' 164. His estate seized by the King; Prince Henry's intercession, 164. Raleigh's companions in the Tower, 165. His health impaired, 166. His correspondence with the Prince, 167. Proposes to the King an expedition to Guiana, 167. Gondomar's opposition, 168. The King's consent gained: Raleigh released from prison, 168. His commission; departure of the expedition, 169. Arrival at Guiana; collision with the Spaniards; young Raleigh killed, 170. Suicide of Captain Keymis; return to England; Raleigh recommitted to the Tower, 171. Order for his execution; his plea overruled; his appeal rejected, 172. Interview with his wife; his last hours, 173. His address on the scaffold, 174. The execution, 175. Effect of the iron rule of Elizabeth, 176.

ASSASSINATION OF THE DUKE OF BUCKINGHAM.
1629.

Motive for the murder: Felton taken to the Tower, 177. His trial and execution, 178. His reply to Lord Dorset when menaced with torture, 178. Aubrey's account of the visits of the ghost of Sir G. Villiers to his friend Mr. Towes, 179, 180.

WENTWORTH, EARL OF STRAFFORD.—1641.

His rigorous government of Ireland, 181. Denounced as an apostate, 182. Impeached by the Commons, and given into custody, 183. Impeachment and committal of Laud, 183. Trial of Strafford, 183. Charges against him, injustice towards him, 184. The impeachment abandoned, 185. Proceedings against him by attainder, 185. His defence; proposal to allow him to escape; the attainder passed, 186. The King signs the death-warrant, and entreats the Houses for a commutation of the sentence, 187. Passage to the scaffold, and execution, 188.

LORD CAPEL.—1649.

His escape from the Tower, 189. Betrayed by a waterman, and recaptured, 190. Debate on his wife's petition, 191. Remarks on Cromwell's conduct, 192. Lord Capel's address from the scaffold, 193. His execution, 194. His character drawn by Clarendon, 194, 195.

COLONEL BLOOD'S ATTEMPT TO STEAL THE CROWN JEWELS.—1671.

The public first admitted to view the Regalia: Blood's visit with his pretended wife, 196. His second visit, 197. Returns with his accomplices, 197. Murderous attack on Edwards, the Deputy-Keeper, 198. Arrival of Edwards's son; flight of the robbers, 198. Blood made prisoner; his effrontery before the King, 199. Remanded to the Tower, with his accomplices; and released, 200. Charles's apology for his ill-timed clemency, 200. Particulars of Blood's former outrage on the Duke of Ormond, 201. The Duke of Buckingham suspected of complicity, 201. Lord Ossory's threat, 202. Blood's after career, 202. Neglect and death of Edwards; discovery of his monumental tablet, 202.

MYSTERIOUS DEATH OF THE EARL OF ESSEX.—1683.

Position of Lord Essex's lodging in the Tower, 203. Commission in William III.'s reign to investigate the matter; evidence relied on to prove that Essex was murdered, 204. Greater probability that he committed suicide, 205. Earl Russell's allusion to Essex's death, 206. Prevalent notion that forfeiture of estates might be evaded by suicide, 206.

THE EARL OF NITHISDALE'S ESCAPE.—1716.

Parentage of the Countess; the Earl a leader among the Jacobites; made prisoner at Preston, and committed to the Tower, 207. Lady Nithisdale's journey to London, 208.

Her endeavour to present a petition to George I., 209. Escape of several prisoners; petitions to Parliament, 210. Address to the King; his reply, 211. Lady Nithisdale's mode of availing herself of the passing of the Address, 211. Enlists aid in her scheme for her husband's release, 212. Her own account of the manner in which the escape was effected. 213-217. Her return to her lodging, and visit to the Duchess of Montrose, 217. Joins Lord Nithisdale, who is taken to the house of the Venetian Ambassador, 218. His escape to Calais; his wife goes to Scotland to secure the family papers. 219. Her return to London; rejoins her husband at Rome, 220. The Countess's picture by Kneller, 221. Question of the locality in the Tower from which Lord Nithisdale's escape was made, 221. Probability in favour of the Governor's house, 222. Condemnation of the other noblemen; intercession for them, 223. Execution of Lords Derwentwater and Kenmure, 223, 224. Trial of Lord Wintoun, 224. His escape from the Tower after condemnation, 225.

EXECUTION OF THE REBEL LORDS OF 1745.

Last occasion of the use of the headsman's block in the Tower, 226. Trial of Lords Cromarty, Kilmarnock, and Balmerino. 226. Execution of Kilmarnock and Balmerino, 227. Trial of Lord Lovat, 227. His behaviour at his execution, 228. Discovery of the coffin-plates of these noblemen, 228.

THE CATO-STREET CONSPIRATORS.—1820.

Career of Thistlewood, 229. His scheme for overthrowing the Government; the loft in Cato Street, 230. Opportunity chosen for the outbreak: details of the plan, 231. The plot betrayed, 233. Consultations in Cabinet on the mode of dealing with the discoveries; proposal of the Duke of Wellington, 234, 235. The Duke's plan rejected, 235. Arrest of some of the gang; a police officer killed; escape of Thistlewood; alarm in London, 236. Capture of Thistlewood;

the leaders committed to the Tower; the trials, 237. Details of the executions, 238. Behaviour of the mob, 239. Alarm during a ball at the Spanish Ambassador's: project of Thistlewood to attack the house on that occasion, 239, 240.

ANCIENT ARMOUR.

Need of inspection and arrangement, 241. Suit of armour presented by the Emperor Maximilian to Henry VIII.; representation of the rack, 242. Indifference produced by habit to the sufferings of prisoners; instance of the torture of Anne Askew, 243.

ORDNANCE.

Curious gun cast by Solyman the Magnificent; supposed alloy of gold in its composition, 244. Skill of the Turks in casting large cannon, 245. Presence of gold in the gun-metal disproved; guns cast from cannon captured at Cherbourg, 246. specimens of ornamental casting; revolver of the reign of James I., 247. Store of rifles for the supply of the army, 247.

CONSTABLES OF THE TOWER.

Early Constables; ecclesiastics who held the office, 248. Mandeville, Earl of Essex: Hubert de Burgh, 249. Hugh le Bigod, Earl of Norfolk; Bishop Stapleton, 250. De la Beche, 251. Edward III.'s prisoners, 252. Sir Thomas Rempston, 253. Peculiar privilege of the Constable, exercised by Sir William Balfour, 253. Disputes between Charles I. and the Parliament, 254. Duke of Bolton; Lord Cornwallis, 255. Question raised, and debate, on the appointment of Lord George Lennox, 255, 256. The appointment since restricted to military officers, 257. Reform of abuses by the Duke of Wellington, 257, 258. Increase in number of visitors, 258. Lord Combermere, 258. Sir John Burgoyne; the Constable's salary abolished, 259.

CLOSING THE GATES.

Ceremonies practised, 260. Seizure of the Tower always an object with the ringleaders in riots; Jack Cade; Lord George Gordon, 261. Colonel Despard: Sir Francis Burdett: Watson: Thistlewood: the Chartists. 262. Precautions of the Duke of Wellington: alarms of fire, 263. Paul Hentzner's account of his visit to the Tower in Queen Anne's time, 263-265.

THE MENAGERIE.

Early custom of keeping wild beasts in the Tower; Henry III.'s leopards, bear, and elephant, 266. Edward II.'s lion; increased importance of keepers, 267. Baiting of lions introduced by James I.: account of an eye-witness, 267, 268. The King's second visit to a like exhibition, 269, 270. A horse worried by dogs; a bear baited to death by the King's order; his niggardly device for saving his own pocket. 271. A popular reason for anticipating the death of George II., 271. Removal of the menagerie, 272.

APPENDIX.

		PAGE
LIST OF CONSTABLES	.. ..	273
,, LIEUTENANTS	.. ..	279
,, DEPUTY-LIEUTENANTS	.. .. ..	280
,, MAJORS	.. ..	281
INDEX	.. ..	283

LIST OF ILLUSTRATIONS.

North Front of St. Thomas's Tower and Traitors' Gate .. .. *Frontispiece.*

Gen. Sir J. Burgoyne (Constable of the Tower) .. *Title.*

Plan of the Tower at present .. *to face Introduction.*

                                                                                                    PAGE

Recess in Upper Part of Wakefield Tower .. 11

> A representation of the south-eastern of the eight recesses in the first floor of the Wakefield Tower, a Decorated addition to a Norman basement. This recess is prolonged into the chamber by lateral walls and buttresses, so as to give it greater depth. It was evidently an Oratory.

Lancet Arch in Wakefield Tower 20

> Shows the tall lancet doorway which occupies the next or eastern recess in the Wakefield Tower, and which led from the royal apartments, and was no doubt closed when the King's Gallery was pulled down, and this tower fitted up as a record-room.

N. Aisle, St. John's Chapel, White Tower *to face* 22

Plan of White Tower 23

Interior of St. Peter's ad Vincula .. .. *to face* 28

Joggled Masonry in Great Arch of Traitors' Gate 37

> A representation of the crown of the very curious arch which spans the Pool, and supports the rear-wall, of brick and timber, of St. Thomas's Tower, better known as Traitors' Gate. The arch, of 61 feet span and 15 feet 9 inches rise, has recently been disencumbered of buildings. The joggled joints have no doubt well fulfilled their object in retaining the voussoirs in their places.

List of Illustrations.

	PAGE
VIEW OF TOWER OF LONDON IN THE FIFTEENTH CENTURY .. .. *to face*	38
PISCINA, ST. THOMAS'S TOWER	40
BLOODY TOWER	45
LANDING-PLACE ON STAIRS IN WHITE TOWER *to face*	46
CINQUEFOIL-HEADED LOOP IN WHITE TOWER	54

One of the very few unaltered windows in the whole fortress. It is the remaining one of a pair which opened from the basement chamber of the Cradle Tower in its rear or north wall.

INTERIOR OF BEAUCHAMP TOWER	57
FIREPLACE IN WHITE TOWER	64

This fireplace has been recently discovered in the east wall of the upper or state-floor of the White Tower. Its ring-stones appear to be original, as is its round back, and it is the only known fireplace in the building. As the vent has not been cleared out, it is uncertain whether it opened on the face of the wall, or ascended to its summit.

PLAN OF TOWER OF LONDON. 1558 .. .. *to face*	70
TRAITORS' GATE	71
SIDE PASSAGE, BYWARD TOWER	81

This is the entrance and perspective of the gallery of the postern appendage to the Byward Gate Tower. It is of excellent Perpendicular work, with ribbed vaulting, as shown in the cut. At the further end of this gallery, but within it, was a portcullis and small drawbridge, the "altera securitas" of the postern. The second bridge was exterior, and crossed the South Moat, dropping upon the Quay.

PASSAGE AND CELL IN BEAUCHAMP TOWER .. *to face*	89
"IANE" (Lady Jane Grey)—name inscribed on the wall of the Beauchamp Tower	97
GUY FAWKES'S DUNGEON (Little Ease)	133
DOOR OF GUY FAWKES'S DUNGEON	134

List of Illustrations.

	PAGE
TABLE AND BOWL IN ORATORY, ST. THOMAS'S TOWER	152

    St. Thomas's Tower is flanked on its southern angles by two cylindrical turrets, which contain octagonal chambers of great elegance. One of these, to the south-east, on the upper floor, has been intended for an Oratory. Of its three eastward openings, the central has been above the altar. The sill of that on the south side is a Purbeck slab with a projecting half-circle containing the bowl. In the north window a similar but thicker slab seems to have projected bodily, as a credence table, but is also hollowed out, as represented in the cut. Both stones must have been broken off when the windows were plastered up, and were discovered in 1866. The Tower is of Early English date.

SIR WALTER RALEIGH'S CELL	166
ENTRANCE TO RALEIGH'S CELL	176
COUNCIL CHAMBER IN GOVERNOR'S HOUSE *to face*	222
VAULT UNDER WAKEFIELD TOWER .. .. *to face*	225
AXE CARRIED BEFORE PEERS GOING TO TRIAL AT WESTMINSTER	257
EXECUTIONER'S AXE, BLOCK, AND MASK	272

THE TOWER OF LONDON.

GENERAL DESCRIPTION.

EFORE entering upon any personal details of the prisoners of historical notoriety who have been confined within the Tower, it may be well to present the reader with a brief description of its actual condition, and of the various Stores, Armouries, Prisons, Offices, and Chapels which are contained within its precincts, especially as many of them have of late years undergone considerable changes and restorations, subsequent to the publication of the work of Messrs. Britton and Brayley. Situated on the Middlesex side of the Thames, about one-third of a mile below London Bridge, and just outside the jurisdiction of the City, the Tower in its general aspects resembles a small fortified town, such as we find in many parts of Germany and Flanders. But it is so hemmed in by a large and populous suburb, that, although a stronghold against surprise by any riotous or insurrectionary assemblage, and even against an attack by regular troops, unless provided with heavy

artillery, yet the Tower could not of course oppose any prolonged resistance to a siege carried on by regular approaches, and with the formidable battering train, which would accompany such an operation in modern times.

A wide dry ditch, capable of being flooded at high tide, runs round the whole exterior of the Tower, commencing from the river at Tower Stairs, on the west, and running round the whole outer wall or scarp, till it again touches the Thames at Iron Gate Stairs, at the eastern extremity of the ditch. Between the outer edge of this ditch, and the open space of Tower Hill (the margin of which represents what in military language would be termed the "glacis"), there is a tolerably wide strip of pleasure-ground or garden, open to the chief inhabitants and residents, and managed by a committee of official gentlemen connected with the Tower and the Mint. The scarp or inner side of the Tower Ditch rises into an elevated wall, with bastions at its angles, and short, but heavy guns, distributed along the rampart, in the positions best suited for command of Tower Hill and its approaches.

The main entrance of the Tower of London is through the Middle Tower on the outer side of the ditch; then across a causeway bridge, and through the fine old arch of the Byward Tower, which leads under the rampart into the interior of the fortress.

The ramparts are "casemated," and contain Store-rooms, Workshops, Magazines, Engine-houses, and Warders' quarters, being complete as far as the western and northern faces. The eastern face was, till lately, in a state of total dilapidation, the result of many years of neglect on the part of the former Board of Ordnance, but is now in rapid progress of restoration.

Immediately within the ramparts, and between them and the inner or "Ballium" wall (a military term of the middle ages), there was until lately a narrow street, known as Mint Street, with houses built at different periods, and without order or arrangement, against the rampart on the one side, and the "Ballium wall" on the other, rendering the rampart of little service, and disfiguring, as well as rendering useless, the ancient wall of the fortress. In this street were situated the Royal Mint, Workshops, Barracks, and Stores, with three or four warders' quarters, in a condition of ruin and dilapidation, forming a great contrast to its present appearance. Among other objections to Mint Street were two taverns, which former Lieutenant-Governors or Lieutenants had allowed to be erected, for the sake of the rents they received from them, amounting at one period to several hundreds per annum, either unknown or unnoticed by Government. The level of Mint Street, though higher by many feet than the outer ditch, is lower than the interior parade, in the middle of which is situated the White Tower, which was the donjon or keep of the ancient fortress, and is celebrated as the scene of some of the darkest tragedies of the Tower of London.

The "Ballium" wall is of great thickness and solidity, and of a height varying from thirty to forty feet. It has every appearance of great antiquity, and is probably of the same date as the White Tower, erected in William the Conqueror's time, by Gundulph, Bishop of Rochester, a prelate famous in his day for skill as an architec, and engineer. The Ballium wall commences just inside the main gate of the outer rampart, with a lofty tower (the Bell Tower) forming the south-west angle of the Governor's house. From thence a massive curtain wall, disfigured unfortunately by modern brick buildings on the top, runs northward for about fifty yards to the Beauchamp Tower, which projects as a bastion about the centre of the west face of the Ballium wall.

State Prison.

The Beauchamp Tower had from the earliest times been appropriated as a state prison for those unfortunate persons who were to be kept in close confinement without indulgence for air and exercise within the outer wall. There are three stories in this Tower, but the middle one, with a small dungeon beyond, was the prison. Its walls tell a truly dismal tale, covered as they are with the sad memorials of the names of successive prisoners of all ranks, engraved in many instances with an elaborate care which bears witness to the dreary weight of time which hung upon their hands, and rendered the inscribing of their names a melancholy resource under the privation of all other interests and occupation. For a number of years previous to the appointment of the late Sir G. Cathcart as Lieutenant-Governor of the Tower, this State prison had been disgracefully neglected, and fitted up by the Board of Ordnance as a mess-room for the Officers of the garrison, the niches being filled with cupboards and shelves, to the concealment, as well as injury, of the inscriptions. Sir George was called from the Tower to active service at the Cape, before his judicious plans for restoring the Beauchamp Tower were yet completed, but he had so efficiently set the work on foot, that no difficulties were found by his successor in carrying them out. The detail was intrusted to Mr. Salvin, the architect, whose admirable taste in restoration had been fully displayed at Alnwick, Warwick Castle, and other historical edifices of baronial times. Certainly a better choice could not have been made, and nothing could exceed the pains and care which he bestowed upon this work, diligently tracing out every nook and corner where restoration was practicable; and where that was no longer possible, from the dilapidations having gone too far, following implicitly the old models before him, till, by the end of the second year, he had succeeded in the perfect restoration of this celebrated tower.

To avoid any future injury to the inscriptions on the inner walls, a preparation of an indurating nature was repeatedly rubbed over them to harden the stone, so that there is every reason to hope that the Beauchamp Tower, and its sad and interesting inscriptions, are now as secure against the effects of age, as skill and care can render them.

A Warder is always in attendance in the prison room during the hours of visitation by the public, and it is his special duty to caution visitors against touching, even with the finger, any part of the walls and inscriptions.

From the Beauchamp Tower, the Ballium wall is continued to the north-west corner of what may be called the inner fortress, where stands the Devereux Tower, designated in Henry VIII.'s time as Robin the Devil's Tower, perhaps a corruption of Robert le Diable. Along the north face we find four towers, namely, the Devereux, the Flint Tower, the Bowyer Tower, and the Brick Tower. The Bowyer Tower is supposed to have been the scene of the murder of the Duke of Clarence, Edward IV.'s brother.

Were there no other notoriety attached to the Tower of London, the fact of our immortal dramatic poet having selected its various localities for some of the finest scenes of his historical plays, should be enough to invest it with a more than common interest.

. It is enough to find in Shakespeare a scene headed "A Room in the Tower," to be certain that what follows will strike our imagination, or excite our sympathy, by some powerful exhibition of the passions and feelings of characters, who have acted conspicuous parts in the history of the early reigns of our monarchs, or the cruel and implacable enmities of the Wars of the Red and White Roses—wars which cut short the lives of nearly a third of the nobility of England, either in the field or on the scaffold. To quote Shakespeare, as an infallible historical authority, would be as absurd, as it would be, on the other hand, unreasonable not to give him credit for faithfully handing down to us the "tale as 'twas told to him," and commemorating in dialogue, as picturesque as natural, those tragedies of real life, with which our early history abounds. Whether he be always as correct in his facts, as he might have been, by a more diligent investigation of the chronicles existing in his day, it is at least certain that he seldom fails to portray with a spirit and fire, unequalled by any who have ventured on the path of historical drama, the chivalrous character of the ancient nobility of England, and the brave and honest nature of the yeomen and soldiers who followed them to those bloody fields, where the flower of English youth were sacrificed to the ferocity of civil war. In proceeding with the description of the interior of the Tower, a reference to the Scenes which Shakespeare has located in some of its most remarkable chambers and prisons, will, it is hoped, be acceptable to most readers. One of the first which occurs has been attributed by tradition to the Bowyer Tower.*

The north-east corner of the Ballium wall is formed by the Jewel Tower, and, following round to the eastern face, we come to the Broad-arrow Tower, at which point, owing to the destruction of the Royal Palace and adjacent buildings by Cromwell, the Ballium wall disappears.

With an utter disregard of the character and requirements of the Tower, whether as an historical monument of unequalled interest, or as a place of security for military stores, for the crown jewels, and for the curious and very valuable ancient armoury, the whole of this south-eastern portion of the Fortress has for many years been given up to degradation by the erection of a modern range of military storehouses and sheds.

Obscured by one of these buildings, stands the

---

* RICHARD III., act i. scene 4. *A room in the Tower.*
 Enter CLARENCE *and* BRACKENBURY.

ancient Salt Tower, lately restored by Mr. Salvin, to whose judgment and skill the public were indebted for the restoration of the Beauchamp Tower before mentioned, as well as for the beautiful inner elevation of the northern and eastern casemates.

The south-east corner of the Tower, where the Salt Tower stands, was the site of the royal palace, an irregular building (to judge from some old prints which are extant), extending from the south side of the White Tower, over the ground now occupied by those modern buildings of the Military Store department, which stand forth as a monument of all that is low and unsightly in modern architecture.

During the Government of Oliver Cromwell, he gave orders to put the Tower in a condition of defence, and is believed to have procured most of the material for this purpose from the ruins of the Royal Palace, which he took early occasion to pull down to the very ground. So effectually was this destruction accomplished, that the buttress of an old archway adjoining the Salt Tower is now the only vestige of a Palace which was the secure and stately residence of so many of our earlier monarchs. The modern buildings of the Military Store department, which resemble a large factory rather than a public edifice suitable to the character of the Tower, are continued along the south or river face, to near the centre, where the ancient Hall Tower, better known as the Wakefield Tower, marks the re-commencement of the Ballium wall.

Next to the Wakefield Tower stands the Bloody

Tower, opposite the celebrated water entrance of the Traitors' Gate; then comes a massive curtain-wall, at the back of which stands the Governor's house, and some Warders' quarters, the windows of which are pierced through the thickness of the wall (in most cases above eight feet), but unfortunately disfigured by modern brickwork at the top. This curtain-wall terminates westward at the Bell Tower, from whence the description of the Ballium wall was commenced.

The exterior defences of the Tower on the southern front consist of a low rampart (a prolongation of the exterior casemated wall with the Tower wharf), between it and the Thames, at the west end of which is a small river terrace, laid down in gravel, and shaded by a row of trees. The eastern part of this wharf is encumbered and disfigured with modern workshops, wooden sheds, and storehouses. Opposite to the Wakefield Tower, in the Ballium wall, stands the fine old tower known as St. Thomas's, under which, the wide stone archway, called by the fatal name of the Traitors' Gate, admitted the barges in which state prisoners were brought to the Tower from Westminster. From this arch there is an ascent of stone steps, by which prisoners were conducted through the Gate of the Bloody Tower to their cells or prison-rooms within the inner or Ballium wall. From the Traitors' Gate, the wharf extends westward to the Queen's Stairs, and thence to the Byward Tower and Main Gate, ending with the Tower stairs, which are just outside the defences of the Tower. A beautiful restoration of St. Thomas's Tower, the Traitors' Gate, and its noble arch, has just been completed by Mr. Salvin, under the authority of the Hon. W. Cowper, First Commissioner of Works, who deserves every praise for this restoration of so curious an historical building, and for intrusting the execution of the work to such able hands as those of Mr. Salvin.

WAKEFIELD TOWER.

The large Hall in the Wakefield Tower has been always traditionally pointed out as the scene of Henry VI.'s murder.

After the total defeat of the Lancastrians at Tewkesbury, in 1471, and the murder of the young Prince of Wales in presence of Edward, the life of Henry VI., a captive in the Tower, became the only stake on which further insurrections of the Lancastrians could be ventured.

Edward was not a man to hesitate in such a case, and on the evening of the day (May 22) on which Edward made his entry into London, Henry was declared to have died in the Tower. Grief and vexation were the causes publicly assigned for his decease; but the common rumour of the day was that he had been stabbed by the Duke of Gloucester, whose after-deeds as Richard III. seemed to authorise the belief of his taking part in any act of blood and cruelty.* The funeral was conducted with little reverence or respect, the body being first taken

---

* HENRY VI., Part III., act. v. scene 7. *The Tower of London. Enter K.* HENRY *with a book, and* GLOUCESTER *with the* LIEUT. *on the Tower walls.*

by torchlight to St. Paul's, and after to Chertsey, where it was buried in the Abbey, "unreverently, without priest or clerke, torch or taper, singing or saying." Shortly after the accession of Gloucester as Richard III., some stories got abroad of miracles wrought at the tomb of the murdered monarch, and the Usurper, in order to prevent any impression being made by these tales upon the public mind, caused the coffin to be disinterred, and removed to the royal sepulchre at Windsor.

RECESS IN UPPER PART OF WAKEFIELD TOWER.
(Supposed to have been used as a Chapel.)

The Wakefield Tower has a gloomy vault under its base, where it was supposed that a number of distinguished prisoners taken at the battle of Wakefield were confined, but there seems to be no good reason for supposing that such was the case; and indeed the barbarous custom which prevailed, during the bloody struggle of the Red and White Roses, of executing the principal leaders of the defeated party immediately after the battle, renders it unlikely that any number of them should have been transferred to London after the battle of Wakefield.

But there is a more recent and better authenticated tradition that sixty or seventy of the Scots prisoners, after the Rebellion of 1745, were here placed in close confinement, and so little attention given to proper supplies of fresh air, and even food, that more than half of them perished from overcrowding and neglect, before the Government, at the instance of the Lieutenant of the Tower, caused them to be removed to less unwholesome quarters.

From the time our Sovereigns ceased to make the royal palace within the Tower their occasional residence (James I. was the last who ever occupied it), great abuses have prevailed in the government and management as well as the necessary repairs within the Tower. The Constables appointed from time to time seem only to have considered how they might derive most income from their high office, which was invested with almost unlimited local authority. They sold the Warderships, allowed public-houses to be erected, even against the most venerable Towers and ancient buildings, and filled every corner with tenants, from whom they collected heavy rents, allowing every sort of encroachment and dilapidation to proceed unnoticed. Besides this, there had existed within the Tower walls, and by royal permission from very early times, a considerable Ordnance and Store establishment for the supplies of the army. The Tower has long been the depôt for the muskets, swords, carbines, and pistols issued to the troops, and the Storehouses contained every article required for the furnishing of barracks and hospitals. During the pressure of the Crimean war, stoves, tables, bedsteads, bedding, and all sorts of clothing, were collected in vast quantities, and fresh warehouses and storehouses were run up on every vacant spot that could be made available, with utter disregard of architectural appearance.

As far back as the reign of Charles II. large barracks, capable of lodging a battalion of Guards, had been constructed in the Tower, without any attempt at preserving the architectural style of the place. But, unfortunately, while the space within the Tower walls was crammed with numerous unsightly buildings in the worst possible taste, the old walls, the ditch, and the ramparts, were suffered to fall into ruin. This state of things would seem incompatible with the security of a state prison; but it must be remembered that all the Bastions and the Ballium or inner wall, and both the Gate Towers, were appropriated to the double purposes of state prisons and Warders' lodgings, each Warder or Gaoler having charge of his prisoner, and being answerable for his safe custody, in strong rooms, with barred windows and iron-plated doors.

The great fire which occurred in the Tower in 1841, and consumed Charles II.'s barracks and storehouse, together with a quantity of modern arms, which were kept in the latter building, gave an opportunity to the Duke of Wellington, who was then Constable, to urge in the strongest manner upon the Government the necessity of constructing a suitable barrack for the troops in garrison, and at the same time of commencing the restoration both of the inner and outer defences and walls of the Tower.

The dilapidation of the Tower of London, as well as the confusion of the records and papers in the Constable's charge, had long been a matter of concern to the Duke, as likewise the unquestionable fact, that the troops stationed in the Tower were much more unhealthy than in any other of the London barracks and quarters. For these reasons, upon the office of Lieut.-Governor falling vacant, he selected the late Sir George (then Colonel) Cathcart, an officer of distinguished talent and merit, and an able man of business, to fill this post, and carry out the improvements he had designed. On careful investigation of the causes of ill-health in the garrison, Colonel Cathcart came to the conclusion, that the mud and stagnant water of the ditch must be the primary mischief, and suggested a project for draining it and converting it for the future into a dry ditch. This scheme was carried out, and answered so well, that this Garrison is now considered as healthy as any of the Barracks in London, and the western portion of the ditch, instead of being a nuisance, affords a dry, gravelled parade, commonly used as an exercising ground for the garrison, as well as for several neighbouring Volunteer corps, who are permitted to drill there, on application to the Lieut.-Governor.

At the Duke's urgent suggestion, it was determined by the Government to insert annually in the Parliamentary Estimates a certain sum to be expended, under superintendence of the Engineer department, for the gradual restoration of the Tower walls and Bastions. During several years this plan was successfully executed, nor was a voice raised in the House of Commons to oppose an expenditure due to the credit of the nation, as well as a wise and needful precaution for the security of valuable national property. However, in the year 1852, a sudden stop was put by the Government to any further repair of the Tower defences, just as the western and northern ramparts had been completed, leaving the whole eastern front in the same ruinous and dilapidated condition as before. But the evil did not end here; advantage was taken of supposed exigencies of the Crimean war by the Secretary for War at the time, to order the construction of extensive stores on the very localities where the further restorations were to have taken place, even filling the dry ditch with accumulations of condemned stores, in the teeth of the protest of Lord Combermere, who had succeeded the late Duke of Wellington as Constable of the Tower. The enormous and ill-managed expenses of the war were still held out as reasons against the resumption of the works, and the dilapidation was becoming worse and worse till 1862, when the Right Honourable F. Lewis, the Secretary for War, resolved, after a careful personal inspection, to bring forward in his estimates the sum necessary for continuing the eastern defences. On Mr. Lewis's lamented death Earl de Grey took up the matter with his usual ability, and under the able direction of Colonel Nicholson great progress has been made in the rampart, which is casemated, in accordance with a characteristic elevation furnished by Mr. Salvin, while the parapet is "arcaded" in the same style, to protect troops from any musketry fire from the lofty warehouses of St. Katherine's Docks. The precaution no doubt is judicious, though, as the late Duke of Wellington remarked on occasion of his last inspection of the Tower, a few heavy round-shot directed at the foot of St. Katherine's wall from the guns on the rampart would very soon induce any venturous rioters who might have occupied the roof, to abandon a post exposed to the risk of the whole building falling about their ears.

Now, as regards the question of the restorations and repairs lately carried on within the Tower, it may be asked why should so much difficulty attend them? It is a matter which requires explanation, if only to defend the Constable and his officers from the charge of negligence. Unfortunately the authorities of the Tower have, of themselves, no power to order the most common repairs; and it is only by persevering application to different Government offices that the most trifling restorations can be effected. For what concerns the "Palatial" portions of the Tower, such as the Jewel Repository, the two Chapels, the Governor's Residence, and the Quarters of the Warders, application is annually made to the Chief Commissioner of Works, for the proposed repairs or restorations to be inserted in the Estimates, and laid before the House of Commons. By his directions (if he approves what is proposed) a survey is first made of the work, and an estimate goes forward to the Treasury; but here, unfortunately, it too frequently comes to an untimely end; because the Chancellor of the Exchequer, if pressed for other public works, or desirous of coming to Parliament with low Estimates, has the discretionary power of striking his pen through any item in the Tower Estimates, however strongly urged upon his notice. Yet it is evident that he cannot be so well informed of the details of such subjects as either the Tower authorities or the Office of Works; and the worst part of the arrangement is, that, by this clumsy routine, many repairs, which would cost very little if done in proper time, become doubly expensive, when allowed to stand over till time and weather have aggravated the dilapidation.

With regard to the military portions of the Tower, such as the ramparts, ditches, guns, storehouses, barracks, hospital, magazines, fire-engines, &c., applications must be made by the Tower authorities to the Secretary of State for War, and are referred by him for the opinion of the Commanding Engineer.

It is on the recommendation of the Commanding Engineer that the Secretary for War enters in the Estimates he prepares for the House of Commons any works or repairs proposed. But here again the Chancellor of the Exchequer can put his veto in action, and the works in question being out of the public view, and not likely to draw attention like improvements in the Barracks, Parks, or Public offices at the west end of London, are too often set aside in favour of other buildings more likely to attract public notice. Thus the eastern walls and rampart of the Tower, facing St. Katherine's, have only lately been approved in the Estimates, having lain for above ten years in a state of ruin and decay disgraceful to public buildings of any kind, but especially to the most venerable and historical fortress of Great Britain.

One great difficulty which the Constable and his officers had formerly to contend with, was the absence of anything like good taste, or appreciation of a suitable style of architecture, on the part of the old Board of Ordnance, as regarded the restoration or construction of military buildings: witness the monstrous Warehouses and Store-offices which disfigure the river front of the Tower, and to which, so late as in 1852, an upper story was added, in the decorative style of the great gin-palaces of London.

A different and more judicious course is now followed, and reference is made to Mr. Salvin, the celebrated castle architect, as well as to the Commanding Engineer, when it is a question of restoration or improvement of the Walls, Barracks, and

Storehouses in the Tower. With no greater expense than was formerly thrown away on absurd modern decoration, the buildings are now treated with due reference to the ancient style of the Tower. A general principle has lately been introduced by Mr. Salvin in making a distinction between the exterior style of building connected with the walls and defences, and the interior edifices of the Tower. According to this principle, the latter should have no defensive character about them, but their fronts and roofs should resemble the common street architecture in London before the Great Fire of 1666. Those readers who happen to be familiar with the appearance of the old parts of the city of Chester, will readily understand the style considered suitable for the interior buildings in the Tower.

The walls and outer defences must of course partake of a military character, though it has been shown, by the effect of the new Rampart and Casemates to the eastward, that it is perfectly possible to combine the requisites of fortification, with the style appropriate to so ancient and historical a pile as the venerable Tower of London.

With deep respect for the memory of one who never meddled but to amend or to improve, it may here be observed that the late Prince Consort, by his discreet intervention on the part of The Queen, in reference to those portions of the Tower which were dependencies of the ancient Palace, first established a proper system of control over the architecture of the Tower, by declaring it to be Her Majesty's pleasure that " no edifice within its walls should be built, altered, or restored, until the plans and elevations should have been officially submitted for her Majesty's personal approval"—a regulation which is now strictly attended to, and which has produced already some very satisfactory results.

LANCET IN WAKEFIELD TOWER.

THE WHITE TOWER.

THE chapel of St. John, in the upper story of the White Tower, was, until a very few years back, most improperly used as a repository for obsolete records. On the erection of the General Record Office in Lincoln's Inn, in the year 1857, the whole of the State Papers were cleared out from this and other parts of the Tower, and removed to the new establishment. It will scarcely be believed that an attempt was made, on that occasion, to take possession of this ancient and historical chapel, as a clothing store for the War Department, and in spite of the remonstrances of Lord Combermere (then Constable), this appropriation would have taken place, but for a change of Government, which occurred within a few days after the order had been issued. General Peel then came into office, and, admitting the propriety of the Constable's objection, saved the Chapel from further desecration. As part of the royal palace, it was at once put in charge of the Office of Works; and when the Hon. W. Cowper became First Commissioner, a complete restoration was undertaken under his auspices by Mr. Salvin, who carried it out with his usual taste and judgment. Perhaps there is nowhere, certainly not in England, a more noble and striking specimen of the grand and simple style of Norman architecture than this Chapel, as now restored. The massive and solemn effect of its huge columns, and the absence of all minor decorations and ornament, give a peculiar character and dignity to its imposing architecture. It is associated with many interesting historical recollections. Here it was that the forty-six noblemen and gentlemen, created Knights of the Bath by Henry IV., on his accession to the throne, performed the ancient chivalrous ceremony of watching their armour from sunset to sunrise. Brackenbury was at his prayers in this Chapel when he received Richard's message to destroy Edward V. and his brother, which execrable deed he, to his honour, refused to undertake. Here the mortal remains of Queen Elizabeth, the White Rose of York, lay in state for some weeks, previous to her splendid funeral in 1503.

The floor or body of St. John's Chapel is on the same level as the Banqueting-hall, which occupies the main story of the White Tower, while the gallery, which runs round three sides of the Chapel, is entered from the Council Chamber, without communication from below. The Royal Palace, of which there is scarcely any vestige remaining, communicated with the White Tower, and this gallery was probably the place to which the English queens and their ladies resorted for the celebration of mass, unseen by the congregation in the body of the Chapel below.

AISLE ST JOHN'S CHAPEL WHITE TOWER

By the late arrangements for throwing open to the public the magnificent Armoury (60,000 stand of rifles) recently fitted up in the Banqueting-hall and Council-chamber, visitors are now conducted through St. John's

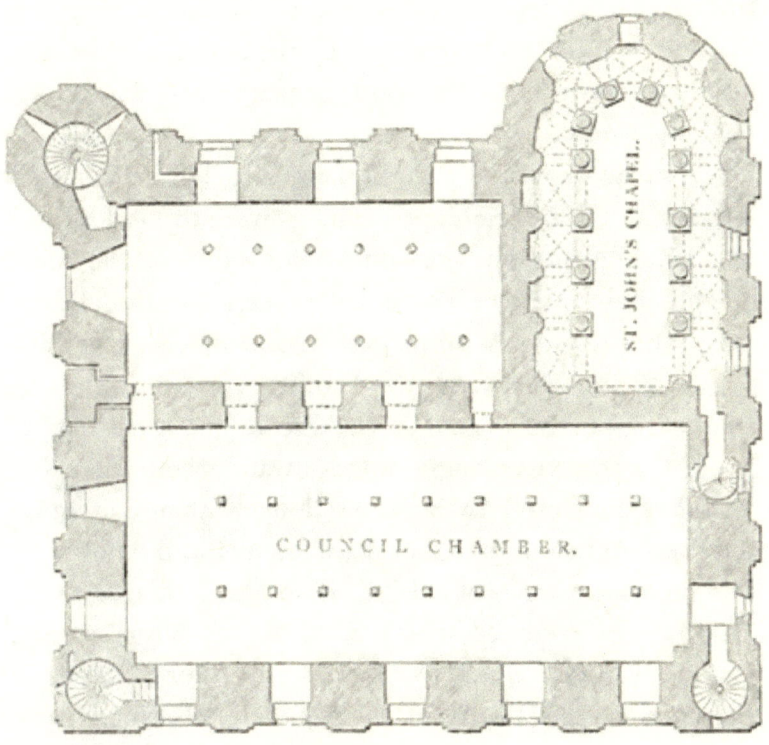

PLAN OF WHITE TOWER.

Chapel by the outward turret stair (at the foot of which the bones of the murdered princes were found in Charles II.'s time), and so through the armouries to the main stairs, by which the White Tower is entered.

Among the curious traditions of the White Tower, it

is said, that in the time of the civil wars a Parliamentary soldier was pursuing a Royalist, sword in hand, up the north stairs, when the latter, finding escape impossible by further flight, suddenly dropped on his knees at the landing-place, close to a window, which has a very low sill, and tripping up his pursuer by the heels, pitched him headlong down into the yard beneath, and broke his neck by the fall.

The underground part of the White Tower was used for confinement of such prisoners as were to be deprived of all indulgence, and contained dungeons of the most gloomy description. These have been mostly cleared away and removed, in making room for the extensive stores of iron bedsteads, and other barrack furniture, which used to be accumulated here by the store depôt; but at the south-east angle of these vaults, there still exists a dark cell, closed by a heavy door, with no aperture for the admission of either light or air, and known by the ominous name of "Little Ease." In this cell Guy Fawkes was confined, previous to his examination and torture, which took place in the Governor's house, in presence of the Lords of the Council, of which particulars are given in another place. There has been lately discovered in the vaults of the White Tower another cell, with this inscription :—

> Sacris vestibus indutus
> dum sacra mysteria
> servans, captus et in
> hoc angusto carcere
> inclusus.   R. FISHER.

Somewhere also in the vaults of the White Tower was the cell mentioned in several of the records as "Cold Harbour," a denomination which has given rise to much discussion, from its having been applied, not only to places of confinement, but to several hamlets in different counties of England, without any apparent similarity of meaning. It is said that there are to be found in old English maps and itineraries, as many as fifteen or twenty "Cold Harbours," but whether they were places of confinement, it is vain now to conjecture. It has been remarked, as somewhat peculiar in the construction of the White Tower, that there is but one portion (that which supports the enormous weight of St. John's Chapel) which is vaulted. The floors of the Banqueting-hall and the Council-chamber are laid on huge oak joists, placed at very close intervals, and so strong and solid are they, that not the smallest deflection has ever been perceived in them, though, at one time, the weight of the stores placed on the floors which they supported, must have tested them severely. In Mr. Salvin's able restoration of this part of the Tower, an open space for admission of light from the council-chamber to the banqueting-hall beneath it has been judiciously left open in the flooring, exactly in its original state, in order to show the great size and perfect preservation of the ancient oak joists above mentioned. Round the whole of the council-chamber, a sort of gallery or corridor is cut in the thickness of the wall, which accords with the details of Shakespeare's celebrated scene of the Protector's sudden condemnation of Lord Hastings at the Council.* Here were probably concealed the armed men, by whom Hastings was hurried down into the court below, and, the block not being at hand, his head struck off upon a beam of timber, accidentally lying on the green.

One of the turrets on the corners of the roof of the White Tower is supposed to have been the scene of the imprisonment and murder of the unfortunate Matilda Fitz Walter, called Matilda the Fair, from her remarkable beauty. "About the year 1215," saith the Book of Dunmow, "there arose a great discord between King John and his barons, because of Matilda, surnamed the Fair, daughter of Robert Lord Fitz Walter, whom the King loved, but could not obtain her, nor her father's consent. Whereupon the King banished the said Fitz Walter, the most valiant Knight in England, and caused his Castle in London, called 'Baynard's,' and all his other dwellings, to be spoiled; which being done, he sent to Matilda about his old suit in love, and because she would not agree, the messenger poisoned an egg, and bade her keepers, when she was hungry, boil it, and give her to eat. She did so, and died."

Miss Strickland, in one of her most interesting Royal Lives, that of Isabella of Angoulême, observes, in speaking of the unhappy fate of Matilda Fitz Walter, "The

---

* RICHARD III., act iii. scene 4. *A room in the Tower.* BUCKINGHAM, STANLEY, HASTINGS, *the* BISHOP *of* ELY, CATESBY, LOVEL, *sitting at a table; Officers of the Council attending.*

abduction of this lady, who, to do her justice, thoroughly abhorred the royal felon, was the exploit which completed the exasperation of the English barons, who flew to arms, for the purpose of avenging the honour of the most distinguished among their class, Lord Fitz Walter."

The White Tower, like other parts of the Tower of London, has been subjected to much modern disfigurement. Even the eminent Sir Christopher Wren so entirely lost sight of architectural propriety in his restoration and repair of the White Tower, that he faced the windows with stone in the Italian style, and so disfigured this venerable building, that, until the stranger has entered within its massive walls, and observed their huge thickness and other evidence of its antiquity, he might suppose the White Tower to date no farther back than the time of Queen Anne or George I.

ST. PETER'S CHAPEL.

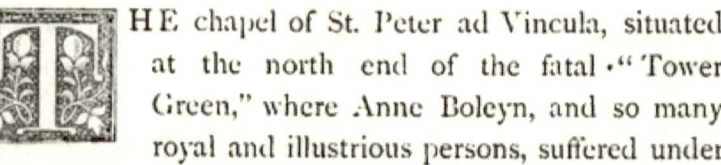HE chapel of St. Peter ad Vincula, situated at the north end of the fatal "Tower Green," where Anne Boleyn, and so many royal and illustrious persons, suffered under the stroke of the executioner, is a building of ancient date, but not remarkable for any architectural merit, beyond that of simplicity, and a certain justice of proportions which is always pleasing to the eye. It is inconceivable what pains have been taken, in comparatively modern times, to disfigure this interesting chapel. During the reign of George II. directions were given to adapt it for the reception of the troops for Divine Service, when, instead of the obvious expedient of throwing out a gallery or clerestory, on the north side and exterior to the main wall, the interior of the Chapel was defaced and encumbered by a projecting gallery along the north and west sides, such as may be seen in the worst style of country church of the last century. The handsome old doorway to the west was built up, and a brick and plaster porch was thrown out from the south front, for the entrance to the body of the Chapel. From this porch was carried up a narrow and inconvenient wooden

INTERIOR OF ST. PETER'S AD VINCULA, IN THE TOWER. 1866.

staircase, giving access to the west end of the soldiers' gallery.

In the year 1862 the old doorway was accidentally discovered concealed by a thick coat of plaster, and on the late Constable's representation, the First Commissioner of Works sanctioned its restoration, and the removal of the unsightly porch and staircase on the south side. One or two modern tablets which had been awkwardly fixed up across part of the windows were shifted, and an inspection being made of the ancient roof, by removal of the plaster over the chancel, brought to view the original woodwork, which was not in a bad condition. The whole of the ceiling was then carefully removed, and the woodwork of the roof now appears as originally intended by the architect. Near the Communion table there are two curious monuments of the Blounts, father and son, who were both Lieutenants of the Tower, and one of Sir Richard Cholmondeley and the Lady Elizabeth his wife, at the north-west corner of the Chapel. But the chief interest of St. Peter's Chapel consists in the number of royal and illustrious persons whose corpses lie buried beneath its pavement.

To enumerate some of the most remarkable :—

Queen Anne Boleyn.

Queen Katherine Howard.

Fisher, Bishop of Rochester.

Gerald, ninth Earl of Kildare, Lord Deputy of Ireland, one of the few who died a natural death. After a long confinement, he had at length every hope of release and restoration to his estates and honours, when the news arrived that his eldest son, "Silken Thomas," deceived by treacherous friends, had broken out into an open rebellion, which so grieved him that he died of a broken heart, 1534.

Thomas Cromwell, Earl of Essex, the leading actor in Henry VIII.'s suppression of papal supremacy.

In Edward VI.'s reign was buried here, after decapitation, Thomas Seymour, the Lord Admiral, brother of the Protector Somerset. The Protector himself fell a victim soon after to the combination of his enemies, and was buried by the side of his brother.

In Mary's reign this Chapel received the headless bodies of Lady Jane Grey and her husband Lord Guildford Dudley.

In Elizabeth's reign, Thomas Howard, Duke of Norfolk; Devereux, Earl of Essex, and other nobles were here interred after execution.

In James I.'s reign, Sir W. Raleigh here found rest after his life of vicissitude and trouble. There also lies among these noble persons, the body of Sir Gervase Elways, a man whose infamy should have excluded him from a spot where so many eminent persons found their last repose. This wretch, who had borne an active part in the poisoning of Overbury, was allowed his last request of being buried in St. Peter's Chapel, after being hanged on Tower Hill instead of Tyburn, a favour granted to his earnest entreaty, and to which in his dying speech he alluded with a singular satisfaction.

A visit to St. Peter's Chapel is recorded by Pepys in his 'Diary' with much complacency:—

"Lord's day, Feb. 28, 1663-4. The Lieutenant of the Tower, Sir J. Robinson, would needs have me by coach home with him, where the officers of his regiment (? of the Tower) dined with him. After dinner to chapel in the Tower with the Lieutenant, with the keys carried before us, and the Warders and Gentlemen porters going before us; and I sat with the Lieutenant in his pew, in great state. None, it seems, of the prisoners in the Tower that are there now (though they may) will come to prayers there."

In the vestry of St. Peter's Chapel may be seen the three leaden coffin-plates of the Scotch lords Kilmarnock, Balmerino, and Lovat (beheaded in 1746, and interred within the Tower). After the great fire in the Tower of 1841, some excavations were found necessary to obtain a solid foundation for the present Barracks, when a great number of old coffins were, with a vast quantity of bones, removed into the vaults on the north side of the Chapel. On that occasion these coffin-plates were discovered, and placed in the vestry, where they are carefully preserved in glass frames.

Against the south wall of the Chapel is affixed a small rough tablet, rescued from among a heap of rubbish when the pavement of the Chapel was repaired, about 1852. It records the burial of Talbot Edwards, the brave old guardian of the Regalia, at the time of the desperate attempt of the notorious Blood to carry off the crown, of which an account will be given in another place.

Plans have lately been submitted for the removal of the modern gallery, occupied by the troops, when attending Divine Service, and for converting the close pews into open seats; and, as this would be a work of no great expense, it may be hoped that, at no distant period, so manifest an improvement may be carried out.

The public take more interest daily in the Tower of London; and the best proof that the restorations effected within the last ten years have given general satisfaction, is the great increase in the receipts for admission tickets at the gate. When restorations and improvements of any ancient and historical building are properly explained, the House of Commons is not disposed to be illiberal, but the difficulty generally arises from the desire on the part of the Chancellor of the Exchequer to cut down the public expenditure in every branch which does not come prominently before the public observation.

RICHARD II. (1377.)

IN the early troubles of Richard II.'s reign the Tower was his chief residence, and on more than one occasion proved his safest protection against the London mob. It was from the Tower stairs that the young King embarked when he first attempted, from his barge on the Thames, to pacify the armed crowds which had assembled on the shore at Rotherhithe. But the tumult overpowered his endeavours to address them, and he had no option but to return to the Tower. The excited mob followed him along the bank, and, crossing the bridge, occupied the ground about St. Katherine's, "hooting," as Froissart tells us, "as loud as if the very devils were in them."

The gallant Mayor, Walworth, who was in the fortress with the King, proposed to make a sally at night, when most of the mob would be drunk; but other advisers induced the King to attempt a further parley, and to meet the leaders at Mile-end, in order to hear their grievances. Scarcely had he passed out of the gate, when a party of rebels placed in ambush made a rush and burst into the Tower. The Archbishop of Canterbury, Sir R. Hales, and other knights, betook themselves to the Sanctuary of

St. Peter, but were torn from the very altar, and their heads struck off upon the spot, after which great plunder was committed, and the King's mother, the widow of the Black Prince, treated with insolence and brutality. Historians have given detailed accounts of the result of the young King's spirited behaviour, after Walworth had struck down Wat Tyler; and there is the following quaint narrative of what passed afterwards, in the 'Chronicle of London:'—

"And on the morrow after, that is to saye Fryday, and than on the Satirday after Corpus Christ.-day, the Kyng anon after, rood into Smythfield, and Willm. Walworth, than beinge Maire of London, Sir Robert Knollys, and Aldermenne, and other citezeins with hym; and there they metten with Jake Straw, leder of the uprysers; and this Jake Strawe spak to the Kyng hoded, as it hadde bene to his fellawe; and John Blyton that bar the Maire's swerd, bad him don his hodde, while he spak to the Kyng; whereat Jack Strawe wax angred and mynte to caste his dagger at Blyton. And than Wm. Walworth drewe his 'baselard' and smote Jack Strawe on his hed; and with that Rauf Standyshe, that bar the King's swerd, roof Jack Straw through his bodye, and there he fel down ded."

At a later period (1387) Richard had to seek safety again within the Tower walls, from his uncle the Duke of Gloucester and the Barons, whom his recklessness and misgovernment had exasperated against him. The Duke of Ireland marched a force to his assistance, while the Barons drew near London with 40,000 men. The Duke secretly sent three of his knights into the city, to test the temper of the citizens. They quitted their horses and followers at Kennington, and, taking boat near Vauxhall, were rowed down to the Tower, and entered by the water-gate unobserved by the rebels. But learning from the Governor, the strong animosity of the citizens of London against Richard, they withdrew, as privately as they had come. The Duke of Ireland was attacked and defeated, and the King besieged again in the Tower, where a parley having been held with the rebel leader in the council-room, the King found himself obliged to accept their terms, and to submit to the sorrow and humiliation of giving up Sir Simon Burley, his oldest and most devoted adherent, to the vengeance of Gloucester and Arundel.

This noble veteran of Edward III.'s wars, who had been placed about Richard's person by the Black Prince, as his governor and tutor, was beheaded on Tower Hill, though the "good Queen Anne" fell on her knees in tears before Gloucester, to obtain his life.

Richard never forgave this outrage; and when Gloucester's party were afterwards overthrown, the death of Burley was one of the chief reasons which led him to take so terrible a revenge on Gloucester, by causing him to be secretly put to death in prison in the Castle of Calais. Richard II. also seized his leading adherents, the Earls of Arundel and Warwick, and both were condemned to die as traitors. Arundel was beheaded in Cheapside, where he was led from the Tower; but so much intercession was made for Warwick, on account of his former military services in France, that Richard spared his life, on the condition (a very curious one it appears in these days) that he should go into perpetual exile in the Isle of Wight; an island, observes Froissart, in his narrative of these events, "where there is room enough for a great nobleman's establishment, only he must take with him every kind of provision and furniture, or he would find himself under much discomfort!"

But Richard's prosperity was of short duration. Henry of Bolingbroke raised an army against him, and after various successes made him prisoner and lodged him in the Tower, where, with a barbarous refinement of cruelty, four or five of his most faithful adherents, accused of having been concerned in the death of Gloucester, were brought under the window of the King's prison, tied to horses' tails, and dragged through the streets to Cheapside, there to suffer an ignominious death. After this humiliation, Richard was compelled to go through a formal ceremony in the Council-chamber of the White Tower, of resigning his crown and sceptre to the Usurper. He was kept close prisoner during the magnificent pageant of Henry IV.'s coronation, when an attempt at a rising having been prematurely made by some who still adhered to him, he was removed to Leeds Castle, and thence to Pomfret, where, according to Hollingshed, he was murdered. Froissart's version is, however, different, for he states that he perished "somehow" in the Tower. His remains however were, as both agree, eventually conveyed from the Tower, in a procession to St. Paul's Cathedral, "where he lay," says Froissart, "his head on a black cushion, and his visage open to view.

Some had pity on him, and some had none, but said he had long ago deserved his death." He was carried to Langley and there buried, but his corpse was afterwards removed to Westminster Abbey.

Shakespeare's pathetic scene of the parting between Richard and his unhappy queen was doubtless drawn with little alteration of fact from the chronicles and traditions current in his day.*

---

* RICHARD II., act v. scene 2. *A Street leading to the Tower.*

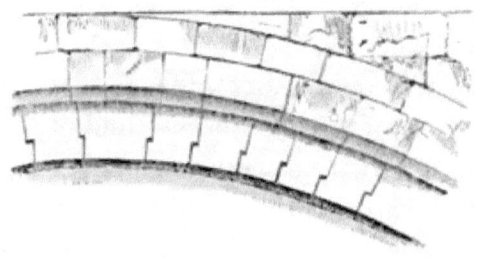

JOGGLED MASONRY IN GREAT ARCH OF TRAITORS' GATE.

PRISONERS OF AGINCOURT, AND CHARLES OF ORLEANS.

THE Battle of Agincourt, that extraordinary victory, gained, against all the usual chances of war, by the cool and deliberate courage which has been from the earliest times the characteristic quality of English troops, filled the Tower with illustrious and noble prisoners.

The Chivalry of the times, though it led the captors to spare the lives of persons of birth and quality, did not prevent them from taking every possible pecuniary advantage of the unhappy position of their prisoners. The personal captivity of a great landed proprietor was consequently a cause of the utmost distress, and damage, to his estates and family. Too often it occurred, that the neighbour encroached; the tenants eluded the payment of their rents and services; the stewards, and all concerned in the property, took advantage of their master's absence; and, worst of all, his feudal chief, or sovereign, frequently increased the evil by his extortions, instead of acting as a protector to the family and estates of the captive vassal.

Though Henry V. probably treated his noble pri-

soners of Agincourt with as much courtesy and regard as was customary at the time, yet he was not a man to scruple at screwing out the utmost amount of ransom which a prisoner of distinction could produce, by heavy impositions on his vassals. Shakespeare's graphic dialogue between Henry V. and the royal herald on the field of battle shows the prodigious number of the French nobility that fell into his hands by that memorable victory:—

"*King Hen.:* What prisoners of good sort are taken?
Exeter: Charles Duke of Orleans, nephew to the King;
John Duke of Bourbon, and Lord Boucicault.
Of other lords and barons, knights and squires,
Full fifteen hundred." *

We find from various authorities, that although these illustrious personages were, in the first instance, treated with the respect due to their rank and misfortunes, yet after time had been allowed them for free communication with their families and territories, in order to collect the vast sums demanded for their liberty, restrictions and hardships were imposed by their captor, as a means of inducing more prompt and effective measures on the part of their friends and dependants for collecting their ransoms. That of Charles of Orleans (who before his capture had the ill fortune to be grievously wounded in the battle) was fixed at an enormous sum, equal to about 50,000*l.* of our present money; and his noble companions the Dukes of Bourbon and Boucicault died in

---

* HENRY V., act iv. scene 8.

the Tower, while vainly awaiting the collection in France of equally large ransoms, levied with much delay and difficulty, on the inhabitants of their exhausted and ruined lands.

It was this Charles of Orleans who, a very few years after the murder of Richard II., married his young widow, Isabella, who had been sent back to France by Bolinbroke. Perhaps there is not in all his plays a more beautiful and touching scene than that in which Shakespeare describes the parting of Richard with his young queen. Isabella did not long survive her marriage to Charles of Orleans, who deeply lamented her death, little aware of the wretched existence which awaited her, had she survived to bewail the long and sad captivity in which he afterwards languished in the Tower, till his ransom was at length paid in the year 1440, after an imprisonment of twenty-five years, the greater part of which was of a rigorous nature, though relaxed a few years before his release.

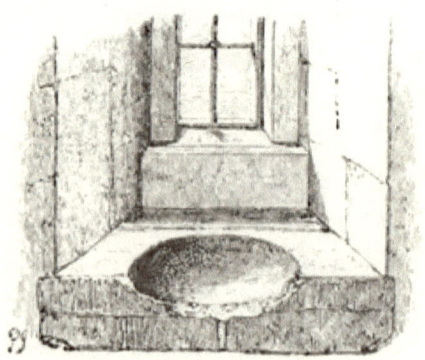

PISCINA, ST. THOMAS'S TOWER.

MURDER OF THE PRINCES. (1483).

NE of the most terrible mysteries of the Tower is the question how Richard III. disposed of his unfortunate nephews, after consigning them to that imprisonment, from which they never issued alive.

Taking the tradition as generally received, Richard, after giving all the necessary orders for the ceremony of his nephew's coronation (there is evidence that even his robes were prepared), somewhat suddenly declared his intention of seizing the crown, and caused the Lieutenant of the Tower, Sir Robert Brackenbury, to be sounded, as to whether he would undertake to make away with the young King and his brother. Brackenbury is said to have received Richard's message while kneeling at his devotions in St. John's Chapel, in the White Tower, and to have rejected so dreadful a task. Richard, in consequence of his refusal, gave authority to James Tyrrell to receive from Brackenbury the temporary charge of the Tower and the prisoners within its walls. This being arranged, Tyrrell employed Dighton and Forest, two unscrupulous assassins, to take the lives of the royal children, which was accomplished by smothering them with the pillows of their bed. Their bodies were then buried within the Tower, nor does it appear that Richard ever at any time alluded to them afterwards, or attempted to account for their disappearance. There was no announcement of their illness, or of their death from natural causes, no ceremony of a funeral, or any further public notice of the fate of the princes.

The appearance at the court of Burgundy, some years afterwards (1492), of the youth who assumed the name of the Duke of York, was the first we hear of the matter from the time of the supposed murder. But though there have been many details handed down by contemporaries and writers who lived no long time after these occurrences, history affords no circumstantial narrative or relation, to show by what means, or by whose assistance, the pretended Duke of York had avoided his brother's fate, and contrived to escape from the Tower and elude the vigilance of his uncle by flight beyond sea. Was Richard a man to neglect any act of caution, or to shrink from any violence in regard to the custody, or in respect to the escape of such a prisoner as the Duke of York? and could it be effected by a boy of such tender years without powerful aid, and the concurrence of a considerable number of influential persons? But if the impostor really was the Duke, what had become of his elder brother? Did those who managed to save the younger make no attempt to rescue the elder and more important victim? If Edward was not murdered, what became of him? Had he died a natural death, would not Richard have given it every notoriety? Would he not have exposed the body to public view, as was done in the case of Henry VI.? and would he not by a public funeral, and by other marks of respect, have tried to convince the world that there had been no foul play, or, at all events, that he had had no hand in the disappearance of Edward V.?

Again, why is there no record of the existence of Edward V. as a prisoner in the Tower, from the momen when Richard usurped the crown? Up to that time we find his uncle's orders for his clothing and provisions on a scale to be expected for the maintenance of a Royal Personage. It has been asked, why should the Duchess of Burgundy, Edward IV.'s sister, have acknowledged Perkin Warbeck as her nephew, if she had any doubt of his identity? Now, supposing her to have been really deceived by his plausible tale, how little opportunity could she have had, in those times, of a thorough scrutiny into events, which it was Richard's whole object to veil in mystery and darkness, and over which his assumption of the regal power gave him a control, amply sufficient to defeat any attempt of a foreign princess to investigate the facts. On the other hand, her personal aversion to Henry, the political state of Europe, and the scanty communication between Burgundy and England, would account for her more readily adopting the imposture, and doing all in her power to damage the character of the King, and his title to the crown.

As the murder of the Princes has been called in question, so the localities attributed to its perpetration have been disputed on various grounds. A small chamber in the Bloody Tower has, by long tradition, been assigned as the spot where the barbarous deed was done; and notwithstanding the professed doubts of Bailey and other writers, no more probable or likely place has been named. We know that this chamber was closely adjoining to the Governor's house, where so many prisoners of rank have been confined, when security, rather than severity of imprisonment, was the object in view. Indeed, in the older accounts of the buildings within the fortress, we frequently find it called the Garden Tower, from its adjoining the Governor's private garden. It is remarkable that, in a complimentary oration in Latin (still in preservation), with which the authorities of the Tower received James I. at the gate, on his first visit to the fortress after his accession, express mention is made of the "Bloody Tower," as the scene of the Princes' murder.

Now this visit of James I. took place within 120 years of the usurpation of Richard; and there could be no necessity, or even plausible reason, for alluding to it in the Latin 'Oration' above mentioned, had it not been a matter of common belief and notoriety, that the Bloody Tower was the scene of the murder, and that a description of the principal features of the Tower by the orator, would have been incomplete without such notice of the fact.

It was always a sequel to the tradition of the murder of the Princes, that "the priest of the Tower" had buried their bodies in some concealed place (Shakespeare puts this fact in the mouth of Tyrrell); and surely it was not unreasonable to infer, when two children's bodies, corresponding in age, and period of decay, with the date of the murder, were discovered in Charles II.'s time, by some workmen, at the foot of a staircase, about seventy yards distant from the Bloody Tower, that these were the bones of the Princes. There were two consecrated burial-grounds within the Tower, besides that of Barking Church on Tower Hill, close by; and what likelihood was there,

THE BLOODY TOWER.

under those circumstances, of two boys being buried in this sequestered nook, under a staircase, unless with a view to secrecy and concealment? Again, had the bones been those of grown persons, it might be conjectured that two unfortunate prisoners had been quietly made away with in those disturbed times, and buried in secret, but there is no probable cause for this having occurred in respect to two boys, even if there were traces or records of any other youthful prisoners, except Edward V. and his brother, having been in the Tower at all.

Charles II. was by no means of a credulous nature; very much the reverse; and he had, moreover, a considerable turn for investigation, and took much interest in all matters of history. His adoption, therefore, of the tradition of the murder of the Princes, as commonly accepted at the time, must surely be regarded as a strong confirmation of the story.

Had not Charles been fully convinced that these bones were those of the princes, why should he have gone to the trouble and expense of transferring them, with all the respect paid to Royal remains, to the vaults of Westminster Abbey? There could be no political or public reason for his doing so; and we must in fairness, therefore, attribute it to his conviction, that he was paying the respect due to the remains of these victims of cruelty and ambition, by consigning their bodies to the resting-place of their royal ancestors.

It was by Charles II.'s orders, as the tradition went, that Sir Thomas Chicheley, his Master-General of the Ordnance, planted a mulberry-tree on the spot where the Princes' bodies were found; but with a vandalism to which the Tower has too often been subjected, a staircase was built up in 1674 against the wall, which caused the

LANDING-PLACE ON STAIRS, WHITE TOWER
Spot under which the Bones of the Princes were discovered.

rapid decay of the mulberry-tree. There was, however, in 1853, an old Warder who well recollected to have seen the stump still imbedded in the landing of the stairs. If the tale be true that Richard ordered their burial in consecrated ground, it accounts for their being laid here, because the stairs leading up to St. John's Chapel would be considered as under the same consecration as the chapel itself.

Miss Strickland, with her usual research and accuracy, has traced out the very important details of the vast rewards bestowed by Richard on Tyrrell and his assistants in the murder. Tyrrell was made Captain or Governor of the town of Guisnes, near Calais, and further received three rich stewardships from Richard, in the Marches of Wales. Dighton was made Bailiff of the town of Ayton, with a pension. Green was named to the Receivership of the Isle of Wight. Forrest's widow had a pension given her on his death, shortly after the murder; and ample general pardons were granted to them, whatever villanies might be laid to their charge; all under the royal hand and seal, not naming for what offence, but covering any, and all. Sir James Tyrrell, according to Miss Strickland's investigation, actually confessed the murder, just before he was beheaded by order of Henry VII., in 1502, for favouring the escape of John de la Pole, on whom his uncle Richard had settled the succession to the crown. Dighton also confessed his part in the murder, when hanged at Calais, soon after Tyrrell's execution; and at the same time declared his knowledge of the old priest having buried the bodies, first under the Wakefield Tower, and a second time in some place of which he had no knowledge.

EARLS OF KILDARE.

ROM the time of Henry II.'s conquest of Ireland disturbances had never ceased to prevail in that country, arising partly from the impatience with which the native Irish submitted to their rulers, and partly from the dissensions constantly occurring among those rulers themselves. The most powerful of the Norman Lords of the Pale, the Earls of Kildare, of Desmond, and of Ormonde, were a constant cause of anxiety to the English Government. In Henry VII.'s reign Gerald Earl of Kildare (Mr. Froude erroneously calls him Thomas) warmly espoused the cause of the two successive pretenders, Lambert Simnel and Perkin Warbeck, and, raising a body of troops, carried fire and sword through the Pale, till the able Sir E. Poynings was sent over as Chief Governor, who succeeded in defeating the Earl of Kildare, and making him prisoner. Uncivilized and brutal as were these half Norman and half Irish nobles, they appear to have possessed a large share of ready wit, and a freedom and chivalry of address, which stood them in good stead when summoned to London to answer for their misdeeds. Gerald, the eighth earl, when brought before the King

and Council, was warned by Henry himself that great crimes were alleged against him, but that he should have a fair trial, and might choose some fit person to plead for him. He answered boldly, "I will choose the ablest in England, for I will take your Highness yourself for my counsel against these false knaves."

In the course of the trial it was laid to Gerald's charge that he had burned the cathedral of Cashel. The Earl did not attempt to deny the fact, but contented himself with declaring, as his defence, that he would never have set fire to the cathedral had he not been assured that the Archbishop was inside of it. This extraordinary plea so amused the King and his Council, that upon one of them observing, "All Ireland could not govern this Earl," the King replied, "This Earl shall govern all Ireland."

So fully did Gerald acquit himself of the charges of treason, and succeed in gaining Henry VII.'s good graces, that he returned to Ireland a Knight of the Garter, and with Elizabeth the daughter of Oliver St. John (a gentleman high in the royal favour) for his wife. Although he ruled over the country with a hand of iron, and little regard to justice or law, yet he maintained a tolerable condition of order; and the Lords of the Pale, as well as the Irish, were kept in a comparatively peaceable state till his death, in 1513, a period of nearly twenty years.

His son Gerald, the ninth Earl, was allowed by Henry VIII. to succeed his father as Chief Governor; but such strong proofs of intended rebellion were brought against him, that, in 1520, the Earl of Surrey was sent over to supersede him, and transmit him prisoner to London, where he was lodged in the Tower. However, by his loyal professions, and the grace and courtesy of his manners, the Earl contrived so to ingratiate himself with the King, that, releasing him from prison, Henry took him in his suite to the Field of the Cloth of Gold, where the young Irish nobleman gained such applause by his skill in the tournament, and noble carriage and behaviour, that, on the King's return to London, he was allowed to become a suitor of Lady Elizabeth Grey, daughter of the Marquis of Dorset, and nearly allied to the blood royal, and, after a short probation, to marry her. Though not immediately restored to the government of Ireland, yet, in consequence of the alleged misconduct of Ormonde, who had succeeded Surrey, he was soon after (1524) again made Governor. It was not long before Henry had reason to repent his choice, for on the breaking out of war with France in that year the Earl of Kildare entered into secret relations with the Earl of Desmond, who had actually commenced a negotiation with Francis I. for the invasion of Ireland by a French army. The peace between England and France having put an end to this project, Kildare opened a similar proposition to the Emperor Charles V. through the Earl of Desmond, pretending all the while to be at enmity with that Chieftain.

Again the King's suspicions were excited, and again was Kildare summoned to London in 1527; but his sagacity and shrewdness enabled him to clear himself, and Henry appointed him to act as a sort of adviser to his natural son the Duke of Richmond, who became

Chief Governor; Sir W. Skeffington, a veteran officer in favour with the King, being appointed to command the English troops.

Allen, one of those able men who owed their first advancement to the discernment of Wolsey, was nominated Archbishop of Dublin, and directed to keep a sharp watch on Kildare. Meantime the most violent feuds broke out between the Geraldines and Butlers, while O'Neill ravaged the province of Ulster.

In consequence probably of Archbishop Allen's reports to the King, Kildare was for the third time summoned to London, and, without any form of trial, thrown into the Tower. The King had got wind of the negotiation with Charles V.; and Pope Clement having proceeded to his sentence of excommunication of Henry, there was every likelihood of the troubles in Ireland assuming a religious character.

The son of Kildare, Lord Thomas Fitzgerald, best known as "Silken Thomas," accompanied his father to London, but was not imprisoned with him, and shortly returned to Ireland. Historians have differed as to whether it was with his father's sanction or not that Silken Thomas, on his return, broke out into rebellion. It is not likely that Kildare would have desired his son to do that which must imperil his own life; and the most probable version is, that his son's rash and hopeless rebellion was not approved or instigated by the Earl. It is at all events certain that Lord Thomas, breaking violently into the presence of the Council, seized the sword of state, and, abjuring all further allegiance to the King, dashed it on the table, and, mounting his horse, galloped off with a large body of his adherents to raise the country in rebellion.

At the head of several thousand men he laid siege to Dublin, and obliged Sir J. White, who commanded the garrison, to withdraw into the Castle. Archbishop Allen endeavoured to escape to England in a small vessel, which, unobserved by the Irish, dropped down the Liffey to the sea; but, unluckily, the master, being attached to the Geraldines, ran her on shore at Clontarf, and, sending a messenger to Dublin, betrayed the unfortunate Archbishop. Silken Thomas rode down to Clontarf with three of his uncles, and caused him to be dragged from the pallet where he had lain down, in a small cabin, for repose; and one of the savage followers of the Geraldine having struck him on the head as he kneeled for mercy, he was instantly despatched with numerous wounds, and his body treated with every indignity.

Although Silken Thomas afterwards attempted to show that he had had no intention of committing this ruthless murder, yet all doubt must be removed by the fact of his having written to boast of the deed, both to the Emperor and to the Pope.

The siege of Dublin Castle was now pressed hard; but Ormonde, with his brave Butlers, made so gallant an assault on the Geraldine forces that he forced his way through their lines and relieved White when at the last extremity.

Sir W. Skeffington arrived a few days after with a considerable body of troops from Wales; and though he acted with little decision or promptitude himself, yet his lieutenant, Sir W. Brereton, entered the Liffey with five or six hundred men, and at once restored confidence in Dublin. Silken Thomas withdrew with his troops in confusion into the country; but not finding himself pursued by Skeffington, who was in a bad state of health, as well as far advanced in years, made some attempts with parties of horse to harass the English posts round Dublin. The inactivity of Skeffington being reported to Henry, he sent over Lord Leonard Grey, brother to the Countess of Kildare, to act as marshal of the army. Roused by the arrival of Lord Leonard, Skeffington marched upon Maynooth Castle, the stronghold of the Geraldines, and, besieging it with heavy cannon (supposed to be the first employed in a siege in Ireland), took the castle by storm, and barbarously hanged the survivors of the garrison.

Meantime the news of these proceedings in Ireland, and the expectation of the King's vengeance, so affected the unfortunate Earl in his prison, that he expired, after a short illness, and was buried in the Tower chapel. Lord Thomas, driven to the last extremities, and deserted by most of his followers, was induced by Lord Leonard to surrender on hopes of pardon. How far Lord Leonard may be said to have entrapped his unfortunate nephew by false assurances was never quite clear; but the result was the seizure and committal to the Tower of Lord Thomas and his five uncles. His name and arms carved on the gloomy wall of the Beauchamp Tower bear witness to his confinement in that dreary prison, which lasted about a year before he was taken to Tyburn and there hanged, with his uncles. It was said that the Duke of Norfolk advised this cruel delay, on the ground that to execute them at once would have cast dishonour on Lord Leonard Grey; while, on the other hand, if a certain time were allowed previously to elapse, other circumstances might be supposed to have transpired concerning their rebellion which would to a certain degree disconnect their execution from the actual seizure and delivery of their persons by their kinsman.

CINQUEFOIL-HEADED LOOP IN WHITE TOWER.

EXECUTION OF ANNE BOLEYN.

N Her present Majesty's first visit to the Tower of London, the spot in front of St. Peter's Chapel, where the unfortunate Anne Boleyn received her death-stroke, was pointed out as one of melancholy interest, and by Her Majesty's personal commands a small brass tablet recording the event was placed in the middle of the space where the scaffold upon which she received the blow of the executioner had been erected. The suddenness of this unfortunate lady's transition from favour to disgrace, and from disgrace to death, is not the least affecting part of her story.

It was on the 1st May, 1536, that during a tournament at Greenwich, she dropped her handkerchief, which one of the courtiers took up and put to his face with such a gesture as to excite the King's suspicions; if indeed those suspicions ever in reality existed, or were other than the pretence for removing Anne, to make way for the new object of his desire. Next day the Queen's brother, Lord Rochford, Norris, Weston, and Brereton, all gentlemen about the Court, and Smeton, a musician, were committed, and Anne herself arrested and placed in the

Tower, under charge of Sir W. Kingston, the Lieutenant, entreating in vain to speak but one word to the King, and solemnly protesting her innocence of any offence against him. That officer, in his letter to Secretary Cromwell, tells him, that as he led the Queen to her lodgings, she asked was she to go into a dungeon? to which he had said, "No, Madam, but to the same lodging where she lay before her coronation."

"It is gude for me, she sayd; Jesu have mercy on me; and kneeled down weeping apace, and in the same sorrow fell into great lawyng, which she hath often done since"—violent hysterics caused by her distress and terror were probably what Kingston described as "lawyng." He further tells the Secretary, of her passionate protestation of her innocence, and of her expressions of sorrow for her brother, and the other gentlemen involved, for no fault of theirs, in the cruel accusations of her enemies.

Sir W. Kingston seems to have been deeply touched with the unhappy Queen's behaviour, and though he was ordered to set Lady Kingston to watch for any unguarded words she might utter, he evidently obeyed these orders with pain, and mitigated the misery of her position as far as he dared.

On the 10th of May, the three gentlemen accused of familiarities with the Queen were tried, and, without a shadow of proof, declared guilty. On the 13th, the Queen and her brother were tried in the Council Chamber of the Tower, and on charges the most frivolous and unreasonable. Rochford was found guilty. The wretched Smeton was, by false hopes of life, induced to confess the guilt of

INTERIOR OF THE BEAUCHAMP TOWER.

the Queen, upon which evidence she was condemned, by direct instructions to the Court from her barbarous husband, to die either by burning or beheading, according to the King's pleasure. On the 17th, Rochford with the other three gentlemen was beheaded on Tower Hill; and Smeton, in violation of the promise of life by which the condemnation of the Queen had been so basely extorted from him, was hanged at the same time.

Kingston's letter, written next morning to Cromwell,

informs him that, according to his orders, he had caused all strangers to be put out of the Tower, suggesting at the same time that it would be best to have a reasonable number of persons admitted to witness the Queen's execution. " This morning," he says, "she sent for me, that I might be with her at such time as she received the 'Gude Lord' (sacrament), to the intent that I should hear her touching her innocency, &c. At my coming she sayd, ' Mr. Kingston, I heare I shall not dye afore noon ; and I am very sorry therefore ; for I thought to be dead now and past my pain. I told her it would be no pain, it was so sotell" (alluding to the skill of the headsman). Then she sayd, ' I have heard the executioner was very good, and I have a lyttel neck,' and put her hand about it lawing hartily. I have seen many men, and also women executed, and they have been in great sorrowe ; but to my knowinge thys ladye has much joy and pleasure in death."

The Queen had afterwards an interview with Lady Kingston, in which she made the most affecting and solemn protestation of her innocence, probably rather to relieve her overburthened heart, than with any hope of mercy from the King. Next day the unhappy Queen was brought out for execution in front of the chapel upon Tower Green.

The exclusion of the public had no doubt been deemed necessary, lest the sight of her beauty and her declarations of innocence might excite a popular tumult. About thirty persons were appointed by the King to be present as witnesses of her death. She behaved with much resignation and self-command, kneeling down to receive the stroke of death, but without any block before her, as the Calais executioner did not use the axe, but one of those long, heavy, two-handled swords, which were formerly used in some cities of Germany, as the instruments of execution. As she could not refrain from turning her eyes on the man, he became nervous and uncertain how to deal his blow, when at last he took off his shoes, and causing his assistant to approach and attract her attention on the right, he stepped up behind her left shoulder, and with one heavy sweep of his huge sword, struck off her head in an instant. No respect was shown to the Queen's body, which was thrown into a chest made for holding bows and arrows, and buried, along with the corpse of her brother, in St. Peter's Chapel. Such was the end of this most unfortunate lady, who but three years before had entered the Tower in triumph as the idol of the King, and the admiration of all around her. Levities which even now would be thought slight and pardonable, but which in that coarse and licentious Court could hardly deserve even a moderate censure, were the only offences proved against her, unless the extorted accusation of Smeton can be regarded as proof of any deeper guilt.

On the other hand, she had by her gentleness and frequent mediation, between her savage husband and those who had the ill fortune to offend him, gained the favour of the nobility and the affection of the people; and the precaution used at her execution showed the likelihood of an insurrectionary movement, had the public been allowed to assemble within the Tower and to witness this cruel scene.

ANNE ASKEW.

THIS young lady was the daughter of Sir W. Askew, of an old Lincolnshire family. She was married early to a Mr. Kyme; but unhappily it was a marriage entirely of interest, and arranged by the two families without any reference to Anne's inclinations, which from the bad character of young Kyme, as well as his religious bigotry, were wholly averse to it. Overruled by her father, she at length reluctantly consented; and though she conducted herself admirably as a wife, and bore to Mr. Kyme two children, his dissipation and neglect prevented any conjugal happiness between them. Having received a learned education, and being of studious habits, she turned readily from her domestic sorrows to the study of the Bible, now for the first time accessible to the English laity, and became a professed follower of Wickliffe. Her husband, who, without any real principles of religion, was an intolerant Papist, took occasion from this circumstance to cast her off, and expel her from his house, when she betook herself to a residence in London, where she had many friends favourable to the reformed opinions. Queen Katherine Parr herself was among the friends of Mrs.

Kyme; and it has been said that Anne was placed in some situation about the Queen's person for a short time. The promulgation of the Six Articles, sometimes called the "Whip with six strings," which the tyrant Henry VIII. had set up as the standard for his subjects' faith, tended to draw closer those friends of Anne Kyme who shared her religious opinions, and who probably foresaw the persecutions which awaited her. There is reason to suppose that her own unworthy husband combined with others to place spies about her in London, who soon found an occasion of denouncing her for expressions which brought her under the general charge of heresy. In March, 1545, she was summoned before an Inquest or Commission at Guildhall, and subjected to a long examination by one Dare, when she displayed an intelligence and shrewdness which, with her modest, gentle demeanour, drew the admiration even of her enemies. Being remanded to the Compter, she was shortly after brought before Bishop Bonner for examination, who exercised all his subtlety to entangle her in her replies; and at length drew out a written summary, in which he had grossly perverted their meaning, and desired her, after hearing it read, to declare whether or not she would subscribe to its contents. Her answer merits to be recorded. "I believe," she said, "as much thereof as is agreeable to the Holy Scriptures; and I desire that this sentence may be added to it." Furious at what he called her obstinate evasions, Bonner was about to proceed to violent extremities, when by the intercession of some powerful friends, and probably for other reasons, she was allowed to be released on the bail of her cousin, one Brittayne, who, during the examination, at which he was present, had judiciously entreated the Bishop "not to set her weak woman's wit to his lordship's great wisdom."

We have no record of the cause, or rather pretext, of her being, about three months afterwards, again arrested. This time her husband, Kyme, was brought up along with her before the Privy Council, sitting at Greenwich.

Wriothesley, the Chancellor, now undertook her examination, and chiefly on the great point of Transubstantiation, on which she firmly refused to abandon her own convictions, and was committed to Newgate; from whence she wrote some devotional letters, which show her to have possessed considerable talent. Her next appearance was before the Council, at Guildhall, when, after an examination by a silly Lord Mayor (Martin), in which she entirely foiled him by her simplicity and good sense, she was plainly told, that unless she renounced her errors, and distinctly declared her acquiescence in the Six Articles, she must prepare to die; and, on her firm refusal, she was condemned, without any trial by jury, to be burned as an heretic. Meantime, instead of being sent back to Newgate, she was committed to the Tower, with a view to subject her to the torture of the rack, for which the gloomy seclusion of that fortress afforded greater convenience than the ordinary prison of Newgate, with the hope of inducing her to criminate the Duchess of Suffolk, the Countess of Sussex, the Countess of Hertford, and other ladies, who were supposed to have assisted her with money for her support in prison. She was too high-minded and grateful to betray them; and whatever might have been the case, she declared that she had been chiefly kept from starvation by her faithful maid, who went out and begged for her of the "prentices and others he met in the street."

The unhappy lady was now carried to a dungeon, and laid on the rack in presence of the Lieutenant of the Tower, Sir A. Knyvett, and Wriothesley, the Chancellor, Rich, a creature of Bonner's, and a secretary, sitting at her side, to take down her words. But when she endured the torture without opening her lips in reply to the Chancellor's questions, he became furious, and seizing the wheel himself, strained it with all his force, till Knyvett, revolting at such cruelty, insisted on her release from the dreadful machine. It was but in time to save her life, for she had twice swooned, and her limbs had been so stretched, and her joints so injured, that she was never again able to walk without support. Wriothesley hastened to Westminster to complain to the King of the Lieutenant's lenity; but the latter, getting into his barge with a favourable tide, arrived before him, obtained immediate audience, and told his tale so honestly, and with such earnestness, that Henry's hard heart was softened, and, approving his conduct, he dismissed him with favour: a stronger reason for this may have been that the rack was regarded with such horror by the people as to be applied only in secrecy; and had Anne expired under it, and the fact become known, some violent outbreak might have been apprehended in the

City. She was shortly afterwards carried to Smithfield, and there burned to ashes, together with three other persons, for the same cause, in the presence of the Duke of Norfolk, the Earl of Bedford, Sir Thomas Wriothesley, the Lord Mayor, and a vast concourse of people. One of the peers, learning that there was some gunpowder about the stakes, became frightened lest any accident should happen to *himself*, from the faggots being blown into the air; but the Earl of Bedford assuring him that no such chance could occur, and it was only to hasten the deaths of the sufferers, he remained looking on with the same barbarous indifference as the brutal mob, who had assembled to witness the dreadful spectacle.

FIREPLACE IN WHITE TOWER.

EDWARD COURTENAY, EARL OF DEVONSHIRE. 1553.

ALTHOUGH this unfortunate victim of the jealousy and caution of Henry VIII. was in no respect a prominent historical character, except as regards the high and peculiar position in which his birth had placed him in relation to the English Crown, yet few have been so unhappily remarkable for one of those long and weary captivities of the Tower which seem almost painful to record.

During the short period he was allowed to emerge from his prison, he had just time to taste those pleasures of life and youth to which his noble manners and handsome person would have given him easy and agreeable access, when he was again confined, and released only to end his few remaining days in a foreign land.

Edward Courtenay, Earl of Devonshire and Marquis of Exeter, was born about 1526, and when his father was beheaded, he being then twelve years old, was committed to the Tower, lest "he should avenge his father's wrongs." He continued there through the reigns of Henry VIII. and Edward VI., being excepted by name from the general pardon proclaimed on the coronation of the latter. On the accession of Mary to the throne she set him free, and showed him much favour, and some say, from his personal beauty and his royal extraction, was disposed to single him out from among her various suitors. He, however, showed a great preference for the Princess Elizabeth, and thus falling into disfavour with the Queen, was again committed to the Tower, whence, after a year's imprisonment, he obtained the Queen's leave to travel to Italy, and died at Padua, October 4th of the same year, 1556.* "This Earl was born to be a prisoner, for from twelve years of age to almost thirty, when he died, he had enjoyed scarcely two years of liberty." He was the twelfth Earl of Devonshire of that name and family, second Marquis of Exeter, and fifteenth Baron of Okehampton.

* See Cleaveland's 'History of Courtenay Family.'

THE PRINCESS ELIZABETH.

THE day after Sir Thomas Wyatt broke out into open rebellion, Sir Richard Southwell, Sir Edward Hastings, and Sir Thomas Cornwallis, were despatched to the house of the Princess Elizabeth, at Ashridge, in Hertfordshire, with a guard of two hundred and fifty horse, to bring her a prisoner to London; and the manner in which these gentlemen executed their commission, reflects but little honour on their names. Elizabeth was at the time confined by severe illness, and, notwithstanding that the messengers did not arrive at Ashridge till ten o'clock at night, they immediately sent her word, that they were bearers of a message from the Queen, and forced their way straight to her bedroom, a rudeness at which her high spirit revolted. Although worn down by sickness, her manner of receiving them marked her indignation at their conduct. She expressed surprise that they should, unbidden, have intruded themselves there at such an hour of the night; inquiring, "Is the haste such, that you could not have waited till the morning?" But their answer was, that they came to do their duty, by orders of the Queen, whose pleasure it was that she should repair with them without delay to London, adding, that "They must take her with them whether quick or dead." Nor could her own remonstrances, or the entreaties of her household, prevail upon them to have any consideration for her state of health. She was strictly guarded that night, and on the following morning, at nine o'clock, was placed in a litter, and compelled to commence her journey towards London; yet, so serious was her illness, that they could proceed no farther than Redburne, where she rested that night. On the following day, they reached St. Albans, where she lay at Sir Ralph Poulet's, and on the next, arrived at "Maister Dodde's house," at South Mymmes, where she remained that night: and thence, on the fourth day, they brought her to Highgate; but her illness was now become so much more dangerous, that it was found necessary on the following morning to delay her further journey, and many messengers in the interim passed to and fro from the Queen and Council, as to the question of her ability to proceed.

During her journey, the people had assembled in crowds upon the road to see her, and Elizabeth had everywhere the gratification of receiving the strongest demonstrations of the interest that was so generally felt in her fate; on the sixth day especially, when she was conveyed from Highgate to London, many gentlemen rode out to meet her, as a mark of their attachment to her person, and multitudes thronged about her litter, "lamenting and bewailing her estate."

Upon Elizabeth's arrival at Whitehall, she was shut up

a close prisoner, under he charge of the Chamberlain and Vice-Chamberlain, without communication with any one for near a fortnight; when, on the Friday before Palm Sunday, the Bishop of Winchester, and nineteen others of the Council, came from the Queen, and charged her with being privy to Wyat's conspiracy, alleging that she had held correspondence with the Carews and other gentlemen in the west; and although she utterly denied these things, and protested her innocence, they informed her that it was her Majesty's will and pleasure that she should go to the Tower, until the matter should be further tried and examined.

At the idea of going to the Tower Elizabeth was struck with dismay; she reiterated the vows of her innocence, and of her truth and loyalty to the Queen; and desired the Lords to intercede with her sister, that, being neither in thought, nor word, nor deed, untrue towards her Majesty, she might not be committed to so notorious and doleful a place. But nothing could avail! The Lords departed, assuring her that there was no remedy, for that it was The Queen's Majesty's determination that to the Tower she should go; and, in an hour afterwards, the Lord Steward and the Earl of Sussex returned with a guard, and, removing all her servants and attendants, substituted a gentleman usher, two grooms of the chamber, and three gentlewomen of The Queen's in their place; "and there were put an hundred of northern soldiers in white coats, watching and warding about the garden all that night; a great fire being made in the midst of the hall, and two Lords watching there also, with their band and company."

On the following morning the Earl of Sussex, and another Lord whose name does not appear, came to inform her, that forthwith she must go to the Tower, and that the tide served, and the barge was in readiness. In great distress, she begged for delay, and implored permission to see or write to The Queen. The unnamed Lord, however, answered sternly, that he durst not permit it, adding, that in his judgment it would rather hurt than profit her in doing so; but Sussex, more courteous and feeling than his companion, kneeled down, and told her Highness, that she should have liberty to write to The Queen her sister, pledging his honour that he would convey her letter, and bring an answer to it; and so for that day her removal was delayed. On the morrow, being Palm Sunday, in order that she might be conveyed to the Tower with more privacy, it was directed throughout the capital, that the people should all repair to church and " carry their palms ;" and in the mean time Sussex and the other lord again waited upon her, declaring that she must immediately accompany them to the Tower.

Elizabeth now began to think that every hope had vanished; she declared she marvelled what the nobility of the realm could mean, in suffering her to be thus led to prison: and, desiring the Earl of Sussex and his companion to proceed, she followed them down the garden to the barge. There went with her, besides the guards, the two Lords, three of the Queen's gentlewomen, and three of her own, her gentleman usher, and two grooms of her chamber. In passing London Bridge, owing to the great fall of water at half-tide, the whole party narrowly escaped with their lives.

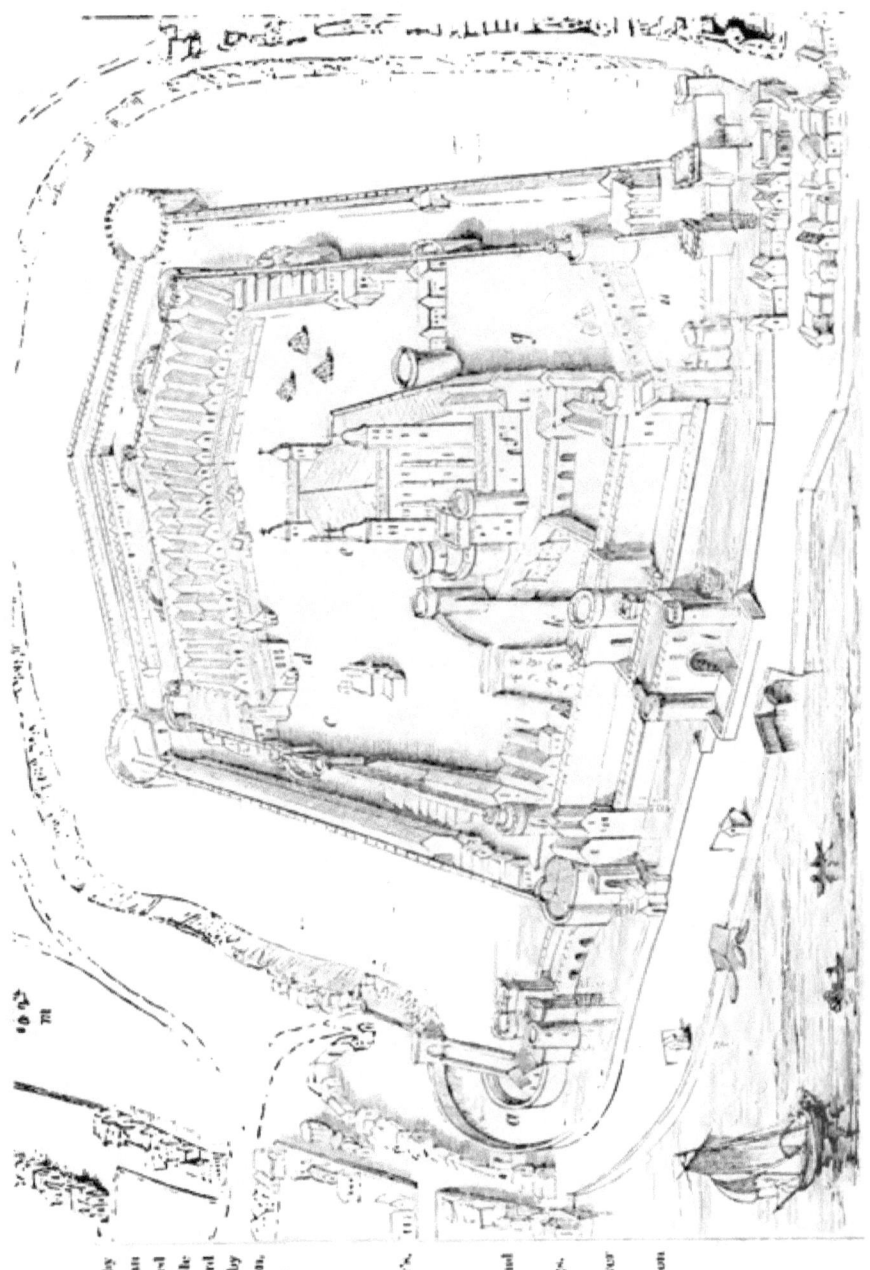

From a Print published by the Royal Antiquarian Society, and engraved from the Survey made in 1597, by W. Haiward and J. Gascoigne, by order of Sir J. Peyton, Governor of the Tower.

a. Lions' Tower.
b. Bell Tower.
c. Beauchamp Tower.
d. The Chapel.
e. Keep, called Cæsar's Tower, or the White Tower.
f. Jewel-house.
g. Queen's Lodgings.
h. Queen's Gallery and Garden.
i. Lieutenant's Lodgings.
k. Bloody Tower.
l. St. Thomas's Tower (now Traitors' Gate).
m. Place of Execution on Tower Hill.

When they came to the Tower, the barge was steered to that dismal entrance, known by the name of the Traitors' Gate, where Elizabeth would fain have avoided the

TRAITORS' GATE.

degradation of landing, till the unnamed lord resolutely told her, that "she should not choose." It rained, and he offered her his cloak, but, "putting it back with her hand with a good dash," she indignantly refused it, and, as she set her foot upon the steps, said with her wonted spirit, "Here landeth as true a subject, being a prisoner, as ever landed at these stairs, and before Thee, O God, I speak it, having none other friends but Thee!" On her ascending into the fortress, she found the Guards and Warders drawn out in order, at which she expressed surprise; and, on being informed that it was the custom, when prisoners entered, she desired that, if it were so, for her cause they might be dismissed: "whereat the poor men kneeled down, and with one voice prayed God to preserve her; for which, on the next day, they were all discharged!" Passing a little further, she sat down on a stone, and there rested herself. The Lieutenant pressed her to rise out of the rain, but she answered, "Better sit here than in a worse place; for God knoweth whither you will bring me;" and, turning to her gentleman usher, she rebuked him: "You ought rather to comfort than dismay me," said she, "especially for that I know my truth to be such, that no man shall have cause to weep for my sake."

She then arose and was conducted to her prison; and when the doors were locked, and she was close shut up, the Lords of the Council "had great conference how to keep ward and watch, every man declaring his opinion in that behalf, agreeing streightly and circumspectly to keep her:" but the Earl of Sussex, who still continued her friend, and was influenced by a nobler soul, said with an oath, "My lords, let us take heed, and do not more than our commission will bear us out in, whatever shall happen hereafter; and, further, let us consider that she is The King's our Master's daughter, and therefore we should use such dealing, that we may answer to it hereafter, if it shall so happen: for just dealing," said he, "is always answerable." This advice in some degree prevailed, and so the Lords departed.

Of the many prisoners accused of sharing in the insurrection of Wyatt, who were confined at this time in the Tower, some were closely examined, while on others every art was tried, either by the torture of the rack, by hopes of pardon, or promises of reward, to obtain evidence that might have afforded Mary any pretext for wreaking her vengeance on a sister who was so much the object of her jealousy and hatred. Nor were any endeavours neglected to entrap the Princess into criminating herself. She had been but a few days in the Tower, before Gardiner, Bishop of Winchester, and many others of the Council, came and examined her, touching a conversation which they charged her with having held at Ashridge, with Sir James Crofts, on the subject of her removal from thence to her castle at Donnington. To which, after a moment's recollection, she answered, "Indeed I do now remember that I have such a place, but I never lay in it in my life; and as for any that may have moved me thereto, I do not remember." Yet, "to enforce the matter," they brought Sir James before her, and Gardiner, who was ever Elizabeth's bitter enemy, demanded what she had to say to that man? She answered that she had little to say to him, or to any others who were then prisoners in the Tower. "But, my Lords," said she, "you do examine every mean prisoner of me, wherein methinks you do me great injury. If they have done evil, and have offended the Queen's majesty, let them answer to it accordingly; and I beseech you, my Lords, join not me in this sort, with any of these offenders. As concerning my going to Donnington Castle, I do remember that Mr. Hobby and mine officers, and you, Sir James Crofts, had such talk; but what is that to the purpose, my Lords? May I not go to mine own houses at all times?" To which the Earl of Arundell, kneeling, replied, "Your Grace saith true, and certainly we are sorry that we have so troubled you about such vain matters." "My Lords," said she, "you do sift me very narrowly; but well am I assured you shall not do more to me than God hath appointed, and so God forgive you all."

The Lords were then about to depart, but Sir James Crofts first kneeled down before the Princess, declaring that he was sorry to see the day that he should be brought as a witness against her; "but I assure your Grace," said he, "I have been marvellously tossed, and examined, touching your Highness, which, the Lord knoweth, is very strange to me; for I take God to witness, before all your honours, I do not know anything of that crime which you have laid to my charge, and will thereupon take my death, if I should be driven to so strait a trial."

Elizabeth's confinement in the Tower was of a harsh and severe description; mass was constantly obtruded upon her in her apartment; for a whole month she was shut up, without the liberty of even passing the threshold of her prison; and, afterwards, when she had obtained permission from the Council to take the air in the Queen's garden, she was always attended by the Constable, the Lieutenant, and a guard; indeed, so rigidly was she watched, that a little boy only four years of age, who was wont to pay affectionate visits to her and other prisoners, and to bring them flowers, was suspected of being employed as a messenger between her and the Earl of Devonshire; and his father, an inferior officer in the fortress, was charged by the Constable and Lieutenant, to prevent his little son from repeating his visits to the prisoners. They strictly examined the child, and, with promises of figs and apples, endeavoured to extract some ground for accusation. After questioning the little fellow when he had been last with Lady Elizabeth and the Earl of Devonshire, they asked him what the Earl had sent by him to her Grace? And notwithstanding the simplicity of the child's reply, "That he would go and know what he would give to carry to her," the Constable, who was also Lord Chamberlain, gravely declared his suspicion that there lurked beneath a plot. "This same is a crafty boy," said he; "how say you, my Lord Chandos?" "Ay, my Lord," cried the child, "but pray give me the figs you promised me." "No, marry," quoth the suspicious officer, "you shall be whipped if you come any more to the Lady Elizabeth, or to the Lord Courtenay."

A quarrel narrated by Hollingshed between the Constable and the Princess's attendants, about her provisions, gives a fair instance of the manner in which prisoners, even of her high rank, were exposed to the extortion of the chief officers of the Tower in those days.

Sir John Gage, the Constable, had given order that the Princess's servants, when they brought her dinner to the gates, were not to be allowed to enter, but were to deliver it to the hands of the " common rascall souldiers." This the servants objected to, on the ground that much of the victuals might be consumed on the way to her Grace's lodgings; but the only answer they received from the Constable to their remonstrance was, that, " if they presumed either to frown or shrug at him, he would sette them where they should see neither sunne nor moon."

An appeal was then made to the Lords of the Council, who appointed, that fourteen of the Princess's own servants should be admitted to superintend the cooking of her Grace's viands. Though forced to submit, the Constable was ill pleased at this decision. "And good cause why," says Hollingshed, "for he had good cheare and fared of the best, while her Grace paid for it."

Though examined closely from time to time by the Commissioners from the Council, the shrewdness and presence of mind of Elizabeth enabled her to avoid every snare that was laid for her, on these occasions; and Wyatt having to the last persisted, to his honour, in asserting her total ignorance of his schemes, she was eventually released from the Tower on the 19th of May, and conveyed to a less rigid restraint at Woodstock, under the charge of Sir Henry Bedingfield.

It was during her stay at Woodstock, that Elizabeth received great kindness from the family of Sir Thomas Williams, and formed that grateful friendship for one of his daughters, which in after life brought out one of the rare instances where Elizabeth was known to exhibit any true tenderness of affection for one of her own sex.

Miss Williams became the wife of the gallant Sir John Norris, and had four sons by him, who were each of them renowned in the land, or sea service of their country. It was on occasion of the younger of these being killed in battle, that the Queen addressed to Lady Norris that touching letter of condolence quoted by Miss Strickland, beginning " Mine own dear Crow," a familiar nickname given by Elizabeth to this lady in the early days of their Woodstock friendship, on account of the raven black of her long and beautiful hair.

There is a tradition that on the removal of Elizabeth from the Tower some of the City churches rang their bells for her deliverance, and that she afterwards, in token of gratitude, presented them with silk bell-ropes. On an inquiry made a few years ago, it was ascertained that some silk bell-ropes, of very ancient date, had long been preserved in a chest in the vestry of the church of Aldgate, but no proof of their present existence could be found.

Upon the death of Mary in November, 1558, Parliament being then sitting, the Commons were summoned to the Bar of the House of Lords, and the event of Elizabeth's accession was announced by the Lord Chancellor, Archbishop Heath, to the whole Assembly. It was received with acclamations, such as had probably never before greeted a new Sovereign. The news spread through London, accompanied by every demonstration of joy, and was carried to every part of the kingdom amidst the rejoicings of all classes of the Queen's subjects.

It was at Hatfield that Elizabeth received the intelligence of this great change in her fortunes. As soon as preparation could be made for her reception, she arrived at Lord North's residence in the Charter-house, and after staying there a few days, to give time for suitable arrangements, she moved into the Tower, the scene of her former danger and captivity, and established her Court with all the solemnity and splendour suitable to the great occasion.

In the early part of the month of December, Queen Elizabeth removed from the Tower, by water, to Somerset House, and sojourned there with her Court till after her sister's funeral, when she proceeded to her palace at Westminster, and there celebrated the festival of Christmas.

In the mean time great preparations were being made for the accustomed cavalcade through the city, and for the ceremonies of the Coronation. The day appointed was Sunday, the 15th of January, and on the Thursday preceding she returned by water to the Tower, where she was welcomed by the nobility and great officers of state, who had assembled to receive her. She was "attended by the Mayor and aldermen in their barge, and all the crafts in their barges, decked and trimmed with the targets and banners of their misteries;" and thus, "with great and pleasant melody of instruments, which played in most sweet and heavenly manner," her Majesty passed the bridge about two o'clock, and entered the fortress at the well-remembered Traitors' Gate, under which, but a few years before, she had been landed an oppressed and calumniated prisoner.

The day of her Majesty's procession from the Tower had been prepared for by the citizens with greater pains and expense than was ever before witnessed; and we are expressly told, that the splendid and more than usually magnificent pageantry and decorations which ornamented the streets on that occasion, were entirely accomplished without the aid of any foreign person.

The procession from the Tower began in the afternoon with trumpets and heralds, and we are informed by a contemporary writer that the Queen, previous to her leaving the royal apartments, lifted up her hands towards heaven, and returned most hearty thanks "to the Almighty and ever-living God, that He had been so merciful unto her as to spare her to see that joyful day, acknowledging that He had dealt as mercifully and wonderfully with her, as He did with his true and faithful servant Daniel, the prophet, whom He delivered out of the den, from the cruel and raging lions." Her Majesty was seated in an open chariot sumptuously adorned, and "most honourably accompanied, as well with gentlemen, barons, and other nobility of her realm, as also with a notable train of goodly and beautiful ladies, richly appointed." The streets through which the Queen had to pass were decorated with costly drapery, and lined with the various crafts or companies of the City, "well apparelled with many rich furs, and their livery hoods upon their shoulders;" and before them stood "sundry persons clad in silks and chains of gold." In several parts of the City stages and triumphal arches were erected. The first of these was in Fenchurch Street, where Her Majesty's progress was arrested by a child in costly apparel, who, on behalf of the City, addressed her with a welcoming oration: the next was a magnificent arch, spanning the street near Gracechurch, and adorned with "goodly pageaunts," representing the union and emblems of the houses of York and Lancaster: a third, in Cornhill, equally magnificent, was denominated "the seate of worthy governaunce;" in which, besides the eight Beatitudes, and other representations suitable to the occasion, were the cardinal Virtues, treading under foot the opposite Vices; among which were Ignorance and Superstition. At the standard in Cheapside, the Recorder, in the name of the City, presented a thousand marks of gold, in a purse of crimson velvet, as a token of their affectionate loyalty to a sovereign "whose prosperity they wished, and whose protection they implored:" there she also received a Bible in English, which was let down to her as if from heaven, by the hand of a child representing Truth; a gift which she accepted with the strongest marks of reverence; declaring that it gave her more real gratification than all the other endearing proofs that she had that day experienced of her people's love.

The last and grandest of all the Pageants was another triumphal arch, on which, represented sitting under a palm-tree, was "a seemly mete personage richly apparelled in parliament robes, with a sceptre in her hand, as a queen," with the superscription, "Deborah, the judge and restorer of the house of Israel." At Temple Bar, the western limit of the City, the two giants, Gogmagog and Corineus, were stationed, with a scroll in Latin verse, expounding the meaning of all the representations that Her Majesty had previously passed: and there, "with her hearty commendations," she bade the citizens farewell. It was observed of Elizabeth that, by her kind and affable deportment on that day, she gained more on the affections of the people than many other princes had been able to do, by more real and substantial acts of grace and favour.

SIDE PASSAGE, BYWARD TOWER.

LORD STOURTON'S MURDER OF THE HARTGILLS.

MONG the many crimes for which offenders have been committed to the Tower, none were of a more savage character, nor more indicative of the loose administration of law at a distance from the capital in the early periods of our history, than the barbarous and deliberate murder in Somersetshire of a neighbouring country gentleman and his son by Lord Stourton, during the reign of Queen Mary, whose determined resolution to bring the murderer to justice, as soon as the facts became known to her, is one of the few acts which reflect credit on her reign.

It appears that this nobleman, who had large estates and considerable influence in Wiltshire and Somersetshire, took violent umbrage at the kind and prudent advice given by a Mr. Hartgill to his mother, Lady Stourton, while she was a guest at his country-seat near Kilmington. Lord Stourton wished to obtain from her a bond that she would not re-marry, and desired Hartgill to assist in persuading her to sign it, but he, being a man of honour and respectability, advised her to do nothing of the ort, unless Lord Stourton would first assign her a fixed income, proportionate to her rank in life. This threw Lord Stourton into a violent fury, and, collecting a party of his tenantry and servants, he repaired to Kilmington, the seat of the Hartgills, one Sunday, while the family were at church in the adjoining village, and began to plunder and spoil the mansion.

The younger Hartgill, being told what was going on by a servant who ran to him in the church, desired his father and mother to remain for safety in the church-tower, while he, running across the churchyard to the mansion, hard by, got safe within the gates, though Lord Stourton's people shot several arrows at him as he passed. He now strung his bow, with which he was an expert marksman, and shot so fast and well at Lord Stourton's party, that, after wounding several, he presently beat them off. The unwarrantable attack on his house was naturally complained of by Hartgill in the proper quarter, and the Lords of the Council directed the sheriff of the county to arrest Lord Stourton, who was committed to prison, from whence he was not released till he had been bound over in due form to keep the peace towards the Hartgills for a year. This lenient treatment, however, did not deter Lord Stourton from taking every occasion to avenge himself on the Hartgills, destroying their crops, driving their cattle, and annoying them by every sort of petty persecution. About this time, the Queen making a journey to Basingend, in Hampshire, the Hartgills took advantage of this visit for a personal appeal to her Majesty, who caused Lord Stourton to be summoned before the Council.

He promptly obeyed the summons, affected deep regret for his conduct, and declared that, if the Hartgills would come to his house and be reconciled to him, he would make full restitution for all the harm he had done them.

Trusting to this assurance, the father and son, accompanied by a friend, proceeded, after the departure of the Queen from Basing-end, to Lord Stourton's house; but their perfidious enemy had placed six ruffians in ambush, in a narrow lane, and, before young Hartgill could draw his sword, they attacked, and so wounded him, that he was left for dead on the ground. Again the Queen was appealed to, and the Star Chamber, causing Lord Stourton to be seized aud brought prisoner before them in London, committed him to the Fleet Prison, and sentenced him to pay a considerable fine to the Hartgills. He contrived, however, by fair promises, to be again liberated on giving a bond for 2000*l.* to appear for trial at the next term, and returned home with his mind fully bent on the destruction of the unfortunate Hartgills at all hazards. In pursuance of his scheme, he sent a messenger to invite them to meet him and receive the fine awarded them by the Star Chamber, at Kilmington Church. This appeared so fair a proposal, that the father and son did not hesitate to repair to the place at the time appointed, but finding that Lord Stourton had already arrived, and was attended by a number of his servants and dependants, the elder Hartgill declared that they would not approach nearer to Lord Stourton's party, nor have communication with him, except in the church itself. As if to show his good faith, Lord

Stourton produced a large purse of gold, and began to discuss the amount of the payment due, but, having gradually approached and got them within reach, he suddenly cried out, "I arrest you both of felony," and, as he was a magistrate of the county, his followers did not hesitate to seize and bind the Hartgills hand and foot, supposing that he had legal warrant for his proceeding.

The Hartgills were then confined in the parsonage-house, and the majority of Lord Stourton's tenants and followers dispersed. In the middle of that night the prisoners were removed, and not without some rough usage on the road, to Bonham, a house near Stourton Caundell; and the next day Lord Stourton induced two justices of the peace to go to Bonham and examine them, on the understanding that they should afterwards be committed direct to the county gaol, and charges substantiated against them. These magistrates, finding that there was no case, but afraid of offending Lord Stourton, contented themselves with ordering the removal of their bonds, and left them, as they supposed, to be sent next day to prison.

No sooner, however, had the two magistrates withdrawn, than Lord Stourton commanded four ruffians, whom he had placed in charge of the Hartgills, again to bind them hand and foot, and at ten o'clock that night they were dragged to the garden of Stourton Caundell, where they were thrown to the ground, and their brains beat out by these villains, while their master stood, with a taper in his hand, at a back door of the house, to witness the completion of this bloody act. The bodies were then carried through the back door, into a gallery, at the end of which was a small vestibule, opening into Lord Stourton's own apartment. Here, the old man's life not being quite extinct, he uttered a deep groan, when Lord Stourton, holding the candle, caused his throat to be cut, for fear, as was afterwards deposed by one of the murderers, that a French priest, who lay in a chamber near, should hear his moans.

In order to the concealment of the bodies of these unfortunate gentlemen, they were buried very deep in a sort of cellar beneath the mansion, and then laid over with a double pavement, upon which a quantity of shavings and sawdust was spread, to hide the spot. But Sir Anthony Hungerford, the Sheriff of Wiltshire, who already knew the malignity of Lord Stourton towards the Hartgills, on being informed of the visit of the two magistrates, and that, instead of the Hartgills being lodged next day in the gaol on the charge of felony, they had mysteriously disappeared, instantly set on foot a strict search and inquiry. Their removal was soon traced to Stourton Caundell, and one of the villains, concerned in the murder, having betrayed his employer, the corpses of the unfortunate Hartgills were discovered and disinterred. Sir Anthony instantly caused Lord Stourton to be apprehended, and on his reporting the facts to the Council, an order came down to send him to London, and lodge him in the Tower. He was shortly after arraigned in the Tower, before a Special Commission, consisting of the Lord Chief Justice, with some of the other judges, the Lord Steward, and the Lord Chamberlain. The four servants who had been his instruments in this barbarous murder were sent for trial to Salisbury.

Lord Stourton had shown, at various times, great zeal for the Catholic interests; and the Hartgills being Protestants, it was rather apprehended that the Queen might favour him; but Mary fully shared the public indignation, at the barbarity of the crime, and rejected all intercession in favour of the murderer.

Lord Stourton was treated with great severity, for he was carried to Salisbury on horseback, with his arms pinioned, and his legs tied under the horse; the first day to Hounslow; the second to Staines; the third to Basing; and the fourth to Salisbury, where he was hanged in the Market Place. His execution is the first instance, where any record appears of the privilege claimed by Peers, of being hanged with a rope of silk, a privilege, be it observed, which was not altogether an empty distinction, for there can be no doubt that a much slenderer cord of silk will bear the weight of a man's body without risk of breaking, than any cord made of hemp, and the smaller the rope, the more sudden and complete is the strangulation, especially as the smoother material causes the noose to close more effectually upon the windpipe.

Lord Stourton's servants were hanged near the scene of the murder, and their bodies were afterwards suspended there in chains. Hanging in chains has been for so many years discontinued, that the manner of it is no longer generally known, and many might imagine that a chain was really used for the execution of the criminal, instead of a rope. But this was not so; the man was in the first instance hanged in the ordinary way, with a hempen cord, and, after he was dead and cut down from the gibbet, a stout canvas dress was put on the body, well saturated with tar; the face, hands, and feet were likewise daubed with it, and then a light frame of hoop-iron was fitted round the legs, body, and arms, with the object of causing the ghastly remains to hang together as long as possible. At the top of this framework, was an iron loop, which went over the head, and to this was secured the chain, by which the corpse was finally suspended to a lofty gibbet made of oak, and studded with tenterhooks, to prevent any one from climbing up to remove the body. The last of these hideous spectacles might be seen, as recently as the year 1816, on the point, formed by the curve of the river Thames, a mile below Greenwich, where the wasted corpses of four lascars, hanged for mutiny and the murder of the captain and most of the crew of an Indiaman, were still hanging in chains from a lofty gibbet.

PASSAGE AND CELL IN BEAUCHAMP TOWER

LADY JANE GREY.

FEW victims of a harsh and cruel exercise of the laws of treason have excited more interest than Lady Jane Grey. Her entire innocence of all personal guilt, her devotion to her ambitious parents, and her position as a young and tender bride, all combine to render her story one of the saddest of those which stain the annals of the Tower. That her father was, to all intents, guilty of a deliberate and determined act of treason, cannot be questioned, nor that he deserved a traitor's doom ; but it seems to have been a needless severity to involve her in the same fate as her father, when no other crime could be alleged against her, than a reluctant obedience to the solicitations and authority of her parents. The extraordinary learning and acquirements of Lady Jane Grey increased the general sympathy for her fate, nor is it very easy in these days to realise the early progress of so young a lady in classical studies. But so many other women of high rank, who lived about that period, were distinguished for what would now be regarded as an abstruse education, that it may be permitted to offer a few observations on this interesting point.

The lives of the nobility and gentry of England in the sixteenth century, with exception of such as were employed in offices of state, or attached to the Court of the Sovereign, were chiefly passed on their estates, in a state and grandeur almost resembling that of petty princes. Hunting and warlike exercises, especially manège horsemanship, were the ordinary occupation of the young men, and many of the ladies took part with them, in the pleasures of the chase. But such ladies as had less taste for outdoor exercises were either devoted to household cares, the management of their large establishments, and the arts of embroidery and the needle, or betook themselves, from early years, to such studies as suited the fashion of the time, and could be attained by study of that narrow compass of literature, which the scanty libraries of their castles and mansions afforded. But a far wider field lay open to them, in the classical and theological collections of books and manuscripts, which were to be found in the monasteries and ecclesiastical establishments of England of that period. The constant discussions and arguments which attended the progress of the Reformation, brought forward a number of men who applied their extensive knowledge of the dead languages, to theological and controversial writing. Many of those, who took leading parts in these learned discussions, were received as honoured guests in the houses of the great; and the poverty of others rendered such asylums their resource and refuge, in distress or persecution. It was natural for their hosts and protectors to avail themselves of the services of such learned persons for the education of their children; and since little distinction then existed between the learning regarded as desirable for youth of either sex, these Preceptors probably obtained more diligent attention to their instructions from the young ladies of the family, than from the wild and spirited youths who looked to the chase, as their present amusement, and to war, for the occupation of their more manly years. No instances, or at all events very rare ones, can be found in the domestic records of the noble families of those days, of any such female instructors as would correspond to our modern notions of a governess. Music was universally taught by masters, and what are now known as female accomplishments can hardly be said to have existed at the period to which we refer.

These and other causes, too long to enumerate, will account for the surprising degree of classical knowledge attained by a girl of such tender age as Lady Jane; and will remove the impression which might at first present itself of any conceit or pedantry in this unfortunate young lady's display of her learning, at a time when the preparation for death in so religious and pure a mind might be supposed to engross every thought. But the calm resignation and unaffected piety with which she prepared for her doom, show that her presence of mind never deserted her, or threw her mind off that natural and equal balance, to which the religious books with which she was familiar, probably contributed.

The ill-concerted Insurrection, generally known as Sir Thomas Wyatt's Rebellion, was the immediate ground upon which Queen Mary and her Council resolved on the destruction of Lady Jane Grey. The dislike of the people of England (especially the Londoners) to the proposed marriage of the Queen with Philip II. of Spain, was the chief point of which Wyatt and his party had taken advantage, for exciting discontent in different parts of England. Wyatt assembled a large body of troops in Kent, which, although hastily collected, assumed a formidable character, and, advancing to meet the Royal Forces, commanded by the Duke of Norfolk, near Rochester, defeated and dispersed them after a short conflict, and marched to Gravesend, a post of considerable importance for the command of the Thames below London. From thence, after refusing the overtures made by the Council, and demanding arrogantly the surrender of the Tower with the Queen within it, as the only terms on which he would treat, Wyatt, instead of crossing the river by boats and barges at Gravesend, marched up the Kentish shore to Southwark, from whence he cannonaded the Tower, with no result except that of alarming the city, and enabling the Queen's troops to assemble and make better preparations for resistance.

After some hours wasted in this idle bravado in Southwark, Wyatt marched up the Surrey side of the river to Kingston, which must have been, at that time, the first practicable place for fording the Thames. The now populous district through which he passed, by Wandsworth, Battersea, Wimbledon, &c., was then a tract of rough commons, with scarce any roads, and must have been in winter a most harassing march. Notwithstanding all difficulties, Wyatt and his army made their appearance at Temple Bar within twenty-four hours of their departure from Southwark; but whether the men deserted on finding themselves unsupported as they entered Westminster after this exhausting march, or were most of them dispersed by panic at the appearance of the preparations to resist them, it is certain that Wyatt reached Temple Bar with so few followers, that he was seized by a party of the Royal Forces almost without a struggle, and lodged in the Tower. Here he was received into custody by the Lieutenant, Sir Thomas Bridges, who with unmanly brutality took him by the collar, unarmed as he stood, saying, " I would sticke thee through with my dagger, but that the law must pass upon thee." To which Wyatt in a dignified tone, and " with a grim look at the Lieutenant," sternly rejoined, "It is no maisterie now;" and passed on to the prison which was to be his last abode. This danger once past, Mary and her Council lost no time in the steps necessary for the execution of Lady Jane Grey and her husband. It has been said, on the authority of Fox's 'Acts and Monuments,' that Mary entertained a personal aversion to this young lady, on account of a conversation reported to her, as having taken place with Lady Wharton, when passing a Catholic chapel. It seems Lady Wharton made a curtsy to the consecrated wafer suspended over the altar, when Lady Jane asked, " Did she believe the Virgin Mary were there?" "No," said Lady Wharton. " I made the obeisance to Him who made us all." " How can that be," replied Lady Jane, " when we know it was the baker who made that to which you paid reverence?"

The trial of Lady Jane, if such it could be called, had taken place before Wyatt's outbreak, and, had it not been for his wild attempt on London and the Tower, it has been supposed Mary would have spared her life, and been content to keep her in close imprisonment; but those were not times when much scruple was made of taking life of any one who might be regarded as a pretender to the Crown. As if in mockery of the known Protestant feelings of Lady Jane, Mary's Confessor, Feckenham, was sent on the 8th of February to prepare her for death, and to exhort her husband and her, to die in the Catholic faith. Four days after this visit, was the day fixed for their execution. Tower Hill was at first intended for the fatal scene; but it was afterwards determined to behead them separately, for fear of the excitement which might be expected from so cruel a spectacle as the simultaneous execution of two young and interesting persons only lately united in marriage.

It was therefore determined that Lady Jane should suffer on Tower Green (within the fortress), and Lord Guildford Dudley upon the Hill, outside. Before his death, he sent to her to desire a last interview, but she entreated him to give up this wish, as liable to produce feelings which might unfit them both for their last hour. He consented to her wish, but begged she would give him a token as he was to pass under the window of "Partridge's house," where she had probably been removed that morning from the Beauchamp Tower, to make her preparations for death. Lord Guildford Dudley was led out to Tower Hill, and suffered with all the firmness and resignation which might be expected from his blameless life and character. His body was placed in a cart, covered with a cloth, and brought into the Tower for burial in St. Peter's Chapel.

As the cart passed under Lady Jane's window, she discovered at once the form which the cloth thrown over it but partially shrouded, and exclaimed, "Oh! Guildford, Guildford, the ante-past is not so bitter that thou hast tasted, and which I shall soon taste, as to make my flesh tremble; it is nothing compared to the feast we shall partake this day in heaven."

When Sir T. Bridges, the Lieutenant of the Tower, appeared to conduct her to the block, she presented him her tablets to keep in acknowledgment of his kindness to her. Arrived on Tower Green, only a short distance from her prison door, she addressed a few modest and simple words to those present, to the effect that, although she had most reluctantly accepted the short-lived dignity forced upon her by the entreaties of her relations, she freely admitted she had no real right to the crown, and that the sentence therefore, under which she suffered, was not an unjust one. Hollingshed's account of her end is very touching. "She prayed fervently, and then stood up and gave to Mistress Ellen, her maid, her gloves and handkerchief, and her book to Master Bridges, the Lieutenant's brother, and so untied her gown. The executioner pressed to help her off with it; but she desired him to let her alone, and turned toward her two gentlewomen, who helped her off therewith, and with her other attire, and gave her a fair handkerchief to put about her eyes. Then the executioner kneeled down and asked her forgiveness, whom she forgave most willingly. Then he willed her to stand upon the straw; which done, she saw the block; and then she said, 'I pray you despatch me quickly.' Then she kneeled down, saying, 'Will you take it off before I lay me down?' Whereunto the executioner answered, 'No, Madam.' Then tied she the handkerchief about her eyes, and, feeling for the block, she said, 'Where is it? where is it?' One of the standers-by guided her thereunto, and she laid down her head upon the block, and then stretched forth her body, and said, 'Lord, into thy hands I commend my spirit;' and so finished her life, her head being struck off by a single blow."

Her body was interred with that of her husband under the altar in St. Peter's Chapel. It has been mentioned above that she was in "Partridge's house" when she gave the token just before his execution to Lord Guildford Dudley; and it may therefore be well to explain, that it was not uncommon to remove prisoners of high rank from the Beauchamp Tower, which was the usual state prison, to the Lieutenant's or to one of the Warders' quarters, in order to make their immediate preparation for death, and more conveniently to receive and bid farewell to such friends and relations as were at the last moment permitted to see and attend them to the scaffold.

The word "Jane," inscribed on the north wall of the Beauchamp Prison Tower, has been always attributed to the hand of this unfortunate young lady, and there is no reason to question it, any more than the inscriptions of other prisoners upon those gloomy walls. Bailey and others, who have taken a strange satisfaction in throwing doubt upon traditions of the Tower, would have it believed, that these names on the walls of the Beauchamp Prison, were not really carved by the persons themselves; but a cursory inspection will show, by the confused and irregular way in which the names are scattered over the surface of the interior, that they were evidently the chance work of the prisoners, who sought by any means before them to occupy their thoughts in some manual employment, and perhaps at the same time to hand down their sorrows to times, when that pity and compassion might be felt for them, of which their relentless enemies or persecutors were incapable.

LADY JANE GRAY.
(Inscribed on the wall of the Beauchamp Prison Tower.)

LADY CATHERINE GREY.

URING the last years of Queen Mary's reign, Lady Catherine Grey, the younger sister of the unfortunate Lady Jane, had been residing, under the care of the Duchess of Somerset, Lord Hertford's mother, at her seat of Hanworth. Lord Hertford, who frequently visited Hanworth, formed an attachment to Lady Catherine: but as concealment was necessary from his mother, to whose charge she was in fact confided, almost in the position of a prisoner, it was to his sister, Lady Jane Seymour, and to her only, that he made known the state of his affections. The Duchess, perceiving, as he afterwards expressed it, "familiarity and good will between them, did often admonish him to abstain from Lady Catherine's company." To these warnings he replied that "young folks, meaning well, might well accompany together, and that both in that house, and also in the court, he trusted he might use her company, being not forbidden by the Queen's Highness's express commandment." Beyond this remark, he never avowed to his mother, or to any of his or Lady Catherine's relations (except his sister), the secret understanding that subsisted

between them. This secrecy was the natural consequence of the fear inspired by the harshness with which both Mary and Elizabeth had treated the branch of the Royal Family to which Lady Catherine belonged.

Soon after the accession of Queen Elizabeth, Lady Catherine Grey and Lady Jane Seymour were both of them placed about the Queen's person, and in waiting upon Her Majesty at Hampton Court.

Lord Hertford, being at that time confined by indisposition to his house in Channon Row, Westminster, wrote to his sister to ask her assistance in forwarding his suit with her friend, and "to feel her disposition for marriage with him." Lady Jane executed this commission faithfully, but Lady Catherine declined to give any positive answer, till the Queen should come to Westminster. As soon as the removal of the Court took place, Lord Hertford obtained an interview with Lady Catherine, in his sister's private apartments; and there, in her presence, he made a direct proposal of marriage. Lady Catherine answered, "that, weighing his long suit and good will borne to her, she was content to marry him, the next time that the Queen's Highness should go abroad and leave her and Lady Jane behind her." They plighted their faith "by giving one to the other their hands," Lady Jane being present throughout the interview; and it was agreed that their marriage should take place secretly at Lord Hertford's house in Channon Row; but as the opportunity depended on the movements of the Queen, no day could be fixed. Lady Jane, however, undertook that a clergyman should be ready at very short notice, whenever his services might be required.

The opportunity occurred shortly before Christmas of the year 1560, when the Queen went to Eltham to hunt. Within an hour after her departure, Lady Jane Seymour and Lady Catherine Grey quitted the Palace, and, descending the orchard stairs, proceeded along "the sands" at low tide to the back of the Earl's house in Channon Row. They had not been able to give him previous warning; but as he knew they only waited for the opportunity of the Queen's departure, which was generally known to those about the Court, he was ready to receive them. The Minister with whom Lady Jane had previously agreed for the purpose, was quickly summoned, and brought with him the Book of Common Prayer. Lord Hertford and Lady Catherine Grey were then married, "with such words and ceremonies, and in that order, as it is there set forth, he placing a ring containing five links of gold on her finger, as directed by the Minister."

This clergyman's name was unfortunately never ascertained by either Lord Hertford or Lady Catherine, though both afterwards affirmed they should know him again if they saw him, and agreed in describing him as "a man of middling stature, fair complexion, auburn hair and beard, and middle age, dressed in a plain long gown of black cloth faced with 'budge,' and a falling collar to the same, such a one as the ministers used when they came out of Germany." The ceremony ver, Lord Hertford thanked the unknown Minister, and Lady Jane dismissed him with a fee of 10*l.* for his services. (Though ready enough to earn this liberal reward for his performance of the ceremony, it was no wonder that this Minister, whoever he was, took advantage of the entire secrecy afforded by the early death of Lady Jane, and declined to come forward and vouch for the marriage when it was question of braving the terrible wrath of Elizabeth.) After the ceremony, Lord Hertford accompanied Lady Catherine and his sister to the water stairs, where he took an affectionate leave of his bride, and the two ladies returned by boat to the Palace, "to Master Comptroller's chambers, whom they found ready to go to dinner" by the time they arrived. Many clandestine interviews took place afterwards between the newly married pair, but they still kept their marriage secret.

Whether Lord Hertford thought that by absenting himself awhile on the Continent, any suspicions would be avoided, or that he had other reasons, he resolved, soon after the marriage, to ask the Queen's leave to go abroad. Lady Jane, to whom alone he confided this intention, imparted it in confidence to her sister-in-law, and the sight of his passport, which soon after accidentally met Lady Catherine's eye, left no doubt of his intention; which was, as she afterwards expressed herself, "of no small grief and trouble unto her."

But a greater cause of anxiety now arose; and she was obliged to impart to Lady Jane and to her husband her fears that she was likely to become a mother. Lady Jane, with that decision which marked her conduct throughout this perilous transaction, told her at once "that, if it were so, there was no remedy but be acknown how the matter stood, and that they must abide it, and trust to the Queen's mercy." To the necessity of this avowal Lord Hertford also agreed, and promised his wife that, if her suspicions proved true, he would not depart the realm; but the unhappy Lady Catherine, young, inexperienced, and timid, seems to have been afraid of speaking confidently on the subject; and Lord Hertford, availing himself of the Queen's leave, sailed for France.

On the 19th of March, 1560-1, Lady Jane Seymour unfortunately died at the early age of nineteen. Unsupported by the presence of her husband, or comforted by the affection and counsels of her friend and sister-in-law, Lady Catherine found herself in a few months reduced to the humiliation of confessing that which could no longer be concealed, and of bearing alone the brunt of the Queen's displeasure. "About six days before Lord Hertford's departure beyond the seas, he did conceive and devise a writing with his own hand in parchment, sealed and signed with his own hand," of which the object was to secure to his wife 1000*l.* per annum in case of his death. This writing he had delivered into her hands, but no other person was privy to the transaction. It certainly showed some consideration for her; but Lord Hertford's conduct in originally seeking her hand in secret, in risking the safety of his young sister, by imposing on her the dangerous responsibility of making the arrangements for their marriage, and still more in his quitting England, and leaving his wife exposed to the risk of braving, alone, the consequences of that union which he had induced her to form, certainly betrayed a selfishness, which, later in life, was manifested by his harsh conduct towards both his son and his grandson.

It was in the beginning of August that Lady Catherine determined to declare the whole truth to Mrs. St. Lo, a lady of the Queen's privy chamber, afterwards notorious as "Bess of Hardwick." Her confidence was received with friendly sympathy by that lady, who wept bitterly on hearing her tale, and expressed her sorrow "that the Queen's Majesty had not been privy thereunto." The following night (August 10th) Lady Catherine, acting under Mrs. St. Lo's advice, resolved on trying to interest the compassion of Lord Robert Dudley, afterwards Earl of Leicester, already in great favour with the Queen. She visited his bedside (he was ill at the time), and, telling him her story, implored his services, to obtain the Queen's mercy. He consented to intercede with the Queen. But neither the sympathy of Mrs. St. Lo, nor the good offices of Lord Robert, availed with the hard nature of Elizabeth. Lady Catherine was at once committed to the Tower, and there closely examined by the Lord Treasurer and others, respecting the circumstances of her marriage. On the 21st of September her first child was born.

Whether Lord Hertford was immediately informed of her imprisonment, does not appear; but as she acknowledged, in one of her examinations, that she had acquainted her husband by letter of the certainty of her situation, it may be hoped that his return to England in the month of her expected confinement was dictated by the wish to be with her, at a time when, not only her life might be in danger, but when her honour might also be called in question. On his landing at Dover in the beginning of September, he was at once arrested by Mr. Crispe, the Captain of the Castle, who showed him the Queen's commission, by which he was charged to bring the Earl immediately to Court; his servants were not to be allowed to accompany him, but were to follow him to London.

On the 5th September he was committed to the Tower, and on the 12th examined before the Lord Treasurer. On the 13th February, 1561-2, both he and Lady Catherine were again examined before Commissioners; and on the 12th of May, in the Bishop of London's Palace; the result being that the marriage was declared null and void. This commission was composed of Parker Archbishop of Canterbury, Grindal Bishop of London, Sir William Petre, and some others.

A decision which could only be grounded on the difficulty of procuring timely evidence of the truth of their statements, was not likely to affect the sentiments of the parties themselves respecting the validity of their marriage; and after a time, by persuasion or corruption of their keepers, the doors of their prison were no longer secured against each other, and the birth of a second child rekindled the anger of Elizabeth. A double fine was imposed on Lord Hertford, and their imprisonment was made so much stricter, that there is reason to suppose they never met again. Sir Edward Warner, the Lieutenant of the Tower, was at the same time dismissed for his negligence in the custody of his charge.

Many letters and petitions were addressed both to Sir William Cecil and to the Queen, in behalf of Lady Catherine, by her uncle, Lord John Grey of Pirgo, and by herself, but the only mercy extended to her and her husband, was during the time when the plague raged in London, and when a thousand in a week were said to die of that malady. Then, in the month of August, 1563, Lord Hertford was delivered (but in the condition of a prisoner) to the custody of his mother, and Lady Catherine to that of her uncle, Lord John Grey, at Pirgo, where she was ordered to be maintained at the expense of her husband.

In January, 1565-6, and again in April, 1566, Anne, Duchess of Somerset, addressed letters to Sir William Cecil, praying for the release of her son, begging his helping hand "to end this tedious suit," and urging "how unmeet it is this young couple should thus wax old in prison, and how far better it were for them to be abroad, and learn to serve Her Majesty."

These appeals were fruitless: and the following year death released the ill-fated Lady Catherine from the sorrows and humiliations to which she had been so heartlessly subjected. She had been for some time in the custody of Sir Owen Hopton, and died at his country house, Cockfield Hall, in Yoxford, Suffolk. There is an account preserved of her last hours which contains some pathetic details of the resignation and courage, worthy a sister of Lady Jane Grey, with which she prepared for her end.

When it is remembered that, at the time of her persecution of this unhappy young lady, Elizabeth was but twenty-five years of age, and had herself so recently endured the bitterness of imprisonment, we cannot but wonder at the severity and harshness which disfigured her naturally noble nature, and led her to actions of cruelty and tyranny unworthy of so great and illustrious a Queen.

MURDER OF THE TWO KEATINGS BY GERALD, 11th EARL OF KILDARE.

AMONG the numerous committals in Elizabeth's reign, were those of Hickey and Barry, the "Harbinger" and "Steward" of Gerald, the eleventh Earl of Kildare, for the murder of the two Keatings in Ireland. The story affords a fearful picture of the barbarity and contempt of law and justice, which then prevailed in that country: but what appears so strange in the matter is, that the Queen, or her councillors, should have thought it worth while to incur all the expence and trouble of bringing over to London such subordinate miscreants as Hickey and Barry, instead of causing them to be executed at once, near the spot where their crimes were committed, to serve as an example to their comrades, which their removal to London must have rendered almost nugatory.

The Earl of Kildare was, it appears, in the habit of keeping up a frequent, though secret, communication with the chiefs of the petty insurrections, which were always smouldering within the English pale, and these Keatings, who were agents and spies of the rebel chiefs, were occasionally received by him as guests at his castle of Kilkea, the residence of the Marquis of Kildare, for whose occupation the present Duke of Leinster repaired and restored this ancient stronghold of the FitzGerald family.

1574.—Being desirous of courting the favour of the Lord Deputy (Sir W. Fitzwilliam), the Earl, by a base and unworthy deception, invited the brothers Keating to his castle, under a safe-conduct, as he had often done before, and, after causing them to be hospitably entertained, by his dependants and servants, allowed Shan, the elder brother, to depart upon the faith and security of his usual " protection or safe-conduct." The Earl afterwards declared that the safe-conduct was only to enable the Keatings to come to his castle in safety, but contained no engagement as to equal safety after their departure.

On this base pretext, he despatched Hickey, his harbinger, and his steward, Barry, accompanied by another ruffian, to waylay Shan Keating, whom they overtook in a lonely spot, where the road led through a dreary bog. It would seem that the unfortunate man at once guessed their errand, for, as soon as he saw them, he dismounted from the " stout black horse" which he rode, and drawing his sword, boldly faced his assailants. They had made up their minds, however, to all hazards, and at once fell upon him, and after a desperate combat, in which, but for the odds of three to one, it is probable his courage might have saved his life, they eventually threw him to the ground, covered with wounds, and, cutting off his head, carried it back to the Earl, who immediately forwarded the ghastly offering to Dublin Castle, as a proof to the Lord Deputy of his zeal for the Queen's service.

Meyler Keating, the brother of Shan, and his fellow guest at Kilkea, remained meantime feasting unsuspiciously in the castle, when the Earl, on the following night, ordered Hickey and Barry to decoy him out into the demesne, despatch him, and cut off his head, as they had served his brother, which these unscrupulous wretches performed, without hesitation, and Meyler's head was sent as a second tribute of loyalty to Sir W. Fitzwilliam in Dublin.

The Deputy endeavoured to disclaim having given the Earl any authority or encouragement to commit these acts of cruelty and treachery, but the Earl, when on his trial, quoted a letter of his, which, if it did not convey any direct order, certainly would bear the interpretation by which he attempted to justify the act.

Whether Fitzwilliam really did write the letter produced by the Earl, in his justification, or whether he was ashamed to confess to any share in these savage murders, it is certain that Hickey and Barry were sent to England, imprisoned in the Tower, and tried and executed for their crimes.

Such, however, was the devotion of Hickey to his Lord, that, when interrogated with a view to bring to light other deeds of violence laid to the charge of the Earl, he said, the only illegal act he could remember of his master's, was the cutting off a man's nose, " which certainly was not to be liked;" but then the man was believed to have stolen some of the deer from the demesne of Kilkea !

Upon the subsequent inquiry by a Commission, into the conduct of the Earl, who was brought to London under an escort (the expense of his journey as a prisoner was no less than 400*l*.), a list of interrogatories was given him to answer or refute. These questions, and the Earl's replies, are preserved in original, and show the wonderful shrewdness, with which he applied himself to his defence, in which he so far succeeded, as to escape the fate of the two wretches, who, at his direct instigation and command, committed the perfidious murders of Shan and Meyler Keating.

PHILIP EARL OF ARUNDEL.

PHILIP HOWARD, Earl of Arundel (called by this, his minor title, on account of the attainder of the Duke of Norfolk, his father), was one of the most unfortunate of men. Queen Elizabeth restored him in blood about 1580, and for a short time he enjoyed her favour, and was among the gayest of the Queen's courtiers; but the Earl of Leicester caused him to be accused of conspiracy, and in 1584 he received an order to confine himself to his own house; his real offence in the Queen's eyes being his reconciliation to the Roman Catholic faith. As no act of treason could be charged against him, he was shortly liberated, but his distrust of the Queen, and the daily severities exercised by her upon those who adhered to the Romish faith, induced him to take steps for flying the country. Before doing so, he, however, resolved to write a full justification of his conduct to the Queen, which was to have been delivered as soon as he should make known to his friends in England that he had reached a place of safety on the Continent. By some mistake or treachery, his letter fell into the hands of Secretary Walsingham, before he had effected his intended flight, and, being betrayed by his attendant, he was seized, when on the point of embarking on the Sussex coast, and at once thrown into the Tower. Charges, as groundless as the former ones, were now brought against him, and, after a very unfair trial before the Star Chamber, he was fined 10,000*l.*, and sentenced to imprisonment during the Queen's pleasure.

While he lay prisoner in the Tower, the Spanish Armada arrived in the Channel (1588), on which event he had the imprudence (as asserted by his enemies) to express his joy and hopes of freedom, and even to have caused masses to be said for the success of the Spaniards, by a priest who was brought to him in disguise. Fresh charges of high treason were now framed against him, one of which was, an intention of serving under the Prince of Parma, against England; and although he ably defended himself, and proved the falsehood of all the accusations against him, except his adhesion to the Roman Catholic faith, he received sentence of death.

This barbarous condemnation seems, however, to have been only intended as a pretence for his perpetual imprisonment, since it was never carried into execution. After he had been some time in the Tower, he petitioned the Queen that his newly married wife might visit him; or at all events, that he might be allowed the sight of his infant son, born since his imprisonment. Both these favours were cruelly refused by Elizabeth, and he continued to languish in his solitary prison for several years. He sent in, however, a second petition, and it was said that the Queen not only offered to grant it, but to release him altogether, if he would renounce the Roman Catholic faith. This he had the resolution and constancy to refuse, and died in 1595, worn out with sorrow and the severe exercises of religious penance, to which he latterly devoted himself, in the fortieth year of his age; his father, grandfather, and great-grandfather having perished on the scaffold, by a far more merciful destiny. His name is roughly inscribed over the chimney of the Beauchamp Tower. He was buried in the Tower graveyard, but afterwards removed, in 1624, to Arundel, where, on opening a vault in 1777, his coffin was discovered, with an inscription in Latin, describing his unhappy fate, and adding that it was suspected that his death had been hastened by poison; but of this suspicion there is no historical record; nor was it likely that Elizabeth would thus have taken the life of an almost forgotten prisoner, who, after so many years' seclusion from the world, could by no possibility conspire, or cabal, against either her throne or life, even had it been in his nature to enter into any such designs, whereas there never was a man more unfit or unequal to take a leading part in such affairs—still less is it likely, that his conscience would have allowed him to lend his hand to the murder even of his bitterest enemy.

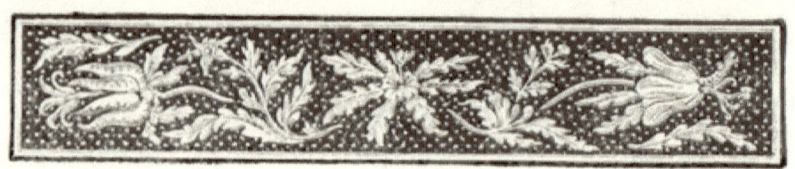

THE GUNPOWDER PLOT.

THE Gunpowder Plot is a subject on which so much has been written, and of which such various versions have been given by historians, that most readers will be acquainted with the principal actors and events of that extraordinary conspiracy; but the arrest and examinations of Guy Fawkes and his associates are matters so connected with Tower History, that it will not be proper to pass the subject, without entering into the question of the origin of the plot, and giving a general account of it, gleaned from the sources which appear the most interesting, as well as the most authentic.

Among the most bigoted of the great Roman Catholic party in England, great disappointment had been felt on discovering that James I. had no intention, after his accession, of changing the Protestant character of the late Queen's government.

Meetings and consultations of a treasonable kind had been privately held in London. Catesby, a gentleman of good family (descended from Richard III.'s faithful follower), took a leading part in these meetings, and in truth was much more the leader of the conspiracy than

Guy Fawkes himself. Catesby had been a profligate in his youth, but later in life had turned his mind to religious questions, and had changed from the Roman Catholic to the Protestant religion; but after reverting to his old courses, and spending the remainder of his estate, had again returned to Romanism in its most bigoted form.

Catesby had taken so leading a part in Essex's insurrection that he narrowly escaped with life, and had been fined 3000*l.* on his release from arrest. It was he who first conceived the scheme of blowing up the King and Parliament. Thomas Winter, a gallant soldier who had served the Dutch against the Spaniards, but gave up his commission from religious scruples, and John Wright, a gentleman of family, were his earliest confidants, the former of whom went over to Flanders, with the object of enlisting into the conspiracy some officers of spirit and daring, who might lead the outbreak. Guido or Guy Fawkes, a Yorkshire gentleman, who had squandered a small estate in Yorkshire and entered the Spanish service, appears to have been the only one of the English officers, serving in the Low Countries, who acceded to Winter's proposals, and returned with him to London, in April, 1604, ready for some desperate undertaking for the overthrow of the government, and assassination of the King.

Being a bold daring man, possessed of some military skill and experience, and deeply imbued with attachment to the Romish faith, Fawkes infused fresh spirit and resolution into the conspiracy. Thomas Percy, a kinsman of the Earl of Northumberland, who had given him a halbert in the Yeomen of the Guard, was another leading character in the conspiracy. He like Fawkes had been a profligate in his youth, and, suddenly changing his habits, was now become a fanatic of the most violent opinions. It was Percy who had been employed by the Catholic party, shortly before Elizabeth's decease, on a mission to James, while yet in Scotland, to ascertain that monarch's views as to the Reformed doctrines; and the wary King having from policy led him to believe he would support the Catholic party, his indignation and fury against James, for the manner in which he had been deceived, knew no bounds.

So active was the part taken by the Roman Catholics to insure the peaceable succession of James, that, immediately on Elizabeth's death, Sir Thomas Tresham, father of Francis, the conspirator, proclaimed the King at Northampton, with some danger to himself, from the excitement of the Protestant population; while his sons Lewis and Francis, and his son-in-law Lord Monteagle, were energetic assistants to the Earl of Southampton, on the occasion of his prompt occupation of the Tower, in the new King's name.

This Francis, like many other of the conspirators, had been a leading man in Essex's insurrection, and was one of those who had been placed on guard in Essex House, over the Lord Keeper, Lord Chief Justice, and other noblemen, during the short time Essex held them in durance.

After binding themselves to secrecy and action, by terrible oaths, which they confirmed by taking the Sacrament together, the conspirators proceeded to examine the localities of the Houses of Parliament, with a view to lay their plan. By a remarkable chance, the house adjoining the Parliament House was untenanted. Percy at once hired it of one Ferris, and, Fawkes's military knowledge being brought into play, a mine was commenced, by which it was expected to effect a passage through the foundation wall, under the House of Parliament. But this undertaking proved more arduous than it at first appeared, for the wall was no less than nine feet in thickness, and built of the hardest materials.

Not to excite suspicion, Winter, John Wright, and Percy, with a few others (seven gentlemen of name and blood as Fawkes emphatically called them in his examinations), were charged with this part of the work. They daily carried down into the vault hard eggs, baked meat, and other durable provision, on which to support themselves, instead of going out to make daily purchases in the market, which might have drawn attention to Ferris's house.

It is almost incredible with what energy these infatuated men persevered in the severe labour of their underground operations, often working by turns through the whole of the night. So extreme was their superstition, that, when some strange sounds were heard in the direction in which they were slowly, but steadily, advancing, they were in the habit, as was afterwards confessed by one of the party, of obtaining from a priest some holy water, with which to sprinkle the sides and bottom of the mine, and persuaded themselves that this caused the strange sounds to cease. The stones and rubbish which they excavated, were carefully spread from day to day, in small quantities, over the surface of a garden in rear of the house.

Contrary to their expectations, the Parliament, instead of meeting this winter (1604), was prorogued to October of next year, upon learning which, they agreed to separate for a month, and to look out for fresh adherents. In February, 1605, they reassembled, and were proceeding with their underground labour, when a noise was heard over their heads, which they discovered, on investigation, was caused by the removal of a quantity of coal, by the tenant of a cellar several feet above the level of their mine, and therefore immediately below the floor of the Parliament House. This discovery greatly facilitated their plans, and made further labour in the mine unnecessary. They at once hired the coal-cellar in Percy's name, and began transferring into it a quantity of gunpowder which they had accumulated in a lone house at Lambeth, to be brought across the river when occasion offered. Upon the barrels of powder, they heaped pieces of iron, crowbars, and all the tools they had used in mining, and then covered the whole with billets and faggots, to avoid any suspicious appearance.

As it was from the first intended, that the blowing up of Parliament was to be the prelude of a general insurrection, it now became necessary to provide a store of arms, and ammunition; with a view to which, Catesby gave out that he had a commission to raise a troop of horse in

London, for the Spanish service; and as he had the full confidence of the other conspirators, he now intrusted the project to several Catholic gentlemen of substance. In order to obtain funds for carrying on the plot, Sir Everard Digby, Ambrose Rookwood, and Francis Tresham, were accordingly admitted into the secret. Meantime the meeting of Parliament was further put off to the 5th November, against which day all the plans of the conspirators were now nearly matured. The great risk was the actual firing of the powder, and this was undertaken by Fawkes, who was familiar with such operations in the wars of the Low Countries, and conversant with the preparations for exploding mines. He prepared a slow match, which he calculated to last exactly a quarter of an hour, thus affording him time to run to the river-side, and embark in a small vessel ready to sail down the Thames with the ebb tide, and convey him to Flanders. Now this part of the plan is somewhat difficult to explain, because, if the conspirators believed that the people would readily join them immediately after the explosion, the natural thing would have been for Fawkes to have appeared at once at the head of the conspirators as their military leader, and to have directed the seizure and occupation of the Tower, and other important points of the city, by the mob and such partisans as they were confident would assemble and join them. This too would have been in combination with the arrangements for the outbreak in the midland counties, where Digby, on the day of the opening of Parliament, was to collect a large party of Catholic partisans and adherents (many of whom were to be kept ignorant of his intentions till the last moment), on the pretext of a great hunting meet at Dunchurch, in Warwickshire.

As soon as they should get the news of the destruction of the King and Parliament, by expresses from London laid along the road, these persons were to detach some men of resolution to seize the person of the Princess Elizabeth (afterwards Queen of Bohemia), then residing at Lord Harrington's house, near Coventry, and proclaim her Queen. Perhaps there is no part of this wild and desperate scheme so unaccountable, or so at variance with the general views and objects of the conspiracy, as this plan for placing the young Elizabeth upon the throne. The tender age of the princess would of course render her a mere puppet in their hands; but what reasonable expectation could they entertain of the country submitting to the nominal government of a child, under the direction of the destroyers of every other member of the Royal Family? Although up to this period the conspirators seem to have acted with great unanimity, a discussion arose, as the time drew near, on the question of warning the Catholic Peers and Members of the House of Commons to absent themselves from Parliament, and thus save their lives, in some way which would not make them acquainted with the conspiracy.

Catesby, and the more violent of the party, had no scruples on this subject, compared with the risk of the secret transpiring; but the greater number, who had friends and connections among the Peers and Members, were strongly in favour of some attempt to warn and save them. The Lords Stourton and Monteagle were married to sisters of Francis Tresham, who recoiled with horror from sacrificing such near relatives, when a word might preserve their lives. But a deaf ear was turned to his entreaties and remonstrances, and there can be little doubt that he then resolved on the anonymous warning, which eventually led to the discovery of the plot.

The other person to whom the information has been attributed was Mrs. Habington, a sister of Lord Monteagle, whose husband was the owner of Hendlip House, where Garnet was eventually arrested after many days' concealment; but certainly Francis Tresham was the person to whom the conspirators themselves attributed the warning. It was about ten days before the day appointed for Parliament to assemble, when Lord Monteagle, son of the Earl of Morley (a Catholic nobleman, and a Peer in right of his mother, the daughter and heiress of Stanley Lord Monteagle), received an anonymous letter delivered by a stranger to one of his servants, who brought it to him while at supper, with some guests, at his house near London. This house was either at Hoxton, or near Barking (where a ruinous mansion still exists, converted into a farmhouse, and said to have belonged to him). The letter ran thus:—

"My Lord, out of the love I bear to some of your friends, I have a care for your preservation. Therefore I would advise you, as you tender your life, to devise some excuse, to shift off your attendance at this Parliament, for God and man have concurred, to punish the wickedness of this time. And think not slightly of this advertisement, but retire yourself into your country, where you may expect the event in safety. For though there be no appearance of any stir, yet I say they will receive a terrible blow this Parliament, and yet they shall not see who hurts them. This counsel is not to be contemned; because it may do you good, and can do you no harm, for the danger is past, as soon as you have burnt the letter. And I hope God will give you the grace to make good use of it, into whose holy protection I commend you."

Monteagle was much puzzled by this mysterious letter, especially at the expression "the danger is past as soon as you have burnt the letter." Though he was not actually alarmed, he knew himself to be somewhat under a cloud, from the part he had taken in Essex's insurrection, and thought best to take the letter at once to the Secretary of State (Lord Salisbury). His house, either at Barking or Hoxton, was not above seven miles from Whitehall, yet it took him four hours to ride there, in such a state were the roads, or rather tracks, in the vicinity of London at that period.

Lord Salisbury, though he did not attach much consequence to the letter, yet deemed it his duty to take the first opportunity of laying it before the King, who was then on a hunting party at Royston, but returned to Whitehall about a week before Parliament was to meet, and being shown the letter, immediately summoned a council to consider its extraordinary contents.

James was just the man to interest himself in a

mystery, and he set to work over Monteagle's letter, weighing and pondering the strange ambiguous terms in which it was worded, with his usual inquisitive diligence. The terrible blow to be struck by unseen hands, the greatness and suddenness of the threatened danger, struck the King as applicable only to gunpowder. It appears indeed very natural that the dreadful death of Darnley, his own father, by the blowing up of the house at the Kirk of Field, may have directed his thoughts immediately to that suspicion. Orders were privately issued for the Earl of Suffolk (Lord Chamberlain) to cause a careful search to be made under the Houses of Parliament, delaying this, however, till the last day before the opening of the session, in order to avoid giving any alarm.

Accordingly on the afternoon of the 4th November, Lord Suffolk, accompanied by Lord Monteagle and a few friends, and attended by a guard, went to the Parliament House, and made a general inspection of all the premises, but especially the cellars below. They saw Fawkes in the coal-cellar, but, as there were many other persons standing about in the passages and other cellars, they took no notice of him at the moment.

But after night had closed in, and all seemed quiet, Sir Thomas Knyvett, an active magistrate, with several armed constables, proceeded, quietly and silently (under the pretence of searching for some furniture which had been abstracted from the King's wardrobe), to the cellar, where Fawkes had been seen in the morning. They met him just as he was quitting his charge for the night, and closing the door. He was instantly seized and searched, as well as every part of the cellar, when, on removal of the billets and faggots, no less than thirty-six barrels of powder appeared, with the tools, iron bars, &c., before mentioned, carefully piled upon them. On Fawkes himself, some slow-match was found, but no weapon or papers.

He was at once taken before the Council, which had already been summoned, though it was near midnight. He did not attempt to deny his guilt; but when urged to name his accomplices, he preserved an obstinate silence, and was committed that same night to the Tower.

Next morning, as soon as the seizure of Fawkes became known, most of the conspirators fled from London in all haste. Some sought the first concealment which offered, but the more determined bent their course for Dunchurch, the rendezvous, before mentioned, of those who were appointed to follow and second Sir E. Digby in the proposed attempt to obtain possession of the person of the Princess. Great consternation prevailed among them, when the news was brought of Fawkes's arrest to Dunchurch; but Catesby, nothing daunted by the danger, collected a number of the boldest, who mounted their horses, and made for Holbeach, a strong mansion of Mr. Stephen Littleton's, about four miles from Stourbridge, in Staffordshire, where he hoped to collect some malcontents from the Welsh border. On mustering at Holbeach, they found their number reduced to less than sixty men, several having deserted them on the road; but as all hope of escape was now gone, they commenced fortifying the house, and prepared to perish rather than surrender.

Their first steps were to put in order what arms they had collected, to block up the lower windows, barricade the outer doors, and take precautions against the danger of their assailants forcing them out, by setting the outhouses and stables on fire. Many of these desperate men had seen enough of foreign war to guide them in adopting the best means for defence; but so reckless were some of the party, that, as was afterwards elicited on their trials, "having spread out two or three lbs. of powder to dry in a platter, before a large fire, and underset the said platter with a great linen bag full of more powder fifteen or sixteen lbs., it so fell out that one coming to put more wood on the fire, and casting it on, there fell a coal into the platter, whereat the powder, taking fire, blew up, scorching Catesby, Grant, and Rookwood, and blowing off part of the roof. The linen bag which was set under the platter, being suddenly carried up through the breach, fell down in the courtyard, whole and unfired, which, had it taken fire in the room, would have slain them all outright."

Not discouraged by this mischance, they continued to make active preparations for defence, and when, on the 8th, the sheriff presented himself with the "posse comitatus" of the county, and a number of well-armed followers, they rejected his summons to surrender, flew to their posts, and opposed a gallant resistance to the assault which instantly took place. But the assailants soon forced their way into the courtyard, where Catesby and Percy, who fought back to back, were struck down by the same shot, which passed through both their bodies, killing Catesby outright, Percy surviving till next day. Thomas Winter, the two Wrights, and Rookwood, being wounded and struck down, were taken prisoners, to undergo the terrible fate they had so desperately striven to avoid.

Tresham, who had ventured to stay in London, and, affecting entire innocence, to appear as usual in public, soon became an object of suspicion to the Government. On the 12th he was arrested and sent to the Tower, but did not live to be brought to trial, being attacked by an illness, during which his unfortunate wife was allowed to attend and nurse him, but which carried him off a fortnight after his committal.

It has been asserted that Fawkes, after three days of sullen silence, made on the 8th November, of his own free will, a full confession of the whole scheme of the conspiracy (saving only the names of his comrades). There is a room in the Governor's house at the Tower, generally known as the Council Chamber, where a large marble tablet, let into the wall, commemorates the names of the Council, and of the leaders of the plot, with other details. The tradition has always existed, that in this chamber Fawkes was examined by the Council, and underwent the application of the rack in its severest form; indeed, so generally was this tradition received in the Tower, that not many years ago the servants of the Major of the Tower, the occupant of this house, were extremely reluctant to enter this apartment after dark, and more than one sentry has declared he had heard terrible groans proceeding from the window of this ominous chamber.

From the determined courage of Fawkes, it might be reasonably inferred that he would endure any torture rather than confess; but experience has shown the fearful power of pain to extort even false declarations from persons exposed to the barbarous extremities of torture. A few days after the seizure of Fawkes, the wretched men taken at Holbeach, some of them badly wounded, were brought to London, and examined separately for several days. In consequence of supposed admissions from them, Garnet, the principal of the English Jesuits, with Gerard and Greenway, two others of the fraternity, were proclaimed, and rewards were offered for their capture.

The trials of the conspirators proceeded, and, the usual sentence of treason being passed, Digby, R. Winter, Grant, and Bates were executed on the 27th, in St. Paul's Churchyard, and the following day, Fawkes, Rookwood, Keyes, and Thomas Winter were executed in Palace Yard, with all the horrible details which followed on the sentence for high treason.

As the awful procession passed along the Strand, Rookwood perceived his wife, a lady of beauty and merit, at a window, and called to her, as he lay on the hurdle, to pray for him. She replied, in a clear voice, "I will, I will; and do you offer yourself with a good heart to your Creator. I yield you to Him, with as full an assurance that you will be accepted of Him, as when He gave you to me!"

Gerard, being found impenetrably silent under verbal examination, was barbarously tortured by suspension from a hook in the wall, by the wrists, till he fainted. Vinegar was poured down his throat to revive him, and the same cruel torment was again applied to him; but on his again swooning with the agony, Sir W. Waad, the Lieutenant of the Tower ("that villain Waad," as Raleigh called him), hard and brutal as he was, refused to allow the torture to be repeated. Gerard being afterwards negligently guarded, on the supposition of his weakness from the torture he had endured, escaped with Greenway, and got safe to Holland.

Garnet had fled for concealment to Hendlip, the country house of Mr. Habington, a Roman Catholic gentleman, near Worcester. Sir H. Bromley, the sheriff of the county, having received positive information that he was there, surrounded the house with a number of armed men, and commenced a strict search through the building; but Habington's house, like many others in those precarious times, was provided with such ingeniously contrived retreats, that the task proved extremely difficult, and walls, wainscot, and partitions without number, were broken through in the search, without success, till, on the fourth day of the search, two wretched creatures, Owen and Chambers, emerged from a secret door in the wainscot of the long gallery, and gave themselves up; having had but a single apple for their sustenance, during the whole time of their concealment. Owen, after committal to the Tower, escaped a dreadful death on the scaffold, by suicide. Indeed, it appears that a certain torture, applied to him for a very short time on his first examination, drove him to this act, from sheer terror of its repetition in a severer form.

Encouraged by the capture of these men, the sheriff and his followers continued breaking down partitions, and searching the large open chimneys of the mansion at Hendlip, till, on the 8th day, a recess concealed in a chimney by a plank covered with mortar and soot, was discovered, from which Garnet the Jesuit, and Oldcorn his companion, were dragged out. They had had time to lay in some store of provision when they first betook themselves to their hiding-place, besides which broth and caudle had been ingeniously conveyed to them by a reed passed through a very small aperture higher up in the chimney, from the sleeping-room of a lady of the family, which scanty supply had enabled them thus to sustain life for so many days.

They were brought to the Tower, where, by James's order, they were tolerably well treated; but subjected to endless separate examinations, the King taking great interest in framing subtle questions himself, by which he expected to entrap and entangle them in their answers.

Among other devices, Garnet and Oldcorn were placed in adjoining cells, with persons concealed behind the walls, to listen and take notes of the conversation which might pass between them.

When their trial came on, although Garnet's line of

defence was to deny everything, till actually proved against him, yet sufficient was elicited by cross-examination, and by the device above-mentioned of listening informants, to satisfy the Council that Catesby had made Garnet privy to the plot, several months before the meeting of Parliament; chiefly, as it seemed, to obtain from him certain religious sedatives for his conscience, especially as to the question, so long disputed among the conspirators, of how far it would be lawful to sacrifice some Catholic Peers and innocent persons in the general destruction of the Parliament.

The trial of Garnet was conducted with the most scandalous disregard of reason and justice, the Crown prosecutor appearing to consider invective and abuse of the prisoner better arguments against him, than any which could be drawn from the evidence, though that evidence was, in itself, sufficient to satisfy any jury of the guilt of the prisoner.

In the report of Garnet's trial (State Trials), the speech of Lord Northampton, one of the Royal Commissioners, occupies some sixteen pages of close-printed folio; and though the editor admits, in a note, that "My Lord had corrected and somewhat enlarged its spoken dimensions," it can hardly have occupied much less than four hours in delivery. Yet it is very little to the purpose, for the chief object of the speaker appears to have been to exhibit his own pedantic learning, by illustrations from the " works of all authors who ever were extant."

Besides quotations from Tertullian, Democritus, Heliodorus, Menenius Agrippa, and Thomas Aquinas, he cited Mahomet, Rahab, Nero, David, Telemachus, Joseph, Valentinian, Pericles, Zedekiah, Trajan, and King John, as instances, in support of the absurd paradoxes of which his oration was composed.

The Attorney-General indulged in the vituperation of the prisoner, usual in state trials of that time, interspersed with sneers at the Roman Catholic religion and abuse of the Pope, but otherwise conducted the prosecution with ability, and placed the guilt of the prisoner on grounds which he did not attempt to controvert, the sacredness of confession being almost his only plea for extenuation of his share in the plot. As there could be no doubt that he was guilty of misprision or concealment of the treason, he was sentenced accordingly, and executed on the 3rd May in St. Paul's Churchyard.

He made a pious and moderate speech on the scaffold, which, together with his meek and patient deportment, so favourably affected the spectators, that when, in pursuance of the horrible ceremony of execution for high treason, the executioner was proceeding to cut him down from the gibbet while yet alive, to perform the frightful barbarities of embowelling and quartering, the people uttered such furious outcries and threats, that the man slunk back in terror of their violence, and allowed him to hang till life was extinct. The King took credit for this afterwards, by declaring, that the executioner had delayed cutting Garnet down by his express order, but the other version is the most probable.

Oldcorn, the unfortunate companion of Garnet in the Priests' Hole at Hendlip, was placed on the rack several times in the Tower, to draw from him further explanations of the conversations between him and Garnet in their adjoining prisons, which had been overheard and reported; but he either knew little of the detail of the plot and those engaged in it, or his courage defeated the cruelty of his tormentors, for he confessed nothing; and after a mock trial was sent to Worcester, and there executed, with the usual barbarities of the punishment for high treason.

On reviewing the circumstances of the Gunpowder Plot, we shall find that in one respect it differs from any other of the wild and desperate attempts of this kind recorded in history. The men who are commonly found to engage in such enterprises are persons who have lost all, or have never had anything to lose, and who venture their worthless lives, for the chance of gaining plunder or power.

But Catesby and his comrades, though they had many of them been licentious in early life, and had taken part in Essex's insurrection and other treasonable schemes, arising out of the great religious and political changes in the government of England, were men of a higher class than those who usually plunge into schemes of violence and murder. Most of them were men who in peaceable times, and free from the strong influence of religious enthusiasm, might have passed through life as respectable country gentlemen, living quietly with their families and friends, and performing with credit the duties and avocations belonging to their position. The Attorney-General, in his speech for the prosecution, did not fail to notice

"Little Ease," Guy Fawkes's Dungeon, in Vaults of White Tower.

this fact, though in aggravation of their offence; for he described them as "gentlemen of good houses, of excellent parts, and of very competent fortunes and estates."

Although several of them expressed, after their trials, a certain degree of contrition for having entered into the wicked scheme of wholesale murder of the Royal Family and Parliament, yet it cannot be doubted that their consciences were lulled into a false repose, by the strong conviction, that the terrible responsibility they had taken on themselves, was a duty they were discharging to their country and to their Maker. Grant, among others, declared on the scaffold, "I am convinced that our project was so far from being sinful, that I rely on the part I have taken in it, for an expiation of all the sins I have ever committed." Finally, it must be observed that, oppressed and insulted as the Roman Catholics had been by laws and penalties disgraceful to any civilized nation, yet the large majority of them showed abhorrence of the massacre proposed by the conspirators, and expressed but little sympathy for the fate of the leaders of the Gunpowder Plot. On the other hand, so violent was the feeling in the House of Commons, that it was actually question of petitioning the King that some " yet sharper pains might be devised than customary in executions for high treason," to mark the public horror of the contrivers of so bloody and atrocious a crime.

Door of Guy Fawkes's Dungeon.

ARABELLA STUART.

HE dismal records of the Tower present hardly any more melancholy story than that of Arabella Stuart, usually called "the Lady Arabella." She was the only child of Charles Earl of Lennox, younger brother of the unfortunate Henry Darnley, and great-grandson of Margaret Queen of Scots, Henry VII.'s daughter. This connection with the Blood Royal of England caused her to be jealously watched both by Elizabeth and James. Her personal charms, and her cultivated mind (she had been carefully educated by her grandmother, the Countess of Lennox, who resided in London), endeared her to all, and made her one of the brightest ornaments of the English Court.

Prompted by hatred of Elizabeth, the notorious Father Parsons collected all the details of Arabella's connexion with the Crown, which he published in a pamphlet dedicated to the Earl of Essex, in 1594, under the name of Dolman; and though he could not maintain any immediate claim of Arabella's, yet by thus bringing forward her name and descent, in a work which had considerable circulation even among foreign courts. she became an object of very general interest, which unhappily served to increase the jealousy with which Elizabeth regarded her. James had made an attempt to obtain Elizabeth's consent to a marriage between Arabella and his cousin Esme Stuart, Duke of Lennox; but the Queen refused, on the ground that the Duke was a Papist. A son of the Earl of Northumberland then became her suitor; but the Queen, as soon as she observed that Lady Arabella viewed him favourably, placed her in confinement, from which she was not released till she had disclaimed any further communication with her admirer.

On James's accession to the English throne her position was by no means improved. The wild schemes of Lord Cobham and his reckless conspiracy, embraced, among other absurd projects, that of raising Arabella to the English throne. On Cobham's trial, at which she was present, Lord Burleigh vindicated her from any knowledge of this treason, by saying in open court, " Here hath been a touch of Lady Arabella, a near kinswoman of the King's. Let us not scandal the innocent. She is as innocent of all this as I or any man here; for when she received a letter from Lord Cobham, she only laughed at it, and immediately sent it to the King;" to which the old Earl of Nottingham, who was standing next her, added, " The lady here doth protest, upon her salvation, that she never dealt in any of these things, and so she wills me to tell the Court."

James appears to have been satisfied for the moment with this solemn denial; but, with his usual meanness, he so scantily supplied her with the means of maintaining her exalted rank, that she was reduced to the most distressing straits and difficulties. Her employments, according to a letter of the Queen's Master of Requests, would seem to acquit her of all ambitious designs, or of meddling in state affairs. "She spends her time," writes Fowler, "in lecture-reading, hearing of preaching and service, and visiting the Princesses."

About the year 1608, James seems to have received her into better favour, for he gave her 1000 marks to pay her debts, and 200*l.* worth of plate for her table, with permission to marry, provided she chose a British subject. Her choice fell upon W. Seymour, grandson to the Earl of Hertford; but whether from doubts of the King's sincerity, or other reasons, Arabella required that their marriage, which took place in 1609, should be kept secret. It was the discovery of the secrecy of her marriage which gave the King a pretext for the persecution, with which he now began to harass his unfortunate cousin. Upon a rumour of her having renewed her intimacy with Seymour, they were both summoned before the Privy Council; but, after a short examination, their denial appears to have been admitted, and they were released from custody. Next year, however, further proofs being obtained by the King, the lady was placed in charge of Sir T. Parry, at Lambeth, and her husband committed to the Tower. One Melvin, confined there as a Nonconforming minister, addressed this distich to him:—

"Communis tecum mihi causa est carceris, Arabella tibi causa est, Araque Sacra mihi."

There is a letter of Arabella's to the King in the Earl of Oxford's collection, which was probably written at this time :—

Extract of Letter from LADY ARABELLA *to* LORD (NORTHAMPTON ?).

"MY LORD,—The long acquaintance between us, and the good experience of your honourable dealing heretofore, maketh me not only hope, but be most assured, that if you knew my most discomfortable and distressed estate, you would acquaint his Majesty withal, and consequently procure my relief and redress, as you have done at other times. I have been sick even to the death, from which it hath pleased God miraculously to deliver me for this present danger. but find myself so weak by reason I have wanted those ordinary helps whereby most others in my case, be they never so poor or unfortunate soever, are preserved alive at least for charity, that, unless I may be suffered to have those about me, that I may trust, this sentence my Lord Treasurer pronounced after his Majesty refusing that trifle of my work [she had worked a piece of embroidery for the King, who refused to accept it]. by your persuasion, as I take it, will prove the certain and apparent cause of my death, whereof I thought good to advertise you, that you both may be the better prepared in case you, or either of you, have possessed the King with such opinions of me as thereupon I shall be suspected and restrained, till help come too late ; and be assured that neither physician, nor other, but when I think good, shall come about me whilst I live, till I have his

Majesty's favour, without which I desire not to live; and you remember of old, I dare die, so I be not guilty of my own death, and oppress others with my ruin too, if there be no other way, as God forbid. . . . . I can get neither clothes nor posset at all, for example, nor anything but ordinary diet, nor compliments fit for a sick body in my case when I call for it."

It was perhaps in consequence of the unhappy lady's reasonable and humble appeal that she was removed to a less rigorous confinement, at a Mr. Conyers's house, near Highgate; and Mr. Seymour obtained "the liberty of the Tower." But the King, being informed by his spies, that they were taking advantage of this relaxation, to renew their correspondence, ordered Lady Arabella to be removed to Durham Castle; and then, driven to despair, they formed that plan of escape which, failing by a most unhappy mistake, they never met again.

For some days Arabella appeared to renounce all hope, and submit herself to the King's will, and thus "induced her keepers and attendants into securitie by the fayre shew of conformitye and willingness to goe on her journey towards Durham," which journey was appointed for the next day. She then put on her disguise, which consisted of a large pair of French-fashioned hose, a man's doublet, a large peruke with long locks, a black hat, black cloak, white, or, as another account says, russet boots with red tops, and a rapier by her side. Thus equipped, on Monday, the 4th of June, between three and four in the afternoon, she boldly went forth, accompanied by Mr. Markham, one of her attendants. They went on foot for a mile and a half, till they reached a small tavern, where Crompton, a devoted attendant, waited for them with saddle-horses. But in the shattered condition of Arabella's health, even the short walk had been too much for her. She turned sick and faint, and could scarcely mount her horse. "That gentleman will hardly reach London," said the ostler, as he held the stirrup for her to mount. As the distance, however, was short, and her attendants were careful not to hurry her, she reached Blackwall by six o'clock. There, at the tavern, they learned that a flaxen-haired man, accompanied by a gentleman, had set off a little before. Arabella waited at Blackwall an hour and a half, her servants arriving one after another. But she waited in vain for Seymour, till delay became so hazardous that she was forced to depart, taking with her only one female attendant. She set off in a boat with "a good pair of oars," followed by another carrying their baggage. The rest waited for Seymour. Arabella and her maid were in the first boat, Crompton and Markham in the second. They rowed down the Thames till nearly opposite Leigh, where they saw a vessel lying at anchor. Upon their hailing her, and asking whither she was bound, Briggs, the master, answered, "For Berwick." Then the youngest of the two servants said to the master, that if he would leave his voyage, and serve him, he would give him any money he chose to ask. The master refused the offer, saying that he was bound to his merchant, and could not break his word. They then asked him if there was not a French vessel lying somewhere near. The master answered that he knew not, unless it might be a vessel that was riding about a mile and a half up the river. They said that, if it were the right ship, they should recognise her by a flag which the master had promised to hold out; so rowing up to her, they found she was the desired bark, and all four went on board, in the sight of the Berwick captain. The latter particularly noticed the company, which he described as consisting of " a man about forty years, with a long flaxen beard, something corpulent, and, as he remembered, in a suit of grey cloth, with a rapier and a dagger gilt. The other was younger, with a little black beard, who was the man that most desired the master to receive them, and carry them for Calais, with large proffers for the passage, who, as he remembered, was in black apparel. The third man he did not notice, and therefore could not describe him. Of the women one was barefaced, in a black riding safe-guard, with a black hat, having nothing on her head but a black hat and her hair. This last he took to be Moll Cutpurse: and thought that, if it were she, she had made some fault, and was desirous of escape. The other woman sat close covered, with a black hood or veil over her head and face, so that he could not see her: only saw that under her mantle she had a white attire (a glimpse of her white boots), and that, on pulling off her glove, 'a marvellous fair white hand was revealed.'"

Arabella had now escaped the greater dangers, and reached the French ship. But where was Seymour? At every station she had lingered with fatal delay, in the hopes of his joining her; and now, having exhausted the last moment of time, she besought the ship to remain at anchor till he arrived. Her followers, more prudent, knew that imminent danger had already been incurred by the time they had lost, and that they risked the whole enterprise by these dangerous delays. Nothing but the dread of her husband's capture, if he did not reach the French ship, can account for her imprudence. Her followers at last refused to listen any longer to her entreaties, and, desiring the master to make sail, proceeded to sea, with their charge, a prey to dreadful anxiety as to whether her husband had eluded pursuit.

In the mean time Seymour's escape from the Tower had been managed with entire success. He had obtained a disguise, consisting of a peruque and beard of black hair, and a tawny suit. A cart had come into the gate early in the morning, bringing his billets of wood, and Seymour " walked alone without suspicion from his lodging, following this cart, as it returned," by the Tower wharf, and passing the warder at the iron gate, where he found one Rodney waiting for him with a boat. With two servants and Rodney, he rowed hard till they came to Leigh, hoping to find the French ship; but as no sign of her was to be seen, and the sea was becoming too rough for their boat, they hired a fishing-boat, for twenty shillings, to carry them to a collier, which was visible in the distance, slowly sailing down the river. The master, seeing "a gentleman in a full suit of satin, laid with gold and silver lace, asked his name; who answered, 'Rodney;'"

and after some talk, the master agreed to put off his voyage to Newcastle, and, for the sum of forty pounds, to carry the boat's crew to Calais. The collier, having received them on board, proceeded down the Thames till they drew near to a place called "the Buoy." Suddenly, Rodney saw a French vessel in the distance, and hurriedly called on the master of the collier to speak with her. The master declared that in the position they were it was impossible to approach her, but promised, if they "anchored near, to send his boat on board the same."

At noon they cast anchor at "the Buoy," and a quarter of an hour after the French bark cast anchor about a mile and a half off. The boat of the collier was then lowered, and boarded the Frenchman, but, finding the vessel was not that of which they were in quest, they again weighed their anchor. The wind preventing them from standing for Calais, they put in near Harwich on Tuesday night; and on Thursday, the wind being still contrary, they made for Ostend. Some of the crew of the collier beginning to ask questions, Rodney said they were leaving England on account of a duel. On Friday morning, at eight o'clock, they reached Ostend; and the master, having received the money for his voyage, returned to Ipswich, carrying with him a letter from Rodney to Francis Seymour.

The moment it was known at Court that Arabella and Seymour had escaped from Conyers' house and from the Tower, one of the King's messengers came galloping from Lord Salisbury to Phineas Pette, at Deptford, the

King's master-shipwright, "to man the Light Horseman with twenty musqueteers, and to run out as low as the Nore head, to search all shippes, barks, and other vessels, for the Lady Arabella." The order was promptly obeyed, but the vessels were searched in vain, as well as every house in the town of Leigh.

On the same day, the following proclamation was made, forbidding any to assist the fugitives, and commanding all, under high penalties, to surrender them:—

"Whereas we are geven to understand that the Lady Arabella and William Seymour, second Sonne to the Lord Beauchampe, being for divers great and haynous Offences committed, the one to our Tower of London, and the other to speciall Guard, have found the means, by the wicked Practises of divers lewd Persons, as, namely, Markham, Crompton, Rodney, and others, to breake Prison and make Escape, on Monday, the third of June, with an intent to transport themselves into forreyne Partes. Wee doe hereby straightly charge and command all Persones whatsoever, upon their Allegiance and Dutie, not onlie to forbeare to receave, harbor, or assist them in their passage anie way, as they will answer it at their Perilles; but upon the like charge and Paine to use the best meanes they can for their Apprehension, and Keeping them in safe Custody, which Wee will take as an acceptable Service.

"Given at Greenwich, the fowerth Daie of June, 1611.

"PER IPSUM REGEM."

Salisbury was then ordered to send a letter, post haste, to the Governor of Calais, to stop the fugitives should they arrive in that port. The French ambassador was also requested to send a message to the Governor of Calais to detain them, till the pleasure of the King of France should be known. James added that he did not think they meant to stay in France, or that they "expected anie good that way," but only to land, and from thence have an easy passage to some place on the Continent.

The next step was to send vessels to sea in pursuit. Admiral Monson discovered, by means of the waterman who had rowed her down the river, that Arabella had gone on board the French ship at about four o'clock in the morning; and that she had been detained two hours by the ebb, which, however, he reckoned would be recovered, for he calculated that she could not fetch beyond the North Foreland; and if the wind were east, it would be impossible to reach Calais that night. He immediately ordered a ship of war to stand over for Calais; and, while the larger vessel was preparing, he seized an oyster-boat, and put six men, with shot, in her, to hasten after the fugitives with all speed. The Admiral himself went out in a light fishing-craft, and sent a vessel, named the Adventure, towards Calais, while another was despatched to the coast of Flanders.

About half-Channel over, the Adventure got sight of a small vessel under all sail for Calais, and crowded sail to pursue her; but so little wind blew that neither pursuer nor pursued could make much way. The Adventure then lowered a boat, with an armed crew, which soon arrived at the French vessel, and, having vainly challenged her, endeavoured to stop her course by firing musketry, while the Adventure was fast gaining on the chase. The French vessel stood thirteen shots before she surrendered, when Arabella—for it was too truly her vessel—seeing that all hope was over, came forward and discovered herself to the officer of the boat, who instantly demanded her husband. She answered bravely, that she had not seen him, but hoped he had got safely over, declaring that her joy at his escape was greater than her grief at her own capture. She was then taken on board the Adventure, and there kept close prisoner till they reached the river, when Monson sent the intelligence to Lord Salisbury, not permitting Arabella to leave the ship till he received orders, though he declared that "in the mean time she should not want anything the shore could afford, or any other honourable privilege." James immediately ordered her to be sent to the Tower. Sir John More, writing to Sir Ralph Winwood, says, "In this passionate hurry here was a proclamation first conceived in very bitter terms; but my Lord Treasurer's moderation seasoned at the print, as now here you find it. There are likewise three letters despatched in haste, written by Sir Thomas Lake to the King and Queen Regent of France, and to the Archdukes, all written with harsher ink than now if they were to do (I presume) they should be, especially that to the Archdukes, which did seem to presuppose their course to tend that way; and all three describing the offence in black colours, and pressing their sending back without delay. Indeed the general belief was that they intended to settle themselves in Brabant, and under the favour of the Popish faction; but now I rather think they will be most pitied by the Puritans, and that their course did wholly tend to France. And though for the former I had only mine own corrigible imagination, yet for the latter many potent reasons do concur: As that the ship that did attend them was French, the place that Mr. Seymour made for was Calais, the man that made their perukes was a French clockmaker, who is fled with them, and in the ship is said to be found a French post with letters from the Ambassador.

"The proclamation for the oath is by divers found strange, for that it is so general; but where love is, loyalty will not be found wanting."

The following persons were now committed to prison:—

> The Countess of Shrewsbury, to the Tower.
> Sir James Crofts, to the Fleete.
> Doctor Moundford, close prisoner in the Gatehouse.
> Hugh Crompton, to the Fleete.
> Edward Rodney, to the Gatehouse.
> William Markham, ditto.
> Bates, to the Bailiffe of Oxford.
> Pigot, sent to the Earl of Shrewsbury to be forthcoming.
> John Baisly, waterman, committed to Davy Rowden, a messenger.

Batten, Mr. Seymour's barber, committed to the dungeon of the Tower by Mr. Lieutenant.

Haladin, a Frenchman, committed to the Porter's Lodge in the Tower.

Mr. Seymour's butler, committed to the Tower.

James Corvé, the French skipper, to Newgate.

Seerson, the skipper of Ipswich, to the Gatehouse.

An examination was shortly held before the Lords of the Council, in which every attempt was made to entrap the prisoners into some confession which should legally justify their imprisonment, and prove them guilty of high treason. Arabella answered calmly; but the Countess of Shrewsbury was so excited and indignant at the unjust and secret tribunal before which she was summoned, that she declared that she would answer nothing in private; if she had offended against the law, she would answer it in public. The chief evidence against her consisted in the large amount of ready money that was found at her disposal—no less than 20,000*l.*, besides bills of exchange for the use of Arabella. All this was supposed to be destined to bribe the Catholic party; and though it was acknowledged that Arabella had "not yet been found inclinable to Popery," yet, says the sagacious More, "her aunt made account belike that, being beyond the seas in the hands of Jesuits and priests, either the stroke of their arguments or the pinch of poverty might force her to the other side. Our Scots and English differ much," he continues, "in opinion upon this point. These do hold that, if this couple should have escaped, the danger was not like to have been very great, in regard that their pretensions are so many degrees removed, and they ungraceful both in their persons and in their houses; so as a hot alarm taken at the matter will make them more illustrious in the world's eye than now they are; and so it is said to fill his Majesty with fearful imaginations, and with him the Prince, who cannot easily be removed from any settled opinion."

In addition to the above arrests, the Earl of Shrewsbury was kept a prisoner in his own house; and the old Earl of Hertford summoned to Court, with the proviso, "if he be found healthful enough to travel, he must not delay his coming."

An appearance of indifference was the only way by which W. Seymour could hope to disarm the King's anger against him; and not only did he abstain from any further endeavour to rescue Arabella, but it appears too sure that he never attempted to soothe her distress by getting any letters conveyed to her. Had he done so, her reason might possibly have been preserved under all her sorrows; and there can be little doubt that subordinate persons, in attendance on the Tower prisoners, might have been bribed for this purpose. But it would seem that, whatever the loyalty and spirit afterwards shown by Seymour, in his gallant adherence to the fortunes of James's son and successor, he was a stranger to that devotion which the conduct of his wife must have inspired in a more tender nature. It is, however, to be remembered, whether from revival of old feelings, or some regrets at his former conduct, Seymour, when an old man, and after many years of marriage to a second wife, expressly desired, in his will, to be buried by the side of Arabella Stuart.

Lady Shrewsbury, though detained a prisoner, was granted many indulgences. She was allowed the liberty of the Tower, and even permitted a short respite to wait on her husband, who was attacked with illness. It was believed that she might have regained her liberty altogether, had it not been for some incoherent accusations made against her by the Lady Arabella, whose sorrows had at length affected her reason. Upon the pretext of these accusations James again ordered her into close constraint till she should answer certain interrogatories; but she still proudly refused to answer anything in private, although she declared her willingness to submit to a public examination. On the 2nd of July, 1612, she was called before the Privy Council and Judges, at the Lord Chancellor's, where she was "charged by the Attorney-General with contempt towards the King by refusing at the first summons to answer all questions." Her persistent refusal, it was said, greatly aggravated her fault, as well as the scornful terms she used towards some of the lords. She again urged "the privilege of her person and nobility," and, after a fruitless discussion, was sent back to the Tower, with a menace of a proceeding in the Star Chamber if she persisted in her wilfulness.

The death of Lord Beauchamp, in July, 1612, brought William Seymour a step nearer to the succession, and rendered it the more important in the King's eyes that Arabella and he should never be reunited;

but there was little fear of that now. At times her intellect showed signs of its former brightness, and a feigned cheerfulness took the place of her despair. "To express her joy" at the marriage of the Princess Elizabeth, she decked herself in courtly robes, and "provided herself with four gowns of the richest description;" but this pretended satisfaction produced no result, as the Princess, in all the joy of bridal pomp and happiness, "had not a thought" for her miserable cousin in the Tower.

Early in March, 1613, Arabella was attacked with convulsions, and declared distracted by the physician—a declaration which probably saved the Countess of Shrewsbury, by invalidating the accusations which her niece had in her frenzy made against her.

On the 13th of May, 1613, Sir William Waad, the Lieutenant of the Tower, was discharged from his place, "to the great contentment of the prisoners," on an accusation of embezzling the lost jewels of Arabella. Whether he or his wife or daughter took them, was not clearly proved, but they had certainly disappeared; and he had acquired such a bad name by his extortions and hard usage of his prisoners that no one regretted his disgrace.

"On the 25th of September, 1615," says Nichols, "that ill-fated and persecuted lady, Arabella Seymour, daughter of Charles Earl of Lennox, cousin-german of Henry Darnley, father of King James, died in the Tower of London."

In the dead of night this daughter of a line of

kings was carried, by water, all pomp and ceremony being forbidden, from the Tower to Westminster Abbey, and there deposited in the royal vault, beneath the coffin of Mary Queen of Scots. The burial-service was read as if by stealth over some felon's grave, "because to have a great funeral for one dying out of the King's favour, would have reflected upon the King's honour."

For more than two centuries Arabella Seymour has lain in her unnoticed grave in Henry VII.'s Chapel. No monument marks her resting-place, and no epitaph records her virtues, her courage, and her misfortunes.

> "Where London's Tower its turrets show,
>   So stately by old Thames's side,
> Fair Arabella, child of woe,
>   For many a day had sat and sigh'd.
> And as she heard the waves arise,
>   And as she heard the bleak wind roar,
> As fast did heave her heartfelt sighs,
>   And still so fast her tears did pour."
>
> <div align="right">EVANS's <i>Old Ballads.</i></div>

TABLE AND BOWL IN NORTH-EAST WINDOW OF ORATORY, ST. THOMAS'S TOWER.

MURDER OF OVERBURY.

THE murder of Sir T. Overbury in the Tower, in 1613, was one of the darkest deeds which stain the annals of James I.'s reign. This man had been raised from a low station by Carr, Lord Rochester, and had become his intimate counsellor and friend. Acting with an honesty towards his patron which deserved a better reward, he had earnestly dissuaded him from his disgraceful connexion with Lady Essex, which, becoming known to that vindictive woman, she induced her paramour to obtain an arbitrary order from the King for the committal of Overbury to the Tower, where he was closely incarcerated, and precluded from any intercourse and correspondence with his friends and family.

Sir W. Waad, the Lieutenant, whom Raleigh, in one of his letters, called "that villain Waad," and who was anything but lenient to his prisoners, was yet a man incapable of lending himself to the iniquitous projects of Lady Essex, and was therefore removed, to be replaced by a creature of Somerset's, ready to undertake any crime to forward his own interest. Sir Gervase Elways, the new Lieutenant, at once entered into the cruel design of destroying Overbury by slow poisons, which for a length of time were mixed with his daily meals. The wretched man's constitution resisted their effects too long for the patience of the Countess, who lived in dread of his finding means to publish the knowledge he possessed of her profligacy. It was therefore determined to put a quicker end to his life, by a strong dose of corrosive sublimate, under the effects of which he died in dreadful agonies. The appearance of his body after death, being such as would have excited suspicion, if seen, it was wrapped in a sheet, and buried privately the same day in the Tower chapel.

Soon after this the favour of the new Earl of Somerset began to decline. Villiers, Duke of Buckingham, was fast supplanting him in the King's good graces; and the rumours afloat as to Overbury's death led to an inquiry which soon left no doubt of his having come to his end by poison.

One Weston, who had been employed as Overbury's gaoler in the Tower, being apprehended, made some confessions which caused the seizure and committal of Sir Gervase Elways, Sir Thomas Monson, and Mrs. Turner, a person deep in Lady Essex's wicked secrets and confidence. Their imprisonment was a prelude to the committal to the Tower of the Earl and Countess of Somerset themselves.

Weston being brought to trial, it was proved that he had been placed in the Tower as Sir T. Overbury's keeper by Sir Thomas Monson, at the instance of the Countess, and that the various slow poisons administered by his means to the prisoner, had been supplied by Mrs. Turner, who was tried, found guilty, and hanged, as was likewise Weston. Monson was shortly after released, partly from want of proof, and partly from some mysterious influence attributed by common report to the King himself.

Elways made so bold and able a defence that it was thought at first he would be acquitted; but one Franklin, being produced as evidence, swore that, being with Mrs. Turner at Lady Essex's house, to receive orders for the purchase and preparation of poisons, a letter chanced to be brought to her from Elways, which from its bad writing she could not well read, and desired Franklin, who knew his handwriting better, to read it to her. This he did; and, in doing so, observed particularly the expression, in reference to Overbury, that "This scab is like the fox, the more he is cursed the more he thrives." Upon this, and other corroborating evidence, Elways was sentenced to death, but permitted, at his special entreaty, to be hanged on Tower Hill instead of at Tyburn. He exercised a curious taste in dress on this occasion. "He was habited in a black suit and black jerkin with hanging sleeves; on his head he wore a crimson satin cap laced round about, and under that a white linen night-cap with a border, and over that a black hat with a broad ribbon and ruff-band, thick couched with lace, a pair of sky-coloured silk stockings, and a pair of three-soled shoes (quære, high-heeled?)." On the scaffold, at Tower Hill, he acknowledged his sentence to be just; but declared, that, though he knew of the murder, he had no actual part in it, and that he had received all his instructions from Sir T. Monson, on behalf of the Countess of Somerset.

He was accompanied to the gallows by two of the King's chaplains, Drs. Whyting and Felton. A large number of persons of condition also attended at his execution, to whom he thus returned his thanks for the compliment: "Nobles and others," he said, "to see your faces here rejoiceth me, whereby you show your love in granting my request to witness my death." After some other remarks to the same effect, he went on to say, "that though his end was a bitter cup, it was mingled with God's mercy in calling him away thus, whereas He might have taken his life in *shooting London Bridge*, or by some fall or accident, and then some unrepented sin had been damnation to him." He said also that he accounted it a favour of the King that he should die on Tower Hill, and not at Tyburn, which was a place of more public reproach, "whereby," said he, "I now see the Tower, wherein of late I had been called to business of the State."

This wretched man seems to have set great value on his office in the Tower, as it came out on his trial, that, so far from his appointment being a gratuitous benefit conferred on him by Somerset, he had paid Waad no less than 1400*l*. to vacate it in his favour, and had further engaged to pay him 600*l*. more. No doubt the emoluments and fees extorted in those days from the state prisoners, produced a large income; but the sum was a very large one, especially when the nomination was conditional on his abetting a murder.

It is recorded of Sir G. Elways's own servant, as proof of his extreme devotion to his master, that he assisted the executioner's man in pulling his legs after he was turned off the ladder; a kindness no doubt in shortning his sufferings, but one which few could have brought themselves to perform.

The trial of the Earl and Countess of Somerset was put off, on different pretexts, till May 1616, when the Countess confessed herself guilty; and as it was evident to the lords who tried the case, that Somerset knew of his abandoned wife's proceedings, they were both sent back to the Tower, where the Earl remained a prisoner till 1621; but, strange to say, the Countess very soon after received the royal pardon. They were both ordered to repair either to Grays or Cowsham, houses of Lord Wallingford, in Oxfordshire, and to remain, on pain of death, within three miles' compass of the same. Here they retired, shunned and abhorred by all, till the year 1624, when, a few months before his own death, the King granted them both a full pardon, leaving them, however, so destitute from the confiscation of their property, that they were compelled to remain in entire obscurity. The Countess died in 1632, but Somerset survived her several years in want and misery.

The Earl of Essex, after his wife's desertion of him, served many years in the Low Countries, where he acquired that knowledge of war so often fatal to the Royalists when he became General of the Parliament's army in the Civil War.

SIR WALTER RALEIGH.

FEW characters in English history have inspired more interest that the gallant and unfortunate Sir Walter Raleigh.

A full narrative of his brilliant career during the reign of Elizabeth would be a history of some of the most glorious passages of her reign. A soldier, a seaman, and a statesman, it was by his advice she was mostly guided in the measures so successfully carried out for encountering the great Armada, and defeating that prodigious armament.

But before this event, his gallant conduct in the Netherlands, his voyages of discovery and conquests, especially the planting of the British flag by one of his captains, Sir Richard Greenville, on the shores of what is now named Carolina, but was then named Virginia by the Queen herself, and his eminent services in Ireland, had raised the fame of Raleigh to a very high standard, not in England only, but throughout all parts of Europe. The Queen loaded him with honours and riches, but, with all her consideration for him as a statesman and a soldier, the delight she took in descending to the most absurd coquetry, led her to encourage the competition of Raleigh and Essex for her favour, and by a show of alternate preference to keep up the farce of a romantic rivalry between them.

After the defeat of the Armada, to which the spirit and skill of Raleigh had so greatly contributed, he had reached the highest pinnacle of court favour, when the discovery by the Queen of his intrigue with Elizabeth Throgmorton, one of her maids of honour, threw her into transports of fury, and she at once consigned them both to a close imprisonment in the Tower. The cell which tradition has assigned to Raleigh on this occasion proves the severity of his captivity, while the Queen's anger lasted.

After a short time, however, Raleigh, by a letter to the Queen of the most fulsome flattery, obtained his release and married Elizabeth Throgmorton, who proved a most devoted and faithful wife, through all the trying vicissitudes of fortune which afterwards befel him. But the Queen still owed him a grudge for having admired any woman but herself, and his first expedition to Guiana seems to have been undertaken while he was yet in disgrace, and in order to keep out of her Majesty's sight till her displeasure should have passed. After his return he was again recalled to Court, where, as Captain of the Body Guard, he was generally near her Majesty's person, and his ability to discourse with eloquence on all matters, from the highest affairs of state, to his own marvellous adventures and perils by sea and land, attracted the Queen's attention and favour, while his display of dress and magnificence flattered her vanity.

His conspicuous wisdom in the very curious parliamentary debates which occurred about this time, on monopolies, on the designs and policy of Spain, and other important national topics, gave him great weight in the country; but his opposition to Lord Burleigh on certain commercial questions, contributed to revive their old dissensions, which proved afterwards a source of serious injury to Raleigh.

The mighty sovereign, who, with all her prejudice and caprices, well knew how to distinguish the best servants of the country and the Crown, and who had made amends to Raleigh, by her late gifts and distinctions, for her former severity, was now drawing near her end, to be succeeded by one who, with far more of personal weakness and vanity, possessed none of her great qualities. King James's antipathy to war rendered him incapable of appreciating the military capacity of Raleigh, which only inspired him with jealousy and distrust. In respect to learning too, James's was a pedantry of the most paltry sort, and was very inferior to the philosophy and extensive range of Raleigh's mind. The late Earl of Essex, who had paid great court to James for years before his accession, had strongly prejudiced him against Raleigh, as a man of dangerous designs, and likely to oppose his accession.

Lord Cobham, brother-in-law of Burleigh, who appears to have been a restless intriguer, with neither heart nor character, had entered into correspondence with Count Aremberg, a Flemish minister of the King of Spain, and had persuaded him, that peace with Spain might be brought about, if Sir W. Raleigh's opposition to it could be overcome, suggesting that this might be managed by a bribe. It was this offer (though rejected by Raleigh as an idle tale of Cobham's own invention), combined with a rumour of his having conspired to place Lady Arabella Stuart on the throne, which formed the basis of the accusations of treason brought against him by James, for the trial of which a commission was assembled at Winchester, Burleigh himself being one of the members. It is scarcely credible to what violent language, and vulgar insult, the Attorney-General, Sir E. Coke, descended, in bringing forward the charges, all of which were met and refuted by the prisoner, with a patience and dignity worthy of his noble nature. The Commissioners, to their disgrace, seldom interposed. Burleigh, on the contrary, made some specious remarks, which tended to prejudice them against the prisoner, and Chief-Justice Popham alone of the Commissioners seemed to recollect his position as a judicial personage, intrusted with the life and honour of an illustrious prisoner.

The evidence on which the Commission found Raleigh guilty of high treason, after a quarter of an hour's pretended deliberation, was such as could never in our times have procured a conviction; and it was even said that when Coke, who had gone out of the Court for air, and was walking in the Castle garden, was told the verdict, he said to his informant, "Surely you are mistaken? I myself accused him only of misprision (concealment) of treason!" Whether from compunction, or that he was content to have Raleigh now wholly in his power, the King did not carry out the sentence, but after a month of cruel suspense at Winchester, ordered him to be removed to close confinement in the Tower. The Lords Cobham and Grey, and Sir G. Markham, were tried and found guilty by the same Commission, and the King, when he signed the warrant for their execution, directed that Raleigh should be informed that a warrant for his death had also been prepared. In order, however, more completely to blast his character, and to give more authority to the verdict, the King had recourse to a paltry stratagem, by which, though he himself regarded it as a masterpiece of policy, no one was deceived. Cobham was brought out on the scaffold at Winchester, and made, what purported to be, a dying speech, asserting the truth of the evidence he had given against Raleigh, at the conclusion of which the Sheriff informed him (as had been preconcerted) that the King pardoned him, and, with loud expressions of feigned astonishment and gratitude, he was reconducted to his prison.

Raleigh, in the mean time, made becoming preparation for the end he daily expected. He received the Bishop of Winchester's prayers and consolations, in a spirit which greatly edified that prelate, and wrote a touching letter of farewell to his wife, some passages of which may here be transcribed :—

"You shall now receive, my dear wife, my last words. My love I send you, that you may keep it when I am dead, and my counsel, that you may remember it when I am no more. I would not by my will present you with sorrows, my dear Bess; let them go into the grave with me, and be buried in the dust; and seeing it is not the will of God that ever I shall see you more in this life, bear it patiently, and with a heart like thyself.

"I send you all the thanks which my heart can conceive, or my words can express, for your many travails and care taken for me; which though they have not taken effect as you wished, yet my debt to you is not the less.

"I beseech you, for the love you bear me living, do not hide yourself after my death, but seek to help your miserable fortunes, and the right of your poor child. Thy mourning cannot avail me when I am but dust."

He then enters into some detail of the condition of his estates, and what he can leave her, and thus resumes:—

"If you can live free from want, care for no more: the rest is but vanity. Love God, and repose yourself on Him, and therein you shall find true and lasting riches and endless comfort. Teach your son to love and fear God while he is yet young, that the fear of God may grow up with him, and then God will be a husband to you, and a father to him.

"I can say no more, time and death call me away."

If any proof were needed that the insinuations of Coke, and even of Chief-Justice Popham, on his late trial, that he was an atheist, were utterly false, surely the pious simplicity and religious trust of this letter at once refute them.

Shortly after the pretended reprieve of Cobham, Raleigh was conveyed from Winchester to the Tower, and, at her earnest entreaty, Lady Raleigh was allowed to share his prison, where their youngest son, Carew, was afterwards born.

Mr. Hawthorn, a clergyman, a physician, and his steward, were allowed occasionally to visit him in prison, and it was under the heavy affliction of disgrace and confinement that he turned his active mind to the composition of his celebrated 'History of the World.'

But the King's persecution did not end yet. Raleigh's estate of Sherborne, which he had been allowed to place in the hands of trustees for his eldest son, was, contrary to all faith, seized, on pretence of a flaw in the deed, and given to the worthless Robert Carr. Lady Raleigh in vain threw herself at James's feet to entreat that her son might not be reduced to beggary. He received her harshly, and merely repeated. "I maun have the land, I maun have it for Carr."

A more powerful intercessor. Prince Henry, who had conceived a great friendship as well as admiration for Raleigh, urged his suit with his utmost zeal, believing it to be of national importance, that so brave and wise a commander should not languish in captivity and disgrace: but his exertions were fruitless. Prince Henry had no wild ambition for distinction in war, but he fully agreed with the views of naval preparation which Raleigh's wisdom and forethought had urgently represented as necessary for

England. "Though the sword," said Raleigh, "is put in the sheath, we must not suffer it to rust, or stick so fast that we could not draw it readily when need requires. If those powerful means, whereby we reduced our enemies to the seeking of peace, were neglected, so that we could not assume the use of them, those proud mastering spirits would be more likely to shake us by the ears as enemies, than to take us by the hand as friends. Therefore, far be it from us to trust more to the friendship of strangers, which is but dissembled upon policy, than to our own strength. Peace is a blessing of God, and therefore, doubtless, blessed are those means whereby peace is gained and preserved. Our defence and safety is in our shipping and sea forces, which should be esteemed as His gifts, and then only available and beneficial, when He vouchsafes us his grace to use them aright."

The hardships of Raleigh's imprisonment in the Tower, were in some degree alleviated by the company of some of his fellow-captives; amongst whom were the Earl of Northumberland, a man of considerable learning, who had been committed on the same charge as Raleigh; Piercy, a great chemist, confined since the Gunpowder Plot for supposed participation in that conspiracy; and Hoskins, a poet and philosopher of his day, mentioned by Ben Jonson as "the man who polished him." Although Sir W. Waad, the Governor of the Tower, was no friend to Raleigh, he does not appear to have put any needless restraint on the meeting of these literary companions in misfortune at Northumberland's apartments, where discourses and experiments on chemistry

were a favourite resource. Still a long confinement in so
damp and cold an abode as the Tower (surrounded as it

SIR WALTER RALEIGH'S CELL IN WHITE TOWER.

then was, by a wide muddy ditch), had now produced
injurious effects on Raleigh's health. In a pathetic appeal
to James's Queen, for her intercession, he complained,
that, after eight years, he was under as much restraint as
the first day, and that " he had in vain petitioned for so
much grace, as to walk with his keeper up the hill within
the Tower." His physician also represented to Lord

Burleigh, the necessity of his lodging in a warmer apartment, which had been built for a laboratory in the garden of his prison. Whether this favour was obtained, does not appear; but there is no doubt that the death of his old and vindictive enemy, Lord Burleigh, about this time, produced some change for the better in his treatment. His release, however, was still opposed by the unworthy Somerset, who had obtained from the King Raleigh's valuable estate at Sherborne. One solace of Raleigh's weary sojourn in the Tower was the correspondence and kind notice of Prince Henry, who was wont to say to his private friends, that "his father was the only man who would have shut up such a bird in a cage." In his 'History of the World,' Raleigh alludes in a touching tone to the early loss of this admirable Prince. "I had written for the Prince, a Treatise on the 'Art of War by Sea,' but God hath spared me the labour of finishing it by his loss; I will therefore leave him in the hands of God, that hath him. ' Curæ leves loquuntur, ingentes stupent.'"

Soon after this misfortune the continued efforts of his friends procured him what was termed the "Liberty of the Tower," which consisted in the free range of the interior of the fortress, and he now brought before the King, the scheme for the expedition to Guiana, where he was convinced that he had ascertained the existence of a gold-mine at the time of his expedition to America during the former reign.

As the expense was all to come from the resources of his friends and himself, and the King was to have a fifth of the profits, he was not likely to resist this bait for his avarice; the only obstacle arose from the remonstrances of Gondomar, the Spanish Ambassador, who, by his address and accomplishments, had obtained much influence over the King's mind. He knew Raleigh's enmity to the Spanish nation, and had no doubt that, if he gained a footing in Guiana, the occupation of the shores of the Orinoco by his countrymen, where a kinsman of his own had been appointed Governor, would soon be put a stop to, by the English expedition. For this reason he made the strongest remonstrances against Raleigh's scheme, and at first succeeded in persuading James that it would lead to a war with Spain.

But although arguments might fail, Raleigh was aware that well-applied bribery would succeed, and by a large present to Sir W. St. John and Sir E. Villiers, the two uncles of Buckingham, he at length, in March, 1615, obtained the King's consent to the project, and three days afterwards the order arrived, for his release from the sad confinement in which he had passed some of the best years of his life, and he at once entered, with all the ardour of his nature, into the preparation for his expedition. Wonderful as it may seem, he had contrived for several years to maintain an intercourse with some of the most civilised of the Indian chiefs, whom he had known on his former expedition, and a deputation from these Indians had actually come to England, and obtained access to him while prisoner in the Tower. As Gondomar continued incessant in his remonstrances to the King, and as little dependence could be placed on any resolution of James, Raleigh deemed it advisable to make a formal protest, that he had no thoughts of attacking Spanish territory, but simply desired to prosecute his search for mines in those portions of Guiana, which, by right of discovery, and consent of the natives, were regarded as belonging to the British Crown.

Gondomar affected to be content with these explanations, and, upon his opposition being withdrawn, adventurers from all parts of England volunteered their services, many of them bringing money and supplies, while several eminent merchants embarked capital in the enterprise.

A commission under the Privy Seal constituted Raleigh Commander-in-Chief and Governor. Some wary friends advised him to press for the formality of a pardon under the Great Seal before he sailed, but this caution was unhappily overlooked; and indeed who could for a moment suppose that his appointment as "Commander and Governor," with power of life and death over those under his orders, would not completely cancel any former sentence? On hoisting his flag on board the 'Destiny,' a ship of thirty-six guns and 200 men (including the Volunteers), and commanded by his eldest son, he issued an order for Divine Service to be daily read in the squadron, and for sundry measures of morality and discipline, showing the religious tone of his mind, as well as his knowledge of the best means of governing the wild spirits he commanded. The weather obliging him to put into Cork, he was generously received, and supplied with many useful stores by the Earl of Cork, who had purchased Raleigh's Irish estates many years before, and improved them with the utmost success. He again put to sea full of hopes and confidence; but though the voyage was neither tedious nor stormy, the ravages of scurvy and fever made sad havoc among his men. He reached Guiana in November, with his numbers reduced by a fourth, and learned, to his mortification, that the Spaniards had established themselves on the shore of the river Orinoco, of which he had formerly taken possession in the name of the Queen.

To ascend that river as far as the supposed situation of the mine, was now his great object; but he found that all his schemes had been betrayed to the Spaniards, and that, so far from any chance of surprising them into granting him a free passage up the river, they had made preparation for giving him a hostile reception, and had occupied in force the access from the river to the mine. Prostrate with illness himself, he at once resolved to detach his son and Captain Keymis, the original discoverer of the mine on the former expedition, with instructions to penetrate at all hazards to the place, avoiding collision if possible; but, if attacked, to repel force by force.

The result was most unfortunate: the Spaniards laid an ambush for the English: and though Keymis and young Raleigh fought most gallantly, the latter was killed, and Keymis, after an unsuccessful attempt to reach the mine, was again surprised, utterly defeated, and obliged to return, without having brought back a single ingot to prove the existence of the mine. The unfortunate man, on being reproached by Raleigh with neglect of his instructions and orders, retired to his cabin and blew out his brains. Harsh as it might appear in Raleigh to condemn so gallant a follower for this unlucky failure, it must be recollected that he had thrown away many valuable lives by his rashness, had given a signal triumph to the Spaniards, and, worse than all, he had never penetrated to the mine, so as to bring back any proof of its existence; a point of every consequence for bearing out the assurances which Raleigh had given to the King. That the mine had never been discovered by the Spaniards themselves, was shown by Keymis's excuse, "that, if he had persisted in making his way to it without force to defend it, he should only have been opening the discovery of it to the Spaniards."

The Adventurers who had followed the fortunes of Raleigh, in expectation of acquiring vast riches, now began to show discontent, and to excite mutiny among the sailors. All spirit and energy was gone; there was not a hope of success, and nothing remained but to abandon the search, and return to England. Raleigh reached Plymouth in July, 1618, where, at the instance of Gondomar, he was immediately arrested by his own relative, Sir Lewis Stukely, and conveyed a prisoner to the Tower. Short and sad is the remainder of the story. His fate was at once resolved; a vain attempt at escape only increased the King's desire for his death; and so base was James's deference to the Spaniards, that he actually offered to deliver up Raleigh to be put to death in Spain, according to King Philip's pleasure. That monarch wisely declined the office of executioner, leaving it to Gondomar, to make sure of his victim in London. Accordingly, an order, under the Privy Seal, was directed to the Judges of the King's Bench, commanding them to proceed to execution against Sir W. Raleigh, under his former sentence. In vain did he plead, that His Majesty's military commission as Marshal, placing him in command of a royal fleet and army, with power of trial for life and death, amounted, both in justice and reason, to a full pardon of any former offence. Chief-Justice Montague overruled the Plea; Yelverton, the Attorney-General, declared, that fifteen years ago the prisoner had been convicted of treason, since which time His Majesty had mercifully abstained from the infliction of the sentence; but it was now the royal pleasure that it should be carried out. Raleigh's pathetic appeal for even a few days' respite was refused.

He said, " My Lords, I desire but this much favour, that I may not be cut off suddenly, but may be granted some time to settle my affairs and my mind, for I have somewhat to do in discharge of my reputation and conscience. I crave not this to obtain one minute of life, for now, being old, sickly, disgraced, and certain to go to death, my life is wearisome to me; and I further beseech your Lordships, that when I go to die I may have leave to speak freely." And he concluded with much solemnity, " I take God to be my judge, before whom I shall shortly appear, that I was never disloyal to His Majesty, which I shall justify, where I shall not fear the face of any King on earth; and so I beseech you all to pray for me."

He was conducted to the Gatehouse Prison, and informed that he was to die next morning at nine, so eager for his death was the heartless King.

A last interview with his wife was the only favour granted him; and we can well imagine what that parting must have been to the loving and faithful partner of his misfortunes. Fearful lest speaking of their surviving son should add to her agony, he shortened this cruel hour by affectionately entreating her to leave him. In floods of tears she told him she had obtained the disposal of his body. "It is well, Bess," he answered, smiling, "that thou mayest dispose of that dead thou hadst not always the disposing of when alive;" and then, tenderly embracing her, he tore himself away, and devoted most of the night to preparing a sort of manifesto of his innocence of every charge which had been brought against him.

His cheerfulness, piety, and resignation, were shown in the few bitter hours which preceded his death next morning. He received the Sacrament, breakfasted, and smoked for a few minutes afterwards, as usual with him.

Shortly before nine he was led to the scaffold erected in Old Palace Yard, dressed in black, and bearing himself with much dignity and composure. So great was the crowd and pressure, that he nearly fainted before he could be got up to the scaffold.

The Earls of Arundel, Oxford, and Northampton, Lords Doncaster, Percy, Sheffield, and other persons of rank, were already assembled, all of whom he saluted with his usual courtesy. In the brief address which he now made, he entreated all present, if they saw any weakness in him, to lay it to his ill-health, and not to fear. "I thank God," he said, "that of his goodness He hath vouchsafed me to die in the sight of so noble an assembly, and not in darkness, nor in the Tower, where I have suffered so much adversity." His weakness here obliged him to pause, and, turning to the Lords who sat in the windows above him, he expressed his fear that they could not hear him, on which Lord Arundel said he would come down to him, as did also Lords Doncaster and Northampton; when, in a firmer tone, he spoke further, from some notes he held in his hand, both generally as to his innocence, and especially as to the slanderous report, that he had stood in a window at Essex's execution, and puffed out smoke from a pipe, in disdain of him. My Lord of Essex, he said, never saw his face at all; for though he was in the Armoury, he had retired back from his view. "It was true," he said, "I was of the contrary faction, and helped to pluck him down, but I knew him for a noble gentleman, and always believed it would have been better for me had his life been spared; for those who set me against him, set themselves afterwards against me, and were my greatest enemies." After some further speech with the Lords present, the scaffold was cleared, and he bid the executioner show him the axe, and, feeling its edge, said, "It is a sharp medicine, but a cure for all diseases."

After a short internal prayer, he examined the block to see the proper manner of placing himself, and then quietly said that he was ready. When the Executioner came forward and asked his forgiveness, Raleigh smiled, and " bade him be satisfied, but desired him not to strike till he gave the signal, and then to fear nothing and strike home." He kneeled, and laid his head on the block; his lips were seen to move a little space as in earnest prayer, and he then lifted his hand as the signal; but, whether from not observing it, or from agitation, the man delayed his stroke till Raleigh said in a clear voice. What dost thou fear? strike, man!" The blow was then given, but, though it deprived him probably of consciousness, it was not till a second stroke, that the head rolled on the scaffold. It was observed that the body never moved, and that the effusion of blood was unusually great. As showing the vigour of his constitution, though lately so enfeebled by care and illness. The head, after being held up to the people, with the words. " This is the head of a traitor," was placed in a red bag, which was immediately wrapped in his velvet gown, carried to a mourning coach, and conveyed to his unhappy wife, who caused it to be embalmed, and preserved it with pious care till her own death, which did not occur for near thirty years after his tragedy.

The records of the time make no allusion to any display of military or other precautions against the chances of tumult or rescue, and yet it seems strange that a man of such renown, and prominent in that daring and love

of adventure so popular with the English, should have
fallen a victim to the Spanish influence over James,
without a hand being raised to save him. So arbitrary
and illegal an exercise of royal power was a signal proof
of the altered power and condition of the nobility, which
the iron hand of Elizabeth, and the unbounded influence
she acquired over her subjects, had effected during her
long reign.

ENTRANCE TO RALEIGH'S CELL—INSCRIPTIONS LEFT BY PRISONERS.

ASSASSINATION OF THE DUKE OF BUCKINGHAM.

HE assassination of the Duke of Buckingham by Felton, which occurred at Portsmouth during his preparation for a second attempt to relieve the Hugonots in Rochelle, in 1628, was at first supposed by the court, to be connected with some general conspiracy, arising from the discontents of the nation. The arbitrary and violent counsels of Buckingham had, at this early period of Charles I.'s reign, excited a spirit of great and deep-seated indignation; and although Felton's act was committed out of personal revenge, for the refusal of promotion when serving in the Duke's previous expedition, it was deemed advisable to make a searching investigation into all the details of the murder, and for this purpose he was brought up to the Tower.

At this period an examination in the Tower was invested with a certain mystery, connected with the known existence of the rack in its gloomy dungeons; and though that dreadful engine had again and again been declared illegal, yet it was little more than twenty years since its terrible powers had been employed, in endeavours to extort confessions from Guy Fawkes. The act of Felton was one, which might be regarded as warranting any means within the limits of custom, if not of law, for arriving at the truth. But on following out the examination, it soon appeared that, although he had excused the deed to his conscience as the justifiable destruction of an enemy to public liberty, yet that revenge for not receiving the promotion he believed to be due to his military conduct, had been his real and only motive, and that he had neither accomplices nor instigators. Felton was tried before a common jury; and as he neither denied the crime, nor made any defence, but, on the contrary, admitted his guilt, expressing the utmost penitence for what he had done, he was condemned and executed in the ordinary manner.

It was currently reported, that during one of his examinations before the Council, when the Earl of Dorset menaced him with the rack, as by the King's order, he stoutly declared he did not believe that so good and gracious a Prince would allow his subjects to be tortured contrary to law. "I do affirm," he said, "upon my salvation, that my purpose was not known to any man; but," he added, "if you do put me on the rack, I will accuse you, my Lord of Dorset, and none but yourself." In that quaint old book, Aubrey's 'Miscellanies,' published in 1721, there is a wild story of the warning or prophecy by the ghost of Sir G. Villiers, father of the Duke of Buckingham, to an old friend of his, which may be introduced here as a sample of the marvellous credulity by which such a tale could gain circulation.

Aubrey tells it as follows, with the remark that he had heard it from others besides Sir W. Dugdale, whom he quotes as his chief authority.

"To one Mr. Towes, who had been schoolfellow with Sir G. Villiers, the father of the first Duke of Buckingham, and was his friend and neighbour, as he lay in his bed awake, and it was daylight, came into his chamber the phantom of his dear friend Sir G. Villiers. Said Mr. Towes to him, 'Why, you are dead. What makes you here?' Said the Knight, 'I am dead; but I cannot rest in peace, for the wickedness and abomination of my son George, at Court. I do appear to you to tell him of it, and to advise and detort him from his evil ways.' Said Mr. Towes, 'The Duke will not believe me, but will say that I am either mad or doat.' Said Sir George, 'Go to him from me, and tell him by such a token' (a mole he had in some secret place, which none but himself knew of). Accordingly, Mr. Towes went to the Duke, who laughed at his message. At his return home, the phantom appeared again, and told him 'that the Duke would be stabbed' (he drew out a dagger) 'a quarter of a year after, and you shall outlive him half a year; and the warning that you shall have of your death will be, that your nose will fall a bleeding.' All which accordingly fell out so. This account I have had, in the main, from two or three; but Sir W. Dugdale affirms what I have here taken from him to be true; and that the apparition told him of several things to come, which proved true; *e.g.* of a prisoner in the Tower that should be delivered. This

Mr. Towes had so often the ghost of his old friend appear to him, that it was not at all terrible to him. He was Surveyor of the Works at Windsor (by the favour of the Duke). Being there, sitting in the hall, he cried out, 'The Duke of Buckingham is stabbed!' He was stabbed, as after was known, at that very moment that Mr. Towes cried out."

WENTWORTH, EARL OF STRAFFORD.

F all the distinguished persons who had shown personal attachment to Charles I., and had most faithfully and devotedly served him, no man was more conspicuous than Wentworth Earl of Strafford. Against him, therefore, above all the servants of the King, was the vengeance of his enemies directed.

As Chief Governor of Ireland, Strafford showed a vigour and energy which had much contributed to the peace of that country; but in his determination to uphold the laws, and to check the violence and anarchy which too often prevailed in that country, it cannot be denied that he had occasionally adopted counsels of an arbitrary and barely legal character, of the notoriety of which his enemies were not slow to take advantage.

Haughty and cold in his manners, and accustomed to have his commands promptly obeyed, the Earl was at little pains to soften the rigour of his government by any arts of conciliation; and his known and open opinions as to the duties of subjects to their Princes, rendered him one of the most formidable opponents to those doctrines of resistance to illegal authority, which were daily gaining ground in the nation.

Before quitting the government of Ireland, for his successes in which country the King had created him an Earl, Strafford left instructions for raising and equipping an army of 8000 men to assist Charles in a fresh attempt to reduce the Scotch to their obedience.

Great complaints were made in England by the Commons that Catholics had been enlisted in the Irish army, and Charles was compelled to give orders for the discharge of the few soldiers of that faith who had joined the new levies. Strafford was not a man to disguise his sentiments on this or any other proceedings of the Commons tending to curtail the King's authority and powers; consequently he was denounced as the "great apostate" from the cause of the people, and so strong was the hatred expressed against him personally, that many of his friends recommended him to avoid the approaching storm by withdrawing from the Court to his government in Ireland; but to his fearless mind such advice appeared unworthy of notice, and, as the King was desirous of his presence and of the aid of his wisdom and firmness, he did not hesitate to continue his attendance at the Court and Council.

The Commons well knew the value of such an adviser to Charles, harassed as he was and uncertain whom to mistrust and in whom to place his confidence. The leaders of the popular party met early in November, 1640, to arrange their plans, and, after a debate with closed doors, the majority of the Commons proceeded to the bar of the House of Lords, where Mr. Pym, their spokesman, impeached Wentworth Earl of Strafford of high treason.

The Earl was informed of what had taken place in the House of Lords while in conference with the King, and hastened to the House; but on entering was met with cries from the Peers of the popular side to withdraw. The Lord Keeper at the same time desired him to kneel at the Bar, and informed him that he was to consider himself a prisoner in the custody of Black Rod till he should clear himself of the impeachment which had been now preferred against him by the Commons. An attempt which he made to address the House from the Bar was instantly silenced, and he was ordered to depart in charge of the Usher.

It was about a month afterwards that Archbishop Laud, who was as obnoxious to the Commons as his friend Strafford, was in like manner impeached by them at the Bar of the Lords, silenced in his attempt to speak, and committed to the custody of Black Rod. A few weeks after this (in January, 1641) Laud was committed to the Tower, from whence neither he nor his unfortunate friend was destined to issue more till they went to their doom on Tower Hill.

It was not till March (1641) that the arrangements were finished and the charges prepared against Strafford, whose trial was as usual to take place in Westminster Hall before the Peers. Places were set apart for the managers on the part of the House of Commons, for the deputation who had come from Ireland with the accusations against him of illegal acts while Governor, and for the Scots Commissioners, who charged him with intentions of transporting his Irish army to Scotland for its subjection and plunder. Galleries were also enclosed behind the throne for the King, Queen, and Court to be spectators of the solemn spectacle.

Without entering into the detail of the charges against the Earl, it may suffice to state that those from Ireland related to illegal quartering of soldiers on the inhabitants, and various acts of military oppression or exaction. On behalf of the Scots, he was accused of levying an army in Ireland expressly for the destruction of constitutional liberty in Scotland; while with strange inconsistency the Commons themselves charged him with intending the Irish army for the subversion of the rights and liberties of England.

A number of minor acts were charged against the Earl, of which no one, of itself, could be called treasonable, yet when accumulated into one charge they were most unfairly represented, as amounting to the guilt of high treason. But the most atrocious injustice towards Strafford was the demand of the Commons that the members of the King's Council, at the deliberations of which he had assisted, should be absolved from the secresy invariably observed there, and subjected to separate examinations as to the illegal tendency of certain advice given by Strafford to the King in Council. A document was produced by Vane the younger, purporting to be a note delivered at the Council Board, to the effect that, as the King had exhausted all ordinary means of bringing his subjects to their obedience, His Majesty was now justified in employing his Irish forces for reducing *this* kingdom to obedience.

It was plain that, if such advice were really given, Scotland, and not England, must have been meant by the words "*this* kingdom;" since it was solely on the state of affairs in Scotland that the deliberation in question had taken place, and the Lords who had been present declared, on interrogation, that there had never been mention that day but of Scotland, and further that they could not remember any such paper as that produced by Vane, being presented by Strafford on the occasion.

As the trial proceeded, the weakness and vague nature of the charges became daily more apparent, while the dignity, moderation, and ability with which Strafford conducted his defence was evidently producing a strong influence in his favour among the majority of the Peers. The managers of the Commons soon perceived the change, and, a debate having taken place with closed doors, it was announced that the impeachment was abandoned, and that the House had resolved to proceed against Strafford by a Bill of Attainder.

Pym read the paper above alluded to to the House, which purported to be the original notes taken by Vane the elder, Secretary to the Council, on the occasion in question, and a Bill of Attainder against the Earl for endeavours to subvert the liberties of the country was formally introduced on the ground of those notes.

Though the King's friends did their best to stem the

torrent of public feeling, it proved too strong for their efforts, and within a fortnight the Bill of Attainder was passed by the Commons. Meanwhile the Lords continued the trial, and Strafford concluded his defence by a pathetic and noble appeal to the sense of justice of his judges, reminding them how his hard fate might befal any of them if they sanctioned such perversion of right as that of which he was now made a victim, and ending with the beautiful words uttered by David in his affliction, " In te Domine confido; non confundar in æternum."

Though the King sent his assurance to Strafford that he would not forsake him, so great appeared the danger of a general rising and tumult, that a proposal was made to Balfour, Lieutenant of the Tower, to admit 100 picked Royalist soldiers, with the secret view of removing Strafford to Newgate, and contriving a rescue by the way. But Balfour stood true to his charge, refusing to open his gates, and rejecting a large bribe which was afterwards offered him to connive at the Earl's escape.

Charles now informed the two Houses of Parliament in a short speech that, had they condemned Strafford on fair proof, he would have allowed the law to take its course; but as he himself knew the falsehood of the evidence which had been brought forward of Strafford's illegal advice to him in Council, he could not give the Royal assent to the Attainder. The Bill had now come up to the Lords, and passed in a very thin House by a majority of 22 to 16, several of the Earl's friends being intimidated from attendance by the violence and menaces of the mob outside the House.

That the King himself should have been affected by fears of insurrection in the City seems hard to believe : still harder is it to believe that he could ever have consented to sacrifice the unhappy Strafford. But where is there a limit to the infirmity of human nature? On receiving from the Earl a letter, generously desiring that no further risk should be incurred for his sake by the King, and freely offering his life as the only means now left for reconcilement with his people, Charles, after consultation with Judges, Bishops, and all whom he deemed fit counsellors in his distress and difficulty. and who proved but too ready, with the bright exception of Bishop Juxon, to avoid the responsibility of speaking in favour of Strafford, yielded his assent to the Bill of Attainder, and the doom of his devoted friend and follower was sealed.

Little did the King suppose that the pious and single-hearted Bishop, who ventured, on this emergency. to give him such faithful and fearless counsel, would be the consoler of his own last hours, when overtaken by the fate to which he had now the weakness to abandon Strafford.

With tears and lamentation he signed the warrant; and if proof were wanting of the distraction of Charles's mind by the interior conflict he had endured, he now took the truly hopeless step of sending the young Prince of Wales to the House of Lords with a letter entreating that both Houses would consent to the sentence of death against Strafford being changed to one of imprisonment for life. It may well be imagined that this petition was treated with scorn, and even a reprieve for a few days refused. The next morning Wentworth Earl of Strafford was conducted to the scaffold on Tower Hill. He had made it his dying request to Archbishop Laud to give him his blessing as he should pass under the windows of his prison (probably a room in the Bloody Tower just above the gate). The venerable prelate raised his hands as his unfortunate friend approached, but grief choked his utterance: he gazed for a moment on the sad but undaunted countenance of the Earl, and sank back insensible on the floor of his prison. Strafford had faced death too often in the field to show fear at its near approach, even in the terrible form of a public execution. He made a brief speech from the scaffold, in which he said that it was some satisfaction to him to know that the King did not think he deserved to die, that he was not guilty of the crimes laid to his charge, and that he forgave, not merely in form, but from his very heart, all his enemies. He then laid his head on the block, and at one blow it was severed from his body. Vast crowds had assembled to witness the execution: they behaved with silence and decency, and those near the scaffold listened to his last words with respect; but in the evening emissaries were sent out into the streets, who excited the mob to make bonfires in the principal streets of the City, and, with huzzas and shouts, to break the windows of those whom they supposed to have been friendly to their victim.

LORD CAPEL.

AS it would be impossible to give a more simple and graphic account of Lord Capel's escape and unfortunate recapture than we find in the pages of Clarendon, his narrative shall be here transcribed without alteration or comment.

"The Lord Capel, shortly after he was brought prisoner to the Tower from Windsor Castle, had by a wonderful adventure, having a cord and all things necessary conveyed to him, let himself down out of the window of his chamber in the night, over the wall of the Tower, and had been directed through what part of the ditch he might be best able to wade. Whether he found the right place, or whether there was no safer place, he found the water and the mud so deep that, if he had not been by the head taller than other men, he must have perished, since the water came up to his chin. The way was so long to the other side, and the fatigue of drawing himself out of so much mud so intolerable, that his spirits were near spent, and he was once ready to call out for help, as thinking it better to be carried back again to the prison, than to be found in such a place, from whence he could not extricate himself, and where he was ready to expire.

"But it pleased God that he got at last to the other side, where his friends expected him, and carried him to a chamber in the Temple, where he remained two or three nights secure from any discovery, notwithstanding the diligence that could not but be used to recover a man they designed to use no better. After two or three days a friend whom he trusted much, and who deserved to be trusted, conceiving that he might be more secure in a place to which there was less resort, and where there were so many harboured who were every day sought after, had provided a lodging for him in a private house in Lambeth Marsh; and calling upon him in an evening, when it was dark, to go thither, they chose rather to take any boat they found ready at the Temple Stairs, than to trust one of that people with the secret; and it was so late that there was one only boat left there. In that the Lord Capel (as well disguised as he thought necessary) and his friend put themselves, and bid the waterman to row them to Lambeth. Whether, in their passage thither, the other gentleman called him 'my Lord,' as was confidently reported, or whether the waterman had any jealousy by observing what he thought was a disguise, when they were landed, the wicked waterman undiscerned followed them, till he saw into what house they went; and then went to an officer and demanded, 'What he would give him to bring him to the place where the Lord Capel lay?' And the officer promising to give him ten pounds, he led him presently to the house, where that excellent person was seized upon, and the next day carried to the Tower.

"When the Petition that his wife had delivered to

the Parliament was read, many gentlemen spoke on his behalf, and mentioned the great virtues which were in him; and 'That he had never deceived them, or pretended to be of their party; but always resolutely declared himself for the King;' and Cromwell, who had known him very well, spoke so much good of him, and professed to have so much kindness and respect for him, that all men thought he was now safe, when he concluded, 'That his affection to the public so much weighed down his private friendship, that he could not but tell them that the question was now, whether they would preserve the most bitter and most implacable enemy they had; that he knew the Lord Capel very well, and knew that he would be the last man in England that would forsake the Royal interest; that he had great courage, industry, and generosity; that he had many friends who would always adhere to him; and that as long as he lived, whatsoever condition he was in, he would be a thorn in their sides; and therefore, for the good of the Commonwealth, he should give his vote against the Petition.' Ireton's hatred was immortal: he spake of him, and against him, as of a man of whom he was heartily afraid. Very many were swayed by the argument that had been urged against Duke Hamilton, 'That God was not pleased that he should escape, because He had put him into their hands again, when he was at liberty.' And so, after a long debate, though there was not a man who had not a value for him, and very few who had a particular malice or prejudice towards him, the question being put, the negative was more by three or four voices: so that, of the four Lords, three were without the mercy of that unmerciful people. There being no other Petition presented, Ireton told them, 'There had been great endeavours and solicitation used to save all those Lords; but that there was a commoner, another condemned person, for whom no man had spoke a word, nor had he himself so much as petioned them; and therefore he desired that Sir John Owen might be preserved by the mere motive and goodness of the House itself;' which found little opposition; whether they were satiated with blood, or that they were willing, by this instance, that the nobility should see that a commoner should be preferred before them."

The picture given in the above extract by Lord Clarendon, conveys a dreadful impression of the dark and gloomy hypocrisy of Cromwell's character, and the unrelenting malice with which, by means of every wile and subtlety, he pursued those persons whom he believed to have been devoted to the unhappy monarch whom he had brought to the scaffold.

The description which follows of the execution of Lord Capel, and the cool and brave composure with which he addressed the bystanders before he met his doom, shows that his virtue and spirit had not been overrated by the friend who has so eloquently praised him, or by the enemy who, with a guile so infernal, contrived to represent his great qualities as so many additional arguments for bringing him to destruction.

"The Lord Capel was then called, who walked through Westminster Hall, saluting such of his friends and acquaintance as he saw there, with a very serene countenance, accompanied with his friend Dr. Morley, who had been with him from the time of his sentence; but at the foot of the scaffold, the soldiers stopping the Doctor, his Lordship took his leave of him, and, embracing him, thanked him, and said he should go no farther, having some apprehension that he might receive some affront by that rude people after his death; the Chaplains who attended the other two Lords being men of the time, and the Doctor being well known to be most contrary.

"As soon as his Lordship had ascended the scaffold, he looked very vigorously about, and asked, 'Whether the other Lords had spoken to the people with their hats on?' and being told that 'they were bare,' he gave his hat to his servant, and then, with a clear and a strong voice, he said, 'That he was brought thither to dye for doing that which he could not repent of: that he had been born and bred under the government of a King whom he was bound in conscience to obey, under laws to which he had been always obedient, and in the bosom of a church which he thought the best in the world: that he had never violated his faith to either of those, and was now condemned to dye against all the laws of the land, to which sentence he did submit.'

"He enlarged himself in commending 'The great virtue and piety of the King, whom they had put to death, who was so just and merciful a Prince, and prayed to God to forgive the nation that innocent blood.'

"Then he recommended to them the present King, who, he told them, was their true and their lawful sovereign, and was worthy to be so: that he had the honour to have been some years near his person, and therefore he could not but know him well; and assured them, 'That he was a Prince of great understanding, of an excellent nature, of great courage, an entire lover of justice, and of exemplary piety: that he was not to be shaken in his religion, and had all those princely virtues which could make a nation happy;' and therefore advised them 'To submit to his Government, as the only means to preserve themselves, their posterity, and the Protestant religion.' And having, with great vehemence, recommended it to them, after some prayers very devoutly pronounced upon his knees, he submitted himself, with an unparalleled Christian courage, to the fatal stroke, which deprived the nation of the noblest champion it had."

Here follows one of those beautifully drawn characters in which Clarendon is so eminently successful.

"The Lord Capel was a man in whom the malice of his enemies could discover very few faults, and whom his friends could not wish better accomplished; whom Cromwell's own character well described, and who indeed would never have been contented to have lived under that Government. His memory all men loved and reverenced, though few followed his example. He had always lived in a state of great plenty and general estimation, having a very noble fortune of his own by descent, and a fair addition to it by his marriage with an excellent wife, a lady of very worthy extraction, of great virtue and beauty, by whom he had a numerous issue of both sexes, in which

e took great joy and comfort; so that no man was more
happy in all his domestic affairs, and he was so much the
more happy in that he thought himself most blessed in
them.

"And yet the King's honour was no sooner violated,
and his just power invaded, than he threw all those
blessings behind him; and having no other obligations to
the Crown than those which his own honour and conscience suggested to him, he frankly engaged his person
and his fortune from the beginning of the troubles, as
many others did, in all actions and enterprises of the
greatest hazard and danger; and continued to the end,
without ever making one false step, as few others did;
though he had once, by the iniquity of a faction that then
prevailed, an indignity put upon him that might have
excused him for some remission of his former warmth.
But it made no other impression upon him, than to be
quiet and contented whilst they would let him alone,
and with the same cheerfulness to obey the first summons
when he was called out, which was quickly after. In a
word, he was a man, that whoever shall, after him,
deserve best of the English nation, he can never think
himself undervalued, when he shall hear, that his courage,
virtue, and fidelity, is laid in the balance with, and compared to, that of the Lord Capel."

COLONEL BLOOD'S ATTEMPT TO STEAL THE CROWN JEWELS. (1671.)

 SHORT time after Charles II. had appointed Sir Gilbert Talbot to be "Master of the Jewel House" in the Tower, several of the allowances of his office were reduced, and permission was given him, by way of compensation, to admit the public, under certain restrictions, to view the Regalia, paying the "Master" a regulated fee as his perquisite.

This liberty of access to the Jewel Office suggested to one Blood, a disbanded officer of Cromwell's army, the possibility of carrying off the crown and other valuables.

Having dressed up a woman of decent and quiet appearance to represent his wife, Blood attired himself as a clergyman, with cloak and cassock, according to the fashion of the time, and took her to the Tower, where they asked permission to see the jewels. While Mr. Talbot Edwards, the Deputy-Keeper, was showing them, the lady pretended sudden sickness, and Mrs. Edwards kindly asked her into their apartments, where she gave her some cordial which appeared to restore her; and with many thanks, the pretended clergyman and his wife took their leave, but not before Blood had availed himself of the occasion, to take a careful view of the localities, and to form his plan for the robbery.

A few days after this he called with a present of gloves from his supposed wife to Mrs. Edwards, in return for her hospitality, telling her that his wife could talk of nothing but the kindness of " those good people at the Tower," and had desired him to mention, that they had a ward (a nephew) with a comfortable little estate in the country, and if such a match for their daughter would be agreeable to the Edwardses, they would with pleasure do their endeavour to forward it. Highly gratified by this plausible offer, the Edwardses invited Blood to dine with them that day, when he had the impudence to say a very long grace, with great appearance of fervour, concluding with a prayer for the King and Royal family. Noticing a pair of handsome pistols hanging against the wall of the parlour, he remarked that he should much like to buy them, if Mr. Edwards did not object to part with them, for a young friend in the army (his real object being to remove any defensive weapons from the house). He took his leave with a solemn benediction, and named a day for bringing his nephew to be introduced to Miss Edwards, requesting to be allowed to bring two country friends at the same time, to see the Jewels, before they returned to their homes. On the morning appointed, May 9, 1671, he arrived with three respectably dressed men, and as Mrs. Edwards and her daughter had not yet come down stairs, he asked Edwards to show his friends the Crown in the mean time. No sooner was this wish complied with, than they threw one of their cloaks over the old man's head, gagged him with a wooden plug with a breathing hole, and tied it tight with a string at the back of his neck. They then said they must have the Crown, Globe, and Sceptre, which if he quietly surrendered, but not else, they would spare his life. Poor Edwards, though eighty years old, instead of submitting to their conditions, made desperate struggles to get free and give the alarm, on which the villains gave him repeated blows on the head with a wooden mallet, and also stabbed him in the body, to silence his attempted cries. Blood now seized the Crown, one accomplice (Parrott) secreted the Globe, and the other proceeded, with a file they had brought for the purpose, to divide the Sceptre into two parts, for easier concealment; but at this moment the third man, whom they had left on the watch at the door below, gave an alarm, and in another moment Edwards's son, who, by a most fortunate chance, had just arrived from Flanders with Captain Beckman, his brother-in-law, hastened up stairs to salute his family. The villains made a rush past him, and, leaving the half-cut Sceptre behind them, escaped with the Globe and Crown, pursued by young Edwards and Beckman, shouting to stop the thieves. A warder at the drawbridge leading to the wharf, attempted to arrest their progress, but Blood firing a pistol in his face, he was so frightened, though the shot missed him, that he fell as if killed, and they got clear away by the wharf, and through the Iron Gate to St. Katherine's. At a place near this gate, they had appointed horses to meet them, and had nearly gained the spot, when Beckman, who was a fast runner, overtook them, and though Blood fired another pistol at him, rushed upon him and seized him, when young Edwards coming up, he was overpowered, after a hard struggle, and brought back prisoner into the Tower.

In this scuffle, the Crown, which Blood kept under his cloak, was knocked out of his grasp on the pavement, and a pearl and large diamond, with some stones of less value, were displaced; but they were nearly all picked up afterwards and restored. Parrott, who had, like his leader, been an officer in the Parliament's army, was captured, as well as two or three others who were waiting with the horses near St. Katherine's. This daring outrage having been immediately reported to Charles II., he took such interest in the matter, that he caused Blood and Parrott to be conveyed to Whitehall, in order to examine them himself.

When brought before the King, Blood's impudence was astonishing; not only did he acknowledge his recent offence without shame, but he boasted of the part he had taken some time before, in dragging the Duke of Ormond out of his coach in St. James's Street, and carrying him off to hang him at Tyburn, which was only prevented by the fortunate chance of his servants overtaking his captors, just in time for his rescue.

But the strangest piece of effrontery in Blood, not unmixed with a good deal of cunning, was his declaration to the King, that he had been engaged in a conspiracy to shoot him, when bathing near Battersea, being hidden with a carbine among some rushes, for the purpose, but "that his heart had been checked by an awe of Majesty, which caused him not only to spare the King's life, but to induce his associates also to abandon any further attempts at his assassination. As to giving the names of these associates, he said he would never betray a friend's life, nor deny a guilt to save his own." He said he knew the risk of such confessions, but "he had a large number of friends bound together by the most solemn oaths, to revenge each other's death, on whoever should bring them to justice. If His Majesty would now spare him and his accomplices in the Crown robbery, he would oblige the hearts of many; and as he and his fellow prisoners had shown that they could be daring in evil, so they would, if pardoned, be found ready to do great service to the King." At the termination of the examination, Blood and his accomplices were remanded to the Tower, but after a short imprisonment, were, to the astonishment of all, released without trial.

For this ill-timed and unwarranted clemency, it is hard to assign any reason. To suppose that Charles was really intimidated by Blood's tale of impending vengeance, is quite inconsistent with his known courage in real danger. Yet he was so fully aware of the wrong he was committing, that he deemed an apology necessary to the Duke of Ormond in respect of the outrage which Blood had owned to having committed against his person. By the King's orders, Lord Arlington conveyed to the Duke a message "that it was His Majesty's pleasure that Blood should not be prosecuted, for reasons which he was commanded to give him;" but the Duke cut him short by saying "that His Majesty's command was the only reason that could be given, and therefore he need give him no others."

The circumstances of the outrage on the Duke of Ormond were as follows :—Blood had been a leader in the attempt to seize the Castle of Dublin, when the Duke of Ormond was Governor, and had narrowly escaped the gibbet on that occasion, by a hasty flight to England. To revenge himself on the Duke, he laid a scheme to attack him at night, when he was passing down St. James's Street in his coach, and so far did he succeed, that the Duke's life was at his mercy; but fortunately Blood was bent on a refinement of vengeance, and forcing the Duke to mount behind one of his associates, carried him off across the fields (now the Green Park) towards Tyburn, with the intention of there hanging him on the common gibbet.

After they had proceeded some distance, the Duke collecting himself for a sudden effort, threw the man behind whom he was bound, from his saddle, and falling with him, a desperate struggle took place in the mud, during which some of his servants arrived to his rescue, and Blood, discharging a pistol at the Duke without effect, galloped off and escaped in the darkness, but not before the Duke had recognised his features. Great suspicion was entertained, that the Duke of Buckingham, who detested Ormond, had set Blood upon this desperate attempt, and Lord Ossory, Ormond's son, was so convinced of it, that in the presence of the King and Court, he told him that he knew he was at the bottom of Blood's attack on his father, "but," added he, "I give you warning, if by any means my father comes to a violent end, I shall consider you as the assassin; I shall treat you as such; and wherever I meet you, I shall pistol you, though you stood behind the King's chair, and I tell it you in His Majesty's presence, that you may be sure I shall not fail of performance."

The strangest part of this affair was, that Blood became a sort of hanger-on upon the Court at Whitehall, and eventually had a pension given him, besides some confiscated land in Ireland.

Towards the close of his life, he became a Quaker, and there was an old house at the corner of Peter Street, Westminster, where the tradition existed that he died in 1680.

Poor Edwards was but ill recompensed for the courage he had shown and the ill treatment he had received, of which he never entirely recovered, but died in 1674, and was buried under the floor of the Tower Chapel, with a small tablet over his grave. In one of those reckless reparations which so often were allowed in the Tower, the masons employed in repairing the Chapel floor threw this tablet aside, but it was luckily observed by Col. Wyndham in a heap of rubbish, and by the Constable's order fixed against the south wall, in safety from future injury.

MYSTERIOUS DEATH OF THE EARL OF ESSEX.

THE fate of the Earl of Essex, who was found with his throat cut in the Tower, July 13, 1683, on the morning of the day that Lord Russell was undergoing his trial for high treason, was one of those mysteries, on which great difference of opinion, or rather of conjecture, for a long time prevailed.

It is not easy to decide at the present time, the exact position of the lodging where Lord Essex was confined after he was brought to the Tower, from Cassiobury near Watford, by the party of horse who were sent down to arrest him. But, as it is described in the depositions before the Commission assembled in King William's time, to investigate the matter, to have been "on the left hand as you go up the mound, after passing Bloody Tower Gate," there can be little doubt but this building must have stood at the southern part of the avenue of trees which shade the paved walk on the parade, in front of the Government House, and was probably pulled down when the present roadway was made, and the steps and terrace formed, opposite the main guard. In the depositions above alluded to, it was stated that a sentinel was posted, within some wooden railings in front of the door of the Warder's lodging, where Lord Essex was confined. This sentinel, when examined, prevaricated a good deal in his evidence; denying at first, that any one had entered the door, during the period of his watch, but afterwards saying that two gentlemen had produced an order for admission. It must, however, be remembered, that the professed object of the Commission was to cast a suspicion of murder on James II., and that any assertion of this sort, however vague, would be received with favour. Not a word was said of these mysterious visitors coming out again, but the next occurrence mentioned by the sentinel was the alarm given by Mr. Bommeney, the Earl's French valet, that he had found his master on the floor of a closet next his bedroom, with his throat just cut, and the body fallen against the door, which opened inwards, in such a manner, that there was much difficulty to push it open, from the weight lying against it. The evidence chiefly relied upon, to prove that Lord Essex did not kill himself, but died by other hands, was the assertion of two children, who declared, that as they were at play near this spot, they saw a hand throw out a razor from Lord Essex's window, and that a woman ran out of the door, a minute afterwards, and picked it up. But the sentinel had said nothing of seeing either the children or the woman; and one of the children was notorious among the neighbours for being untruthful. It should be here observed that Charles II. and the Duke of York had this same morning visited the Tower, to make an inspection of the works, which coincidence was much dwelt upon, as an evidence of foul play in respect to Lord Essex. But in the first place, the proofs which had come out lately of the intention of the contrivers of the Rye House Plot, to attack and seize the Tower, as part of the plan for an insurrection in London, were very likely to have induced the King and his brother (who had much experience, from his service in the Low Countries, of the strength and requirements of a fortress) to examine the condition of the Tower defences. On the other hand, could anything be less probable, if they really had employed assassins to murder Lord Essex, than that they should have visited the Tower at the very hour, when their doing so might have induced suspicion, and when common prudence would have suggested to them to keep out of the way, if they had authorized the commission of a crime, which would make so much noise in the world? Even admitting the evidence of the children, which was anything but clear or decisive, to have some weight, it must be recollected that numerous instances have occurred of persons retaining the power of moving, and walking about, in a surprising manner, after inflicting injuries on themselves which very soon after proved fatal. One case happened lately, of a woman in Lambeth, whose husband had cut her throat, running down stairs, and walking for a considerable distance along the street, before she fell and expired. To have thrown the razor, with which he had killed himself, from a window, would therefore have been by no means inconsistent with the fact of the Earl having committed suicide.

In the 'Life of Lord Russell,' by the present Earl Russell, he makes allusion at some length to the mysterious end of the Earl of Essex in the Tower, and states that he had once been told by the late Earl of Essex (who died in 1839) that Mr. T. Grenville had assured him, that he had seen in the old Treasury books, the entry of a pension to Bommeney, the French valet; but he adds that he had never been able to trace this entry, nor did Lord Essex say what was its amount; neither did it appear, whether it was granted before, or after, the death of the Earl. If such a pension had existed, surely the active exertions of Mr. Braddon the barrister, who got up the evidence laid before the Commissioners in King William's time, would not have allowed so material a fact to pass unnoticed, especially as the new government of King William would have had every facility of placing in Braddon's hands the details of the supposed grant or pension.

It may be observed of the death of the Earl of Essex, as of that of the Earl of Northumberland in Elizabeth's reign, that there existed a prevalent notion that a prisoner accused of high treason, might evade by suicide the forfeiture of his estates to the Crown, inasmuch as he died, without guilt being actually proved against him. How far any such supposed evasion of the severity of the Treason Laws really availed against the arbitrary powers exercised by the Sovereign, before the Revolution of 1688, it is not easy to determine, but certainly there was such an impression, and one can hardly suppose it would have existed, without some foundation or precedent.

THE EARL OF NITHISDALE'S ESCAPE.

HE escape of the Earl of Nithisdale on the 23rd of February, 1716, the evening before the day fixed for his execution, is one of the most interesting events of the dark history of the Tower. It is hard to say whether the wonderful ingenuity exercised by his heroic wife, in contriving his escape, or her presence of mind under circumstances of anxiety, sufficient to have shaken the most undaunted courage, are most to be admired. Winifred, Countess of Nithisdale, was the daughter of W. Marquis of Powis. She was born about 1690, and married early to Maxwell, Earl of Nithisdale.

This Earl was one of the noblemen who were first intrusted by the Earl of Mar, with the Pretender's intended attempt on the crown of England; and took a leading part in the assembly of the Jacobite nobles at Braemar, where the plans for the invasion were finally discussed and determined.

After the action at Preston, the Earl of Nithisdale was made prisoner, and conveyed on horseback with his arms tied, and other indignities, to London, where he arrived on the 9th December, 1715, and was committed at once to the Tower, with several of his friends and associates.

Lady Nithisdale was residing with her two young children at the family seat of Terregles in Dumfriesshire, when the terrible news reached her of the defeat at Preston, and of her husband's captivity and imprisonment in the Tower. Instead of giving way to the terror and distress with which such news would have overwhelmed an ordinary mind, her first step was immediately to collect, and bury in the garden, all family papers, which regarded the estate; and then, attended only by her faithful maid Evans, and a groom in whom she could place trust, she set out on horseback (though she had never been much accustomed to riding) for Newcastle; from whence a public stage conveyed her to York. But here the snow was so deep, that it was found impossible for the stage to proceed. Nothing daunted, she betook herself again to the saddle, and made her way, exposed to all the inclemency of the winter, and through roads which, bad at all times, were then choked with snow, till she arrived in London. From her rank and connexions, she had many friends of rank and influence in the capital, among whom were the Duchesses of Buccleuch and Montrose, who at her request ascertained for her, through their friends at court, whether there was any chance of intercession for Lord Nithisdale succeeding with George I. The King had a great objection to him on account of his profession of the Roman Catholic faith, and the report of the two Duchesses was very unfavourable.

Lord Nithisdale, however, could not be persuaded

but that a petition to the King would have effect in his favour. To use her own words, Lady Nithisdale says:—
"I was convinced in my own mind that it would answer no purpose; but as I wished to please him, I desired him to have it drawn up, and I undertook that it should come to the King's hands, notwithstanding all the precautions he might take to avoid it. So the first day I heard there was to be a drawing-room, I dressed myself in black, as if in mourning, and sent for Mrs. Morgan, the same who afterwards accompanied me to the Tower, because, as I did not know his Majesty's person, I might have mistaken some other of the court for him. She stayed by me, and told me when he was coming. I had also another lady with me, and we all three remained in a room between the King's apartment and the drawing-room, so that he was obliged to go through it; and as there were three windows in it, we sat in the middle one, that I might have time enough to meet him before he could pass.

"I threw myself at his feet, and told him in French that I was the unfortunate Countess of Nithisdale, that he might not pretend to be ignorant of my person. But seeing that he wanted to go off, without taking my petition, I caught hold of the skirt of his coat, that he might stop and hear me; he endeavoured to escape out of my hands, but I kept such strong hold, that he dragged me, upon my knees, from the middle of the room to the very door of the drawing-room. At last one of the Blue Ribands who attended his Majesty, took me round the waist, while another wrested the coat from my hands. The petition, which I had endeavoured to thrust into his pocket, fell to the ground in the scuffle, and I almost fainted away from grief and disappointment."

Although the Rebellion had been entirely suppressed, yet there were so many persons interested in the cause of the Stuarts, even among those whom the King believed most faithful to him, that already several prisoners had made their escape from prisons in the country, and some had even succeeded in London.

An escape from the Tower being the only chance now left for her husband's life, Lady Nithisdale bent the whole force of her mind to this object, resolving to have no confidant of her scheme, except the faithful maid, who had attended her on her venturous ride from Scotland. No time was to be lost, for the trial of the rebel lords had commenced on the 9th of February, and sentence having been passed on the 19th, they now lay in the Tower awaiting their execution, which was fixed for the 24th.

Numerous petitions were however prepared and presented to both Houses of Parliament, for intervention with his Majesty. The petition to the Commons was stopped, by a motion for adjournment, carried by the small majority of seven votes.

In the House of Lords, where some of the unfortunate nobles had many personal friends, the motion for reading the petitions was carried against the ministry by nine voices.

A question was then raised whether the King had power to reprieve in cases of impeachment? This was carried in the affirmative, and strong hopes were consequently entertained for the prisoners; but when it came to the wording of the Address to the King on behalf of the prisoners, the Whig Ministry prevailed (though only by five voices) for the adoption of terms, which, in point of fact, left the matter much as it stood before; for the Address only petitioned his Majesty to "reprieve such of the condemned lords as deserved his mercy," the period of respite being also left to his Majesty's discretion.

The stern reply of the King to this Address left small hopes for the prisoners, for he merely answered that on this and all occasions he would do what he thought most consistent with the dignity of his Crown, and the safety of his people. Nor did he confine himself to this virtual rejection of the Address; for shortly afterwards he commanded several persons who had taken part in both Houses for the prisoners to be dismissed from offices which they held under the Crown. The issue of this debate, on the very eve of the day appointed for her husband's execution, would have overwhelmed a less bold and elastic spirit than that of Lady Nithisdale, but, with incredible presence of mind, she hastened to avail herself of the fact of the Address, even such as it was, having been carried at all; and taking coach directly for the Tower, presented herself at the gates, with a face of gladness, telling the warders, as she passed to Lord Nithisdale's apartment, that there was now no longer fear for the prisoners, since the motion to address the King had just passed in the House of Lords, giving them, at the same time, some money to drink to its success. She remained with Lord Nithisdale no longer than was necessary to explain to him the real truth, and to instruct him as to the part he was to play in her plan for his escape, and then returned quickly to the lodgings which she had hired in Drury Lane.

It was not the least remarkable part of this lady's character, that, delicate and feminine in appearance as she is represented in the picture by Sir G. Kneller, in possession of the family, she possessed that power over the minds of others which belongs more usually to men early accustomed to command, and long versed in the vicissitudes of life. With that self-reliance so peculiar to her, she resolved on a step, which seemed as rash and imprudent at first sight, as it afterwards proved the contrary. Having observed pretty closely the character of a Mrs. Mills, of whom she had hired lodgings in Drury Lane, she sent for her to her own apartment, and informed her that, all hope of pardon being now lost, she had determined on a scheme to effect Lord Nithisdale's escape from the Tower. "This," she said, "is the last night before his execution;" and then passionately appealed to her feelings, to assist her in the attempt she meditated, by accompanying her at once to the Tower, in order that Lord Nithisdale might escape in one of her dresses, for which scheme she had arranged every detail, and had even secured the dress and carried it to the Tower.

Meantime she had sent for another person (who appears to have been of the same station in life as Mrs. Mills), a Mrs. Morgan, who presently was hurried into similar consent as the kindness of her feelings had exacted from Mrs. Mills. "Their surprise and astonishment," to use Lady Nithisdale's own words, "made them consent, without thinking of the consequences." A coach was called, and all three started for the Tower, Lady Nithisdale talking all the way, for fear they should have time for reflection, and change their minds. As they drove along she explained the details of her scheme, namely, that Mrs. Morgan was to wear over her own clothes a dress of Mrs. Mills's (who was a large woman), for Lord Nithisdale to put on, with other disguise, and so pass the warders stationed in his outer room and at the gate.

Lady Nithisdale's own account, in a letter to her sister, of what now took place, shall be literally transcribed. "On our arrival, I first brought in Mrs. Morgan, for I was only allowed to introduce one at a time, calling her a friend of my lord's, come to take leave of him. When Mrs. Morgan had taken off the dress of Mrs. Mills's which she had brought for my purpose, I conducted her back to the staircase, and, in going, I begged her to send my maid to dress me, as I was afraid of being too late to present my last petition that night, if she did not come immediately. I despatched her safe, and went partly down stairs, to meet Mrs. Mills, who held her handkerchief to her face, as was natural for a person going to take a last leave of a friend before his execution; and I had desired her to do this, that my lord might go out in the same manner. Her eyebrows were inclined to be sandy, and as my lord's were dark, and thick, I had prepared some paint to disguise him.

I had also got an artificial head-dress, of the same coloured hair as hers, and rouged his face and cheeks, to conceal his beard, which he had not time to shave. All this provision I had before left in the Tower. The poor guards, whom my slight liberality the day before had endeared me to, let me go quietly out with my company, and were not so strictly on the watch as they usually had been; and the more so, as they were persuaded, from what I had told them the day before, that the prisoners would obtain their pardon. I made Mrs. Mills take off her own hood, and put on that which I had brought for her. I then took her by the hand, and led her out of my lord's chamber; and, in passing through the next room, in which were several people, with all the concern imaginable I said, 'My dear Mrs. Catherine, go in all haste, and send me my waiting-maid; she certainly cannot reflect how late it is. I am to present my petition to-night, and if I let slip this opportunity I am undone, for to-morrow is too late. Hasten her as much as possible, for I shall be on thorns till she comes.' Everybody in the room, who were chiefly the guards' wives and daughters, seemed to compassionate me exceedingly, and the sentinel officiously opened me the door. When I had seen her safe out I returned to my lord, and finished dressing him. I had taken care that Mrs. Mills did not go out crying, as she came in, that my lord might better pass for the lady who came in crying and afflicted; and the more so as he had the same dress that she wore. When I had almost finished dressing my lord, I perceived it was growing dark, and was afraid that the light of the candles might betray us, so I resolved to set off. I went out leading him by the hand, whilst he held his handkerchief to his eyes. I spoke to him in the most piteous and afflicted tone, bewailing bitterly the negligence of my maid Evans, who had ruined me by her delay. Then I said, 'My dear Mrs. Betty, for the love of God, run quickly and bring her with you; you know my lodging, and if you ever made despatch in your life, do it at present; I am almost distracted with this disappointment.' The guards opened the door, and I went downstairs with him, still conjuring him to make all possible despatch. As soon as he had cleared the door, I made him walk before me, for fear the sentinel should take notice of his walk, but I continued to press him to make all the despatch he possibly could. At the bottom of the stairs I met my dear Evans, into whose hand I confided him. I had before engaged Mr. Mills to be in readiness before the Tower, to conduct him to some place of safety in case we succeeded. He looked upon the affair as so very improbable to succeed, that his astonishment, when he saw us, threw him into such a consternation that he was almost out of himself, which, Evans perceiving, with the greatest presence of mind, without telling Lord Nithisdale anything, lest he should mistrust them, conducted him to some of her own friends on whom she could rely, and so secured him, without which we certainly should have been undone. When she had conducted him, and left him with them, she returned to Mr. Mills, who had by this time recovered himself from his astonishment. They went home together, and having found a place of security, brought Lord Nithisdale to it. In the mean time, as I had pretended to have sent the young lady on a message, I was obliged to return upstairs and go back to my lord's room in the same feigned anxiety of being too late, so that everybody seemed sincerely to sympathize in my distress. When I was in the room, I talked as if he had been really present. I answered my own questions in my lord's voice, as nearly as I could imitate it, and walked up and down, as if we were conversing together, till I thought they had time enough thoroughly to clear themselves of the guards. I then thought proper to make off also. I opened the door and stood half in it, that those in the outward chamber might hear what I said, but held it so close that they could not look in. I bade my lord formal farewell for the night, and added, that something more than usual must have happened to make Evans negligent, on this important occasion, who had always been so punctual in the smallest trifles; that I saw no other remedy than to go in person; that if the Tower was then open, when I had finished my business, I would return that night; but that he might be assured I would be with him, as early in the morning, as I could gain admittance into the Tower, and I flattered myself I should bring more favourable news. Then, before I shut the door, I pulled through the string of the latch, so that it could only be opened in the inside. I then shut it with some degree of force, that I might be sure of its being well shut. I said to the servant, as I passed by (who was ignorant of the whole transaction), that he need not carry in candles to his master, till my lord sent for them, as he desired to finish some prayers first."

So far the courage and ingenuity of Lady Nithisdale had succeeded beyond expectation; it now remained for her and her husband to gain some safe retreat, as the deception must, within a few hours, be discovered, and an active search was sure to be set on foot.

Lady Nithisdale got the first coach she could find, and drove to her lodging in Drury Lane, where Mrs. Mills had already arrived.

It must be observed here, that one of the cleverest parts of Lady Nithisdale's scheme, was the employment of assistants totally unknown, and who, from the insignificance of their position, ran no real risk when once clear of the Tower Gates.

At Mrs. Mills's she found Mr. Mackenzie, a friend by whose hands she had intended originally to send her petition to the Lords—" There is no need," she joyfully exclaimed to him, " of a petition now; my lord is safe out of the Tower, and the hands of his enemies, though as yet I know not where he is."

She now took a chair, and proceeded to her faithful friend the Duchess of Buccleuch; but learning she had company with her, went on to the Duchess of Montrose, who had also company, but, being privately told who was arrived, quitted them instantly to see and console, as she supposed, her unhappy friend. The Duchess, to her astonishment, found Lady Nithisdale in a transport of joy, and, supposing her sorrows had affected her mind, was both distressed and alarmed. From the Duchess, whom she quietly reassured by her story, Lady Nithisdale presently learned the danger in which she herself stood, as the King had been furious at the steps taken in Parliament, and now, as soon as he should hear of Lord Nithisdale's escape, would doubtless use every means to get her into his power.

Every moment was precious, so, taking an affectionate leave of the kind Duchess, our heroine sent for another chair, and hurried to an obscure house, where she was to meet Evans, and learn the place of Lord Nithisdale's retreat. By Evans she was told, that Lord Nithisdale had been first conducted to a lodging belonging to one of her own friends, but afterwards removed, for better safety, to the house of a very poor woman, opposite the Guard House (could this mean the Tower Guard House?). Here she now repaired, and found him concealed in a very small garret at the top of the house. This place of concealment was so precarious, that they did not even venture to move about the room, lest any noise should attract attention. They subsisted on some bread and wine, supplied by Mrs. Mills, for three days, when Mr. Mills, who seems now to have recovered his energies, arrived to conduct Lord Nithisdale to the house of the Venetian Ambassador in London. No part of the scheme appears more surprising than this; for Lady Nithisdale in her narrative says—" We did not communicate the affair to His Excellency, but one of the servants (probably bribed through Mills) concealed Lord Nithisdale in his own room, till Wednesday (a period of three days), on which morning the Ambassador's coach and six was to set out for Dover, to fetch his brother to London.

Lord Nithisdale put on a livery, and went down in the retinue, without the least suspicion, to Dover, where Mr. Mickel, which was the name of the Ambassador's servant, hired a small vessel, in which, accompanied by Lord Nithisdale, he immediately sailed for Calais. The passage was so remarkably short, that the Captain made the remark "that the wind could not have served better, if the passengers had been flying for their lives," little thinking such to be really the case. To return to Lady Nithisdale: the solicitations of her friends, and the interest taken in her cause by persons on both sides of politics, prevailed no further with the hard nature of the King, than to obtain the assurance, that unless seen in England or Scotland, she should not be molested. But this concession would in no way protect her son's estate from waste and plunder. The family papers, as we have seen, she had buried in the garden at Terregles; and to get them safe out of the country was now her object. "As I had hazarded my life for the father," she wrote to her sister, "I could not do less than hazard it once more for the son."

Whether she adopted any disguise does not appear, but she bought three saddle-horses, and attended only by her faithful Evans and the trusty groom she had brought before from Scotland, she left London for the north, putting up at small roadside alehouses, for fear of recognition in the English towns. Could she once reach her own county, she relied on the attachment and respect of her neighbours for not betraying her; nor was her ingenuity and resource ever at fault, for, on arriving in Traquhair, she announced that she had come home, with the leave of Government, and on arriving at her own house, she issued invitations to her neighbours to come and visit her. That same night however she dug up the buried papers, and despatched them by a trusty hand for London; and not a moment too soon; for the magistrates of Dumfries, beginning to doubt her story, had resolved to insist on her producing the passport which she pretended to possess. Before daybreak this indefatigable lady was again in the saddle, and made her way to London, with the same secrecy as she had left it.

> "Spotless without, and innocent within,
> She feared no danger, for she knew no sin."

Rumours, however, of her journey had reached the ears of the King, who, to his shame, was only roused to greater anger than before against her. He declared "that Lady Nithisdale did whatever she pleased in spite of him; and that she had given him more trouble than any woman in Europe." A strict search for her retreat was, by his orders, again set on foot, and to have remained longer in London, would have been to tempt that Providence which had watched over her safety in so marvellous a manner. She accordingly made up her mind to abandon any further ideas of intercession, and to rejoin her husband abroad, with whom she lived a retired life at Rome till his death in 1744. His admirable wife did not long survive him, and died also at Rome, but her remains were brought to England, and were buried at Arundel Castle.

Her picture, by Sir G. Kneller, in the bloom of youth, is still at Terregles, and has been thus described by a lady of the Maxwell family. "Her hair is light brown, slightly powdered, with large soft eyes, regular features, and a fair pale complexion. Her soft expression and delicate appearance give little indication of the strength of mind and courage she displayed. Her dress is blue silk with a border of cambric, and over it a cloak of brown silk."

As doubts have existed as to the locality in the Tower, from whence Lord Nithisdale's extraordinary escape was made, some pains have been taken to ascertain a point of such interest, by examination and comparison of the probable places of his confinement. It would appear from Lady Nithisdale's letter, that the chamber in which the Earl was imprisoned, opened into a sort of lobby, where the Warders in charge were stationed, and that from this lobby or antechamber, there was a staircase leading down to the outer door of the house, or prison, where Lord Nithisdale was confined.

Now this description would not apply at all to the State Prison, known as the Beauchamp Tower; nor indeed was it the custom at this period to confine noblemen in any of the ordinary prisons or dungeons of the Tower. They were usually given in charge to a Warder, and lived in his quarters, the windows and doors of which were barred securely with iron, as may still be seen in the quarters of the Middle Tower, and other old residences of the Warders. The custom of giving prisoners in charge to individuals prevailed also in France, as appears by the Memoirs of the seventeenth and eighteenth centuries, where we read of persons of distinction being placed " aux arrêts," in the custody of an Exempt of the Royal Guard (from which word Exempt that of Exon in the Queen's " Body Guard" is no doubt a corruption, the meaning being an under officer " exempt" from sentinel's duty).

But in the Tower, prisoners of rank were often received as inmates of the Governor's own house, where, besides several upper rooms, from which escape would be difficult, there is in the Bell Tower connected with the upper story, a strong vaulted prison-room, known as the scene of the harsh confinement of Bishop Fisher in Henry VIII.'s reign. Now in this upper story of the Lieutenant's house, there are two rooms opening into a large apartment known as the Council Room, either of which rooms would answer the local description given by Lady Nithisdale in her narrative; supposing the Warders on duty to have been posted in the large Council Room, where she mentions that several of their wives and daughters had assembled from compassion, or curiosity, to see her, and her friends, pass into the inner chamber to visit Lord Nithisdale.

From the " Council Room," there is a lobby or passage about twenty-five feet long leading to the head of the stairs, which descend to the lobby of the first floor, and thence down into the Entrance Hall; every part of

COUNCIL CHAMBER IN GOVERNOR'S HOUSE.

Where Guy Fawkes was examined and tortured, and from whence Lord Nithisdale is believed to have made his escape in 1715.

which localities correspond, so closely, with the details of Lady Nithisdale's narrative, that there can be little doubt of the Governor's House having been the scene of this truly wonderful escape.

Lord Nithisdale's unfortunate friends, Lords Derwentwater, Widdrington, Wintoun, Carnwath, Kenmure, and Nairn, who had all pleaded guilty except Wintoun, were condemned to die as traitors. They had been brought into London on horseback with every degradation, their arms tied behind them, their horses led by soldiers and preceded by drums and music as a sort of triumph over their misfortunes. Lord Nairn was saved by the friendly efforts of Lord Stanhope, who had been his schoolfellow at Eton; but all the interest made for the rest was vain.

Steele, the friend of Addison, pleaded eloquently for mercy in the Commons; but Walpole, though naturally a humane man, held that example was indispensable, and declared "that he was moved with indignation to see that there should be such unworthy members of this great body, who can, without blushing, open their mouths in favour of rebels and parricides." The efforts made for the prisoners in the House of Lords have already been alluded to; and though the Minister would concede nothing as regarded the other noblemen, Lords Carnwath and Widdrington were respited in deference to the feelings expressed in the Commons.

Finally, none but Derwentwater and Kenmure were left for execution, and appointed to suffer on Tower Hill. Derwentwater, who was the first to suffer, behaved with much composure and firmness. He declared that he died a sincere Catholic; that his intention had been what he believed best for his country; that he died in charity with all, even with those of the Government who had been most forward for his death.

It is recorded that on trying his neck upon the block he found a rough place which hurt his chin, and quietly asked the headsman to chip off the projection with his axe before he laid him down to receive the blow. He desired the man to strike when he should hear him say "Lord Jesus receive my soul;" and taking off his coat and waistcoat, placed his neck carefully on the block, and then giving the signal, one blow caused his head to roll on the scaffold.

Lord Kenmure then ascended the platform, and, behaving with the same courage and resolution as his friend, made a declaration to the same purport; but added that he regretted having admitted himself guilty on his trial, and offered a short prayer for King James III. It was not till the second stroke that his head fell; but the first had probably extinguished all sensation.

Lord Wintoun contrived to retard his trial by various pretexts and delays; when at last these resources were exhausted, he declared that he had witnesses in his favour who were retarded by the badness of the roads from Scotland.

With the injustice usual in trials for treason at that time, no counsel was allowed him, against which hard rule he urgently but vainly remonstrated. Lord Cowper, the High Steward, having checked him with some harsh-

VAULT UNDER WAKEFIELD TOWER

ness, he said, "I hope, my Lord, you will give me justice, and not make use of *Cowper-Law*, as we used to say in Scotland—hang a man first and then judge him."

He was found guilty, and sent back to await his doom in the Tower; but the same cunning and shrewdness which had enabled him to stave off his trial, stood him in such good stead, that shortly before the day fixed for his execution he managed to escape from prison, and, being well seconded by friends of the cause in London, was conveyed safely to the Continent. There is no record, or tradition, of the manner of Lord Wintoun's escape; though it was probably even more difficult to accomplish than that of Lord Nithisdale, from the better precautions we may suppose to have been adopted in the Tower to prevent escape of State prisoners.

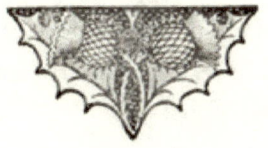

EXECUTION OF REBEL LORDS OF 1745.

HE last occasion on which the headsman's block, still preserved in the Tower, was used for its dreadful purpose, was the execution of the celebrated Simon Fraser, Lord Lovat, for the part taken by him in the Rebellion of '45. The three other Lords sentenced for their part in the same rebellion had given little trouble at their trials. The Earls of Cromarty and Kilmarnock, seeing the strength of the evidence about to be brought against them, pleaded guilty at once, and humbly entreated that their lives might be spared. Cromarty pathetically appealed to the Lords on the plea of his unhappy wife and eight children; Kilmarnock appealed for mercy on grounds which seem far more extraordinary, for he attributed to the excellent principles of loyalty, in which he had educated his eldest son, that the young man had actually fought against him on the Royal side at Culloden! and argued that this fact should be considered in his own favour.

Cromarty received a pardon, but Kilmarnock was ordered for execution.

Balmerino, a man of high spirit, and convinced in

s heart that he had fought in the good cause, made no submission, and after an attempt, which was overruled by the Judges, to disprove his presence in Carlisle on the day named in the indictment, gave up any further defence, and prepared to die with the same courage as he had shown through life.

Kilmarnock and Balmerino suffered upon Tower Hill in August, 1745, the former avowing his error and expressing remorse for his offence, while his companion boldly cried out "God save King James!" on his way through the gates to Tower Hill, and declared, before he laid his head on the fatal block, that if he had a thousand lives he would lay them down in the same cause.

The trial of Lord Lovat was delayed till March of 1746, owing to some difficulties of procuring evidence; for though no one had shown more energy in the Pretender's cause, Lovat had never been seen in arms against the Crown, nor in the commission of any overt act of treason. But John Murray, who had been Secretary to Prince Charles, had the baseness to place in the hands of Government, as the price of his own safety, a number of letters from Lovat to the Prince, which, with other corroboration, furnished unquestionable proofs of his guilt.

He conducted his own defence with a mixture of shrewdness and buffoonery which produced anything but a favourable impression upon the Peers who tried him. H. Walpole, who was present at the trial, observes, "I did not think it possible to feel so little as I did at so melancholy a spectacle; but tyranny and villany, wound up by buffoonery, took off all edge of compassion." At his execution Lord Lovat behaved with wonderful coolness, remarking to the crowd who pressed round the coach of the Lieutenant of the Tower, in which he was carried through the gate to Tower Hill, that they need not be in a hurry, for there would certainly be no sport till he himself arrived.

He appeared to pay serious attention to a Catholic priest who administered to his last moments, and repeated from Horace, " Dulce et decorum est pro patriâ mori;" though, as Lord Stanhope has justly observed in his History, no man was ever less strongly imbued with that noble sentiment, except perhaps its writer.

The coffin-plates of Lords Kilmarnock, Balmerino, and Lovat were discovered about twenty-five years ago, when a quantity of bones were disinterred for the purpose of excavating the foundations of the present barracks.

They were thrown aside with the same carelessness as the gravestone of Talbot Edwards; but fortunately discovered by an officer of the Tower and placed in the vestry, where they are now carefully secured from accident in glass cases.

THE CATO STREET CONSPIRATORS.
(March, 1820.)

AMONG the last State prisoners confined in the Tower were some of the desperate men, who had engaged in what is commonly known as the Cato Street Conspiracy. The leader was one Thistlewood, who had been in Paris at the time of Robespierre, and had probably there imbibed those revolutionary opinions which eventually led him to the gallows. He had served a short time as an officer of the militia, and afterwards in the army. After quitting the service he had made himself notorious in Watson's attempt at a riot in London, in the year 1818 (on which occasion he was brought to trial at the same time as Watson, but obtained an acquittal. On his release he sent a challenge to the Home Secretary, Lord Sidmouth, who placed the case in the hands of a magistrate, and he underwent a short imprisonment in consequence). On his release in 1819, he did not take part in the ordinary mobs and riots of that year, but, entertaining more determined views, he contrived to collect around him thirty or forty discontented followers, from the class of workmen and London idlers; and by his influence and popular discourses at meetings of a treasonable description, obtained great authority over them.

It never appeared that he had any definite plan for organising a provisional government in event of success; he relied upon the state of extreme confusion which he expected to produce in London, in order to overthrow the existing authorities; and his scheme for this purpose was of a nature as bloody and cruel as it was absurd. Having hired a loft over an uunoccupied stable, in a court called Cato Street (the name of which has since been altered to "Homer Street"), near the Edgeware Road, and communicating with John Street and Queen Street, he proceeded to hold nightly meetings there, which were attended, at most, by twenty-five or thirty persons; the loft being too confined to contain larger numbers. He had managed to persuade these men that if they could accomplish a wholesale and simultaneous murder of all the Cabinet Ministers, the executive would be so totally paralysed, that possession might be taken of the Tower, the Bank, and Government Offices, by which time the numbers and force of their partisans would be so increased, that all further opposition might be easily overborne. He assured his followers that the troops in the barracks would retire or be overpowered, and that London would in a few hours be in the possession of the conspirators.

As the first step, it was resolved to collect arms, and to prepare hand grenades and other explosive machines, while those who were most in Thistlewood's confidence were charged to be on the look-out for active and determined associates, who should be ready, on a preconcerted signal, to take a lead in the riot, and guide the mob in the proper direction for their purposes.

A Cabinet dinner appeared to Thistlewood to be the best opportunity for the outbreak. All the Ministers would then be assembled, and being, many of them, elderly and infirm persons, defenceless and unprepared, might be slaughtered without noise, and in a very short space of time. Having ascertained that one of these dinners was about to take place at the Earl of Harrowby's, in Grosvenor Square, a part of the town very quiet at that time of day, and removed from any civil or military protection, he laid his plan in the following manner :—

Soon after eight o'clock in the evening the party selected for the attack were to issue, by twos and threes, from the loft in Cato Street, armed with daggers, pistols, and combustibles of a portable nature, and moving by different routes, so as not to attract notice, were to assemble along the railings on the south side of Grosvenor Square. One man was to keep watch near the dining-room windows of Lord Harrowby's house (No. 39), with a view of ascertaining when the servants should withdraw, after putting the dessert upon the table. On a certain signal two of the stoutest of the gang, armed with daggers, were to ring the bell, and, on the porter opening the door, were instantly to stab him, and, followed by eight or ten of their comrades, to rush into the dining-room. Each of the conspirators was then to seize and despatch one of the Ministers, while one or two others should place themselves with pistols, at the top of the stairs leading down to the offices, and thus prevent any of the servants coming up, to the rescue. Not a moment was then to be lost in cutting off the heads of their victims, which they were to fix on poles, prepared for the purpose, and they were immediately to form a procession, and parade through the streets, with the heads carried in front, by Charing Cross, along the Strand, and eastward towards the City. Strange as it must now appear, there can be no doubt, from various evidence adduced upon their trial, that these misguided wretches were firmly convinced that an immense mob would at once follow and join them, and that before midnight the Bank, the Tower, the Mint, and all the important points of London would be in their possession.

Now if one thing could be devised more likely than another to set against them even the most turbulent of the London mob, it would have been that on which they chiefly relied, the exhibition of a number of bloody heads in the front of their procession. Nevertheless, whatever failure might have attended their schemes, there can be little question, that these desperadoes would have destroyed many valuable lives, and thrown the town into frightful confusion, had not a providential revelation caused the detection and prevention of their scheme at a critical stage of their proceedings.

About a week before the day fixed for the Cabinet dinner above mentioned, as the Earl of Harrowby was riding slowly through the Park on his way to his office in Downing Street, a man of respectable appearance stepped from the foot-path, and, touching his hat, requested a few minutes' conversation with his lordship, on a matter, which he averred was of great consequence to the Government.

Lord Harrowby paid little attention to the man, and telling him he could not listen to such matters there, trotted on, supposing his request to be a mere preamble to some begging imposture.

But a day or two afterwards, at about the same time and place, the man again presented himself, and was so urgent in his assurance, that it was a matter of deep importance to Government, and regarded a great impending danger to the State, that Lord Harrowby was induced to appoint an hour next morning to receive him, and hear what he had to say. Meantime he deemed the communication of sufficient importance to mention it at a Cabinet Council which happened to meet the same afternoon. Most of the Ministers were disposed to treat the matter as unworthy of serious notice, with the exception of the Duke of Wellington and Earl Bathurst, who, having heard rumours from various quarters, of secret meetings for some dangerous object, strongly urged the propriety of further investigation, by placing the matter in the hands of the Magistrates and officers of Bow Street, who at that time were the detective, as well as executive, police of London. Through their means a communication was opened with the person (one Hidon) who had addressed Lord Harrowby in the Park, and on promise of personal safety and reward, he disclosed the whole plot, averring that it was from scruples of conscience, that he had resolved to give warning to the Ministers, as soon as he learned from Thistlewood that the insurrection (to which he had at first been a ready adherent) was to commence with a wholesale and atrocious murder. The Cabinet, having met to consider the fittest means of dealing with these discoveries, and of arresting as many as possible of the conspirators, it was proposed by the Duke of Wellington, as the surest plan of seizing the whole gang in the very act of outrage, that the Cabinet dinner should not be given up, but that, during the previous night, a party of twenty picked men of the Foot Guards, and a few of the most active Bow Street officers, should be introduced privately into the Earl of Harrowby's House, and concealed in the garrets; that two hundred men should be warned for duty at Portman Street Barracks, late in the afternoon, on some pretence not likely to cause suspicion, and that a squadron of the 1st Life Guards then in Hyde Park Barracks should be ordered as if for an escort of the King to the theatre; both detachments to be in readiness at seven o'clock. Two officers, in plain clothes, were to ride slowly through Grosvenor Square at half-past seven, as if returning from a ride in the Park, and to loiter in Grosvenor Street and Audley Street, till they perceived the approach of the conspirators. Meanwhile the Ministers were to arrive in their carriages as usual, each having pistols in his despatch-box, and the dinner was to be served up. But after the second course, the servants were to close the dining-room shutters, and the Ministers to remove quickly, by the back stairs, up to the drawing-room, the front stairs being previously blocked up, at the first landing-place, with chairs and furniture, and the twenty Foot Guards concealed in the garrets brought down into the entrance-hall.

At a quarter before eight, the hour fixed by Thistlewood for the attack of the house, these officers were to proceed, slowly at first, but, as soon as out of sight from Grosvenor Square, at full gallop, to summon the two hundred men from Portman Street, and the Life Guards from Hyde Park barracks. The Guards were to come at double quick, and to form a cordon across the square in front of Lord Harrowby's house, while the Life Guards were to gallop across the Park, pass quickly along Mount Street, and occupy it, as well as Charles Street, and the upper part of South Audley Street, so that the whole block of houses of which Lord Harrowby's formed a part, should be instantly and completely surrounded, and all escape, for those within the space enclosed, rendered impossible. Such was the Duke's scheme, and, had it been carried out, there can be no doubt that every one of the gang must have been killed or captured; but except Lord Castlereagh, none of the Ministers deemed it prudent to allow matters to go so far, considering the desperation of the conspirators, and the risk of mistake, or delay, by the troops. It was therefore determined, that steps should be taken to attack and seize the gang, in their own rendezvous in Cato Street, as late as possible before the moment of their start for Grosvenor Square, which seizure might be effected by a small force, and with less chance of the secret transpiring. No warning was therefore given to the troops, but at seven o'clock two Bow Street officers, with a warrant and authority from the Home Secretary, arrived at Portman Street, and called for the officer on barrack duty for the day, and a party of forty men of the Coldstream Guards. Leaving directions for this detachment to follow them as fast as possible, the Bow Street officers hastened on to Cato Street, to keep a look-out, till the soldiers should arrive. Unluckily it had not occurred to them to provide a guide for the soldiers; and neither Mr. F. Fitzclarence, who was the officer, nor any of the men, had a distinct knowledge of where Cato Street lay, beyond a general notion of its being near the Edgeware Road. They had already missed their way, when they accidentally met a lad who had been in Mr. Fitzclarence's stable, and who, at his desire, undertook to guide them to the place. They arrived but just in time, for the Bow Street officers, hearing a considerable stir in the loft, and fearing lest some of the conspirators might escape, had rushed up the ladder, and one of them, Smithers, was just falling, having been stabbed to the heart by Thistlewood. Mr. Fitzclarence and Sergeant Legge rushed up into the loft followed by the men, and, the lights being struck out, a desperate struggle ensued, in which Mr. Fitzclarence's cap was cut through with a sword, close to his head, and though the greater number of the gang were captured, yet a dozen or more escaped and made for Edgeware Road and the Park, among whom was their leader Thistlewood.

Within two hours after this, the alarm had spread through London in a manner almost incredible. The troops were all placed under arms in their barracks; dinner parties, assemblies, and balls, were quickly dispersed; the wildest reports flew about in all directions;

nor was anything like tranquillity restored in London till long after daybreak next morning; when the astonishment of all, was great, at learning how few were the conspirators, and how quickly and completely their sanguinary plot had been frustrated. A strict search was now commenced for Thistlewood, and his capture was effected a few days afterwards, by Bishop, an active Bow Street officer, in the garret of an obscure lodging in White Street, Finsbury, by the treachery of one of his associates, who gave information of his hiding-place to the Magistrates. A man named Edwards also came forward with evidence against his fellow conspirators, and another named Adams, who had formerly been a soldier. A special commission was immediately issued for the trial of the conspirators, and their leaders were committed to the Tower, and placed in custody of the Warders in different parts of the fortress: Thistlewood in the Bloody Tower; Ings and Davidson (who was a negro) in St. Thomas's Tower; Harrison, Brunt, Tidd, Monument, and Wilson in the Byward and Middle Towers; and Hooper in the Salt Tower. The trials were proceeded with on the 17th of April; and the evidence of their guilt was so plain, that their sentences soon followed. Nor indeed did most of them deny the facts, but assumed a tone of bravado, and endeavoured to blame, and damage, those who had betrayed them. The five first were ordered for execution in front of Newgate, and the rest were transported for life.

It was determined to keep up to a certain degree the terrors of an execution for high treason, and yet to mitigate the details of the ancient executions, especially in respect to the frightful protraction of the criminals' sufferings. On the 1st of May a scaffold was erected from the window over the gate of Newgate, and at eight o'clock the five men were brought out. In reply to the exhortations of the clergyman, Thistlewood said in a surly tone, " We shall soon know the great secret ; " the rest assumed a look of bravado, and Tidd, one of the most savage of the gang, actually attempted to dance on his way to the scaffold; but they were all evidently under the influence of extreme terror, when they took their places under the gallows, and the Executioner attached the ropes to their necks. The fall of the drop took place at exactly eight o'clock and in dead silence. They were left hanging till nine, when a coffin was brought to the front of the scaffold, and placed on tressels about two feet high. At one end of it, was placed a block, on the same level as the upper edge of the coffin. A man now made his appearance, with his face covered with crape, and a broad knife in his hand like that used by butchers, and placed himself by the side of the block. The Executioner and his assistant then cut down one of the corpses from the gallows, and placed it in the coffin, but with the head hanging over on the block. The man with the knife instantly severed the head from the body, and the Executioner receiving it in his hands, held it up in front, and on each side of the scaffold, saying in a loud voice, "This is the head of a traitor." He then dropped it into the coffin, which being removed, another was brought forward, and they proceeded to cut down the next body, and to go through the same ghastly operation.

It was observed, that the mob, which was very large, gazed in silence and fear at the hanging of the conspirators, and showed not the least sympathy; but when each head was cut off, and held up, a loud and deep groan of horror burst from all sides, which was not soon forgotten by those who heard it.

The people dispersed so quietly, that it was evident the conspiracy had found no favour among the masses, and had been confined entirely to Thistlewood's followers. In fact, this was so well known to the authorities, that although all the troops in London were kept in readiness in their barracks, 150 of the Life Guards, and the Bow Street constables, were the only force stationed in the neighbourhood of the scaffold during the execution.

It will be in the recollection of several persons yet living, that some months before the Cato Street Plot, a strange alarm took place at a grand full-dress ball given by the Spanish Ambassador in Portland Place, which was attended by the Regent, the Duke of York, the Duke of Cambridge, and the Duke of Wellington (all of whom wore Spanish Generals' uniforms in honour of the occasion), as well as by the ministers and other distinguished persons. At about one o'clock, just before supper, a sort of order was circulated among the younger officers, to draw towards the head of the stairs, though no one knew for what reason, except that an unusual crowd had collected in the street. The appearance of Lavender, and one or two well-known Bow Street officers, in the entrance-hall, also gave rise to surmises of some impending riot. While the officers were whispering to each other as to what was expected to happen, a great noise was heard in the street, the crowd dispersed with loud cries in all directions, and a squadron of the 2nd Life Guards arrived with drawn swords at a gallop from their barracks (then situated in King Street) and rapidly formed in front of the Ambassador's house. Lavender and the Bow Street officers now withdrew; the officers who had gathered about the stairhead were desired to return to the ball-room. The alarm, whatever it might have been, appeared to be over, and before the company broke up, the Life Guards had been withdrawn to their barracks.

Inside of the Ambassador's house all had remained so quiet, that very few of the ladies present were aware till next day, that anything unusual had happened; but it became known after a short time, that the Duke of Wellington had received information of an intended attack upon the house, which the precautions taken had probably prevented; and upon the trial of Thistlewood and his gang, it came out, among other evidences of the various wild schemes they had formed, that Thistlewood had certainly entertained the project, at the time of this ball, to attack the Spanish Ambassador's house, and destroy the Regent, and other Royal personages, as well as the Ministers, who were sure to be most of them present on the occasion.

ANCIENT ARMOUR.

HE valuable and extensive collection of armour in the Tower, is an object of deserved admiration and interest to visitors: but according to the judgment of antiquaries and persons conversant with the subject, it is beginning to require a fresh inspection and arrangement, similar to that made by the late Dr. Meyrick, about twenty-eight years ago, under the direction of the Duke of Wellington, when Constable of the Tower. In the mean time, however, it is attended to and cleaned with much care: and, if some confusion of the detail has arisen since Dr. Meyrick's inspection, there is no doubt it may at any time be rectified, at little pains and expense. Still it is a subject of reasonable regret, that in so large and fine a collection, any moderate outlay should be spared to classify and to arrange the armour, in a manner suitable to a great national collection of such value and interest.

It would be out of place here to introduce even an abstract of the very long published Catalogue of the Tower Armoury, but it may be mentioned that among other remarkable suits of armour, there is a very handsome one, complete both in the armament of horse and man, which was presented by the Emperor Maximilian to Henry VIII., after their celebrated meeting at the siege of the town of Terouenne. The equipment of the horse is of the finest steel, engraved in every part with rich patterns, interspersed with representations of the martyrdom of several saints of the Romish Church. But the most curious is, a very elaborate delineation of a female, undergoing the terrible torture of the rack, and portraying every detail of the mechanism of that frightful engine. The Rack seems to have consisted of a strongly framed wooden trough, like a horse-trough, in which the sufferer was extended at full length; at each end of the trough was fitted a transverse cylinder, round which, in the fashion of a windlass, a stout rope was passed, after being secured to the wrists of the person under torture. This cylinder projected beyond the side of the trough, sufficiently to admit of the insertion of four wooden bars, into holes pierced through its diameter, by which it could be powerfully turned, so as to tighten the rope, and produce a strain upon the sufferer's arms, so severe as not unfrequently to dislocate the shoulders.

A similar windlass at the other end of the trough, produced a fearful strain upon the joints of the knees and hips; so that it is hardly possible to conceive a more universal distension and agony to the whole human frame than this infernal engine must have caused. The expression of the female's countenance, though a mere outline, conveys a most painful impression, while the deliberate coolness with which the operator at the windlass is forcing round the bars which he grasps, conveys a frightful idea of the indifference produced by habit to the performance of so barbarous an office.

An instance of this indifference occurred at the torture of the unfortunate Anne Askew, who was accused of denying the real presence in the administration of the sacrament.

The mock ceremony of her trial took place in Guildhall, where, after repeated exhortations to confess the error of her belief, she was, by Henry VIII.'s own order, twice placed on the rack. The first time, she was lifted off, after repeatedly fainting under her sufferings. The second time no such mercy was shown, and when Sir Anthony Knyvett, the Lieutenant of the Tower, unable to endure any longer the sight of the unhappy young lady's agonies, ordered the executioner to desist from turning the wheel, Wriothesly, the Chancellor, seized the bars, and recommenced the torture with his whole strength. On his complaining to the King afterwards of Knyvett's leniency, the latter only saved himself from the loss of his place, by begging pardon on his knees, for his praiseworthy act of humanity.

ORDNANCE.

HERE are a great number of cannon of all kinds and periods in the Tower, a correct list of which will be found in the Guidebooks, and only a few of them can here be noticed. One of the most curious is a very long and heavy gun, placed on the west side of the White Tower. By the inscription upon this gun, it appears to have been cast under the immediate auspices and direction of Solyman the Magnificent, for the express purpose of his meditated invasion of India. It is about eighteen feet long; and as it is evident that some portion of the muzzle has been sawn off, it must have been originally cast of longer dimensions than any even of the monster guns of our time. The reason assigned by tradition for the amputation of the extremity of this gun, was a supposition that from its peculiar yellow colour there was an alloy of gold in the metal, and it would seem, from the clumsy way in which the muzzle was cut off, that this portion had been stolen, in order to melt it down, and extract the gold it contained by chemical process. In his very interesting description of the military power and armament of the Turks,

Montecuculi observes, that they excelled all nations in the art of casting large cannon, and gives some remarkable details as to their bringing their gun-metal up the Danube, on the occasion of one of their invasions of the Austrian dominions, and actually casting cannon before the towns which they invested and besieged. This he tells us was done by sinking pits in the earth, and lining them with a composition which formed a mould for the gun. The casting of any very large piece of ordnance was treated by the Turks as a grand ceremony; the Sultan himself often attended, and on such occasions the great officers and pachas present were in the habit of casting purses of gold into the liquid metal, as a special homage and compliment to the presence of their sovereign. It is difficult to believe that large sums of gold should thus have been wasted, in what at best was an absurd piece of adulation; but the prodigality and ostentation of the Turks of that period, when, in the insolence of their riches and military power, they threatened to overrun the finest countries of Europe, would account for almost any display in honour of Solyman, whose ambition, ability, and spirit had elevated the military character of the Turks to a higher standard of renown than it ever attained before or after his long and glorious reign.

In order to clear up the question, and ascertain the existence or not of the supposed alloy, the Lieutenant-Governor of the Tower applied in June, 1865, to Mr. Graham, the Master of the Mint, who obligingly deputed Mr. Field, an experienced officer of that department, to make the trial, by chipping off a small piece of the muzzle, where it had been, as before mentioned, sawn off, and subjecting it to the scientific tests so well understood at the Mint. After a close examination, it turned out that there was not a particle of gold in the metal, but a large proportion of copper, which had given it the colour by which the thieves, who sawed off the extremity, had probably been deceived into the belief that it contained gold.

There are two handsome guns on the Parade which were placed in the Tower at the end of the Seven Years' War, having been cast at Woolwich from some cannon captured from the French in the second expedition to Cherbourg in 1758. It was a strange notion thus to commemorate that affair, for, although the surprise of Cherbourg placed the French cannon from which these two guns were made in the hands of the English, yet the troops, when they afterwards sailed round and landed near St. Malo, which they found too strong to attack, behaved with such irregularity, and such gross carelessness and bad arrangements occurred on their march to St. Cass, that the Commander, General Bligh, surprised by a superior force hastily collected by the Duc d'Aiguillon, was in his turn defeated with loss, and his soldiers driven into the sea in attempting to regain their transports. General Dury, the second in command, made a gallant endeavour to rally a battalion of the Foot Guards, who were covering the rear, but the confusion was irretrievable, and, being much weakened by a wound received in the conflict, he perished in trying to swim off to a boat.

In the Tower collection there are many fine specimens of ornamental casting, but that which specially attracts notice from an admirer of art, is a superb 12-lb. gun captured at Malta, in the upper room above the Horse Armoury. Nothing can be more bold and masterly than the shape of the dragon which forms the main portion of the carriage, and it is evidently from the design of a master-hand.

As a proof how few inventions have not had some former origin in one form or another, there is preserved. in the upper chamber of the Horse Armoury, a revolver, which dates from the reign of James I. It is of course a clumsy affair, but the principle is exactly similar to Colonel Colt's celebrated invention.

The banqueting-hall and council-chamber of the White Tower have been admirably fitted up (and without any sacrifice of their original architectural features) as armouries for the conservation of the store of rifles for the direct regimental supply of the army; nor is it by any means a mere display, for every musket (and there are 60,000) is in the best of order, and fit for immediate use. For practical purposes this is in every respect a far better arrangement than the old plan of keeping the arms in chests, for whatever care might be bestowed on the packing, it was hardly possible to make sure of the exclusion of damp; and it is needless to observe on the mischief which arises with so delicate a machine as the present musket, from the smallest effects of rust on the highly finished steel-work of the lock.

THE CONSTABLES OF THE TOWER.

HE office of Constable of the Tower dates from the Conquest. One of the first on record was Geoffrey de Mandeville, a famous warrior, who came over with William the Conqueror and received from him large possessions in various parts of England.

His grandson, created Earl of Essex by King Stephen, and appointed by him to the government of the Tower, was confirmed in that post by the Empress Maud.

The office of Constable was not confined to military persons in the earlier reigns. Longchamp, Bishop of Ely, was Constable in Richard I.'s time, and was succeeded by   , Archbishop of Rouen. In the reign of John, we find Langton, Archbishop of Canterbury, holding this office. In Henry I.'s time, Pandulph, Bishop of Norwich, and William, Archbishop of York, appear in the list of Constables, and also Walter, another Archbishop of York. In Edward II.'s reign, Stapleton, Bishop of Exeter, became Constable, but he appears to have been the last clerical dignitary to whose custody the Tower was confided.

To notice a few of the most celebrated and remarkable on the List of Constables. Mandeville, Earl of Essex, who was Governor of the Tower in Henry II.'s reign, surrendered his office to the King, and deliberately adopted the life of an outlaw, robbing abbeys, and committing dreadful outrages in all directions, till, encouraged by success in his restless career, he laid siege to a Royal Castle at Burwell, in Cambridgeshire. While making a reconnaissance of this fortress, the heat of the weather induced him to take off his helmet, when an archer from the battlements sent an arrow through his head, and killed him on the spot. As Mandeville had been excommunicated by the Pope, none of his followers dared to bury him; but the Knights Templars of London, from regard to his rank, and some services he had rendered to their Order, brought his corpse to the Temple, clothed in the habit of a Templar, and, placing it in a leaden coffin, slung it up with ropes, to some trees in their garden, till an opportunity occurred for interring it privately. in front of the west door of their Church.

Hubert de Burgh, whose long and eminent services to his country should have secured for him the support of his Sovereign Henry II. against the malice of his enemies, was forced to seek sanctuary in the Priory of Merton, upon a false accusation of treason made against him by the Bishop of Winchester. But the King, in his fury, sent an armed force to drag him from the Altar, causing him to be brought to London, with his legs tied, like a malefactor, under his horse's belly, and threw him into a dungeon. This outrage of the right of sanctuary having produced a threat of excommunication from the clergy, Henry sent De Burgh back to Merton, with orders to the Prior to restrict his daily food to one loaf and a cup of ale, to allow no one to speak to him, and especially to deprive him of a Psalter, which he had always carried about him. As the unhappy prisoner still adhered to his sacred refuge, this scanty supply of food was soon after withdrawn, and he was forced by hunger to come forth and submit. Henry caused him to be loaded with irons and confined in a vault of the Castle of Devizes for several months; but, whether from a late conviction of his own injustice, or from deference to the favour of De Burgh with the barons, he at last released and restored him to the full possession of his titles and honours, which he enjoyed till his decease in 1243.

Hugh le Bigod, Earl of Norfolk, Earl Mareshal of England, and Constable of the Tower in Henry III.'s reign, was one of those turbulent nobles who held the royal authority of such small account, that on the King's desiring him to lead a body of troops on a foreign expedition he flatly refused. "Fore G—, Sir Earl," said the King, "you shall go, or hang!" "Fore G—," replied the sturdy Earl, "I will neither go nor hang!" nor did the monarch venture to urge him further.

Bishop Stapleton, who was Constable in Edward II.'s reign, paid dearly for his misconduct in the exercise of his high office. As Constable of the only fortress of London, he had many opportunities for oppression and exaction. Besides the fines and fees paid by State prisoners, 20*l.* for a duke, 10*l.* for a baron, 5*l.* for a knight, as a sort of bargain for relieving them from fetters, the Constable exacted all kinds of fees and tolls, of wines, and "any dainties" brought to London in foreign merchant ships. Even swans which were drifted through London Bridge by the strength of the ebb-tide; bullocks, pigs, and sheep, which by any accident fell into the river and swam towards the Tower, were the Constable's perquisites. A cart rolling into Tower-ditch, the fines accruing from "outreys and affrays" in the neighbourhood, a portion of every boatload of oysters, muscles, and cockles, were all subject to the grasping claw of the Constable. Bishop Stapleton appears to have been well aware of all his rights, and to have applied the screw so unsparingly, that at length the citizens were roused to insurrection, and, rising in a body, plundered the Bishop's residence in the City, and soon afterwards, meeting him as he was returning past St. Paul's on horseback, dragged him from his saddle and carried him to Cheapside, where, after going through the form of proclaiming him an "open traitor, a seducer of the King, and a destroyer of their liberties, they cut off his head, and set it on a pole upon London Bridge." Nor does it appear that any retribution was exacted by the King for this murder and outbreak, so general was the indignation against the Bishop.

De la Beche, who was Constable in Edward III.'s time, was in so much favour with the King, that he confided the royal children to his charge, while he was absent a the wars in France. De la Beche proved unworthy of this confidence, and absented himself from his post, during which his subordinates, taking example from their chief, neglected their attendance on the royal children, leaving them almost without proper food and clothing. Edward, whom De la Beche supposed to be fully engaged with his military operations in France, returned unexpectedly to England to obtain supplies, and sailing up the Thames, accompanied by his Queen, made his appearance at the gate of the Tower, and called for the Governor. To his indignation he found him absent, and the fortress guarded by a few only of the warders, while De la Beche and his officers were nowhere to be heard of. The alarm of the King's arrival soon brought them however to their posts, when they were immediately deprived of their offices, and committed to the prisons of the fortress they had so negligently guarded. It was soon after this, that Queen Philippa was delivered in the Tower of a daughter, Blanche, who died in infancy.

The King, returning to the prosecution of his wars in France, soon afterwards filled the Tower with prisoners of distinction from that country, including John de Vienne, the brave defender of Calais. Charles of Blois was added to the list of captives; and John, King of France, with his son Philip, captured at Poictiers in 1358, after being imprisoned at the Savoy and at Windsor, were eventually transferred, for safer custody, to the Tower, and detained close prisoners till the peace of Bretigni, which was concluded two years afterwards.

To go through the whole succession of Constables would not be of sufficient interest, but in Richard II.'s reign, the fate of Sir Thomas Rempston may be mentioned as connected with a curious privilege of the Tower Governors. Sir Thomas had been in his barge to the court at Westminster, to solicit a reprieve for a State prisoner under sentence of death, and was unfortunately overset and drowned in shooting old London Bridge on his return to the Tower.

The privilege peculiar to the office of Constable, of which Sir Thomas had on this occasion availed himself, was that of access to the Sovereign at any hour of day or night. Of this privilege the latest instance on record is that of Sir William Balfour, in Charles I.'s reign, who, at the entreaty of Lord Loudon, one of the Scotch Covenant Commissioners discovered in a treasonable correspondence with the King of France, and lying prisoner in the Tower, proceeded late at night to Whitehall, accompanied by the Marquis of Hamilton, to seek an interview with the King, and make a last intercession for Lord Loudon's life, carrying with him the warrant for his execution, which had that evening reached his hands at the Tower.

Sir William, having gained admission to the Royal presence as Lieutenant of the Tower, though the King had retired to bed, fell on his knees, and urgently represented the uproar that would arise in Scotland if one of their Commissioners should be put to death, in spite of the protection with which his mission vested him. The King at first refused to hear these arguments, declaring that Loudon was a traitor, and the warrant must have its course. But the Marquis now came forward, having obtained admission along with Balfour, and added his entreaties for a reprieve. The King, however, still refused. "Well then," said the Marquis, "if your Majesty be so determined, I will ride post for Scotland to-morrow morning, for before night, the whole city will be in an uproar, and they'll come and pull your Majesty out of your palace. I'll get as far as I can, and declare to my countrymen that I had no hand in it." Struck by the resolution of the Marquis, the King hesitated, tore the warrant, and sent back Balfour with the reprieve, which was followed a few days later by an order for Lord Loudon's release. It must be here observed that, although this story has been received as History, there is a glaring improbability in the fact of Lord Loudon having been sentenced without trial, and the probable solution is, that Hamilton and Balfour made their way to the King's presence, not to plead for Lord Loudon's life, but to entreat the King not to bring him to trial; which view is confirmed by the fact of his being so soon afterwards released.

Among the first disputes between Charles I. and his Parliament, the custody of the Tower was a sorely contested point, and the greatest jealousy was shown concerning it by the Commons. Not content with having driven the King, by their remonstrances, to displace Lunsford, whom he had appointed Governor of the Tower, they never ceased to press him, till he had also removed Sir John Biron, a man of character and loyalty, and replaced him by Sir J. Conyers, in whom alone they declared they could place confidence for so important a trust. In 1647 the Parliament appointed Fairfax

Governor of the Tower. At the Restoration, Sir J. Robinson succeeded, and after him some others of less note. Lord Dartmouth was Constable for some years. On the abdication of James II., Lord Lucas was appointed by the Lords Commissioners, and confirmed by William III.

In George II.'s time, Charles, third Duke of Bolton, was for a short time Constable. This nobleman is mentioned by Sir C. Hanbury Williams in one of his political satires, with his usual bitterness towards his political adversaries :—

> " Now Bolton comes with beat of drum,
> Though fighting be his loathing,
> He much dislikes both pike and gun,
> But relishes the clothing."

Lord Cornwallis was appointed Constable of the Tower in 1770, and upon his resignation of this office in 1783, Lord George Lennox, brother of the third Duke of Richmond, and a general officer at the time, was nominated by George III. to succeed the Duke.

Upon his appointment a question was raised in the House of Commons, by Lord Maitland, "whether the acceptance of the office of Constable did not render it incumbent upon Lord George Lennox to vacate his seat for Sussex, for which county he was one of the members? Several speakers on the Opposition side of the House supported Lord Maitland, who moved for the reading of Lord Cornwallis's warrant ; and, as it appeared by the wording of that document, that the Constable drew his pay from the " Exchequer," Lord Maitland and his supporters argued, that it must be regarded as a " Civil

Office" under Government, which would necessitate the vacating of his seat, by any member of that House who should receive the appointment.

But here Mr. Steele, who was Secretary to the Treasury, interposed, and declared to the House, that, strange as it might seem, the wording of Lord Cornwallis's warrant was altogether wrong, and that all the warrants of his predecessors for the last eighty years had been drawn under the same error; for the Constable's salary was not payable from the Exchequer at all, but had been, for the whole of the above period, invariably included in the vote for garrisons. Mr. Pitt then rose, and in a few pithy sentences, showed the manifest inconvenience and absurdity of requiring Lord G. Lennox to resign his seat, since the appointment was plainly military (though derived straight from the Crown, and not through the Commander-in-Chief); for, said he, " if such a precedent were once established, you might have a regimental Captain called upon to vacate his seat, preparatory to his promotion to a Majority. From this debate, and from an examination of the List of Constables, it would appear however, that Mr. Pitt was not quite correct in arguing that the appointment was exclusively military, because certainly neither Lord Carlisle, Lord Lincoln, Lord Northampton, nor Lord Leicester, all of whom had been Constables within the eighty years quoted by Mr. Steele, were military men. The fact of drawing their salaries from the military purse of the country, could no more convert them into military men, than it makes the Chaplains of the army regimental officers. The effect, however, of this parliamentary discussion has undoubtedly been, to restrict the office of Constable to military officers, from that time to the present; and the authority delegated by the Sovereign to the Constable, in respect to all persons within the walls of the Tower, including the battalion of Guards or Line, and the detachment of artillery which form its regular garrison, appears on all accounts to render it advisable, and necessary, that the Constable of the Tower should hold a high military rank.

The Duke of Wellington, who was Constable from 1824 to 1852, regarded the office of the Constable to be by no means a mere honorary position, and set himself seriously to reform and correct many abuses, which the neglect of his predecessors had permitted to accumulate at the Tower. One of the most notorious of these abuses was the mode of selecting and appointing the Warders. These places of trust used formerly to be sold, as vacancies occurred, for 300*l.* each, which sum was paid by the purchaser to the Constable. Therefore the more death vacancies occurred in the year, the more purchase-money the Constable received, and young and able-bodied men were rarely allowed to become purchasers. Most of the Warders were in consequence unfitted by age and

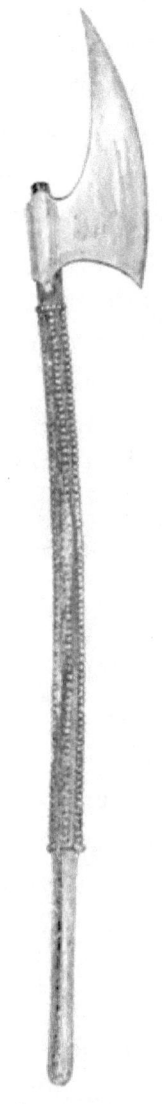

AXE CARRIED BEFORE PEERS GOING TO TRIAL AT WESTMINSTER.

infirmity for the charge of prisoners, the custody of the Tower, and going round the armouries with visitors, from whom they were in the custom of demanding fees amounting often to 5s. or 6s. a head.

The Duke at once stopped the purchase of Warderships, at a loss to himself of from 900*l.* to 1200*l.* a year, and presented these appointments to the Household Cavalry, Foot Guards, and Regiments of the Line, as rewards for non-commissioned officers of merit and good service, to be recommended direct from those regiments, without intervention of private influence.

He also established the present low price of tickets to view the Tower (6d. a head), and granting a liberal allowance of 5s. 6d. to each Warder on such days as it is his turn to conduct visitors, entirely stopped the vexatious system of fees. So greatly has the abolition of fees increased the number of visitors, that for several years they have averaged 1000 persons a week, and since the new armouries and Norman Chapel in the White Tower have been restored and added to the exhibition, this number has considerably increased, producing 1200*l.* or 1300*l.* a year, which is paid into the Exchequer by the Store Department of the War Office.

On the decease of the Duke of Wellington, Lord Combermere, one of his oldest and most distinguished followers, whose discretion and judgment, when commanding the cavalry of the army in the Peninsula, had obtained the highest approval and confidence of the Duke, was named by the Queen to succeed him as Constable. The pay of the post of Constable was co tinued to Lord Combermere, but on his death, in 1865, the place was conferred on another very eminent officer of the Duke's school, Sir John Burgoyne, without any salary, in pursuance of a new and not very considerate arrangement, because the Constable's duty, though not onerous to a man of business habits, yet imposes on him a large amount of correspondence and trouble, both as regards the Tower itself, and the duties of Lord Lieutenant of the Tower Hamlets, entailing many little incidental expenses which custom had rendered almost unavoidable for the person holding this distinguished appointment.

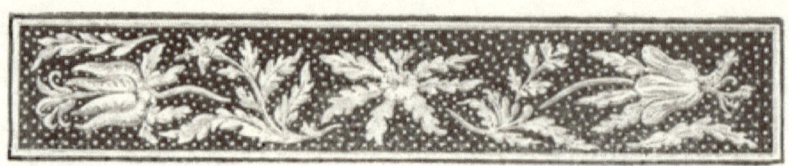

CLOSING THE GATES.

HE ceremony which accompanies the closing of the Tower Gates is of very ancient origin, and had reference to the safety of the Royal Palace, as well as to the security of State prisoners. A few minutes before midnight the Yeoman Porter attends at the Main Guard, and applies for the "escort for the keys." This consists of a party of six privates commanded by a sergeant, who accompany the porter to the outer gate, and assist him to close it. Having locked both the gate and wicket, the Yeoman Porter returns bearing the keys, and followed by the escort. As he passes the sentries, on his way back to the Main Guard, each of them challenges, and in reply to " Who goes there?" is answered "The keys." The sentry rejoins " What keys?" to which the reply is given "The Queen's keys," and the escort passes on, till it arrives at the Main Guard, which now turns out, and after the same questions and answers as to the " keys " and what keys they are? the officer opens the ranks, and presents arms to " The Queen's keys," which are then carried by the Yeoman Porter to the Governor's House, and placed in his Office. All this ceremony and precaution

may seem superfluous, but it is a remarkable fact, and not the less so from the late Duke of Wellington having caused much inquiry to be made on the subject, at the Home Office, and elsewhere, that there has never been any riot or serious disturbance in London, without some plan being laid by the ringleaders, for the attack and seizure of the Tower, from the days of Jack Cade to the Chartist Riots in 1848.

> HENRY VI., Part II. Act IV., Scene 5. *The Tower.*
> *Enter* LORD SCALES, *and others, on the walls.*
> *Then enter certain Citizens, below.*
>
> *Scales.* How now? Is Jack Cade slain?
> 1st *Cit.* No, my Lord, nor likely to be slain; for they have won the bridge, killing all those that withstand them.
> The Lord Mayor craves aid of your honour from the Tower, to defend the city from the rebels.
> *Scales.* Such aid as I can spare you shall command:
> But I am troubled here with them myself;
> The rebels have essay'd to win the Tower.
> But get you to Smithfield, and gather head,
> And thither I will send you Matthew Gough:
> Fight for your King, your country, and your lives:
> And so farewell, for I must hence again.
> [*Exeunt.*

In Lord George Gordon's Riots, in 1780, a scheme of this kind was in contemplation by the mob. Lord George himself solemnly declared it was without his connivance, and very possibly that may have been true;

but this is the common apology of those who place themselves at the head of riots, and it ought never to be received as any extenuation of their guilt and responsibility. The seizure of the Tower was also a chief feature in the wild and desperate conspiracy for which Colonel Despard and several of his followers were hanged in 1803. He had seduced from their allegiance, by plausible falsehoods and delusions, some unfortunate soldiers of the Foot Guards, who, having been in garrison at the Tower, were well acquainted with its localities, of which knowledge he proposed to take advantage, for more readily surprising the gates. Despard's object was not only to seize the large stores of arms and ammunition usually kept in the Tower, but he held out to his followers the chance of obtaining the valuable plunder of the Crown Jewels, and other precious deposits within the Tower walls. On the occasion of Sir Francis Burdett's Riots in 1816-17, plans were proposed for exciting and organising the mob to make an attack on the Tower, by some of his followers, though Sir Francis himself disclaimed, of course, any participation in them, nor was he at all the man to enter into any such absurd and desperate measure.

Discoveries of plans for seizure of the Tower were made on occasion of both Watson's and Thistlewood's conspiracies; also at the Riots in 1831, and the more serious demonstrations of the Chartists in 1848. It was from consideration of these facts, that the late Duke of Wellington, during the many years he held the office of Constable of the Tower, was extremely particular in maintaining the old rules, and very strict about all the precautions for closing the gates at night, and refusing admission during the day to persons, who presented themselves, without ostensible business. It was by the Duke's desire, that a force of twelve constables from the Metropolitan Police was specially appointed to the Tower for prevention of pilfering in the public Stores, and also for security against the danger of fire. The number of old and dilapidated buildings within the Tower, and the numerous warehouses in the neighbourhood, require much vigilance in respect to fires, and although no serious accident has occurred since the great fire of the storehouses in 1841, yet in spite of all the watchfulness of police and sentries, it is a remarkable fact that no year passes without two or three alarms of fire in the Tower. The danger it is true has been quickly arrested by the immediate aid of the troops in garrison, and the excellent organisation of the Artillery in working and manning the four fire engines, but the cautions are very necessary and should never be relaxed.

It appears from the following account of a foreigner's visit to the Tower about 160 years ago, that at that time the precaution was taken of requiring visitors to leave their swords at the gate. The description of the royal furniture and stores in the Tower is so peculiar, that no apology is necessary for its introduction.

Extract from Knight's 'London.'

"Paul Hentzner's account of his visit to the Tower in Queen Anne's time.—Upon entering the Tower of London, we were obliged to leave our swords at the gate, and deliver them to the guard. When we were introduced, we were shown above a hundred pieces of arras belonging to the Crown, made of gold, silver, and silk; several saddles covered with velvet of different colours; an immense quantity of bed-furniture, such as canopies and the like, some of them richly ornamented with pearl; some royal dresses, so extremely magnificent as to raise any one's admiration at the sums they must have cost. We were next led to the Armoury, in which are these particularities:—spears out of which you may shoot; shields that will give fire four times; a great many rich halberds, commonly called partisans, with which the guard defend the royal person in battle; some lances covered with red and green velvet, and the suit of armour of King Henry VIII.; many and very beautiful arms, as well for men as for horse-fights; the lance of Charles Brandon, Duke of Suffolk, three spans thick; two pieces of cannon—the one fires three, the other seven balls at a time; two others made of wood, which the English had at the siege of Boulogne in France, and by this stratagem, without which they could not have succeeded, they struck a terror as at the appearance of Artillery, and the town was surrendered upon articles; nineteen cannons of a thicker make than ordinary, and in a room apart thirty-six of a smaller; other cannons for chain-shot, and balls proper to bring down masts of ships; cross-bows, bows and arrows, of which to this day the English make use in their exercises. But who can relate all that is to be seen here? Eight or nine men employed by the year are scarce sufficient to keep all the arms bright.

"The mint for coining money is in the Tower. N.B. It is to be noted that, when any of the nobility are sent hither, on the charge of high crimes punishable with death, such as murder, &c., they seldom or never recover their liberty. Here was beheaded Anna Bolen, wife of King Henry VIII., and lies buried in the chapel but without any inscription; and Queen Elizabeth was kept prisoner here by her sister, Queen Mary, at whose death she was enlarged, and by right called to the throne.

"On coming out of the Tower we were led to a small house close by, where are kept variety of creatures, viz., three lionesses, one lion of great size called Edward VI., from his having been born in that reign; a tiger, a lynx, a wolf exceedingly old; this is a very scarce animal in England, so that their sheep and cattle stray about in great numbers without any danger, though without anybody to keep them; there is, besides, a porcupine and an eagle: all these creatures are kept in a remote place, fitted up for the purpose with wooden lattices, at the Queen's expense.

"Near to this Tower is a large open space: on the highest part of it (Tower Hill) is erected a wooden scaffold for the execution of noble criminals; upon which they say three princes of England, the last of their families, have been beheaded for high treason. On the Thames close by are a great many cannon, such chiefly as are used at sea."

THE TOWER MENAGERIE.

FROM the earliest times it appears to have been the custom of our kings to collect and keep in the Tower wild beasts of various descriptions, as a sort of appendage to the Palace. The first we hear of this in our Historical Records, was the sending of three leopards to be kept in the Tower, by Henry III., these animals having been presented to him by the Emperor Frederick, in reference to the royal armorial bearings of England. Soon after, the same King placed a white bear in the Tower, with a pension of 4d. a day for his keep, and orders to provide him with a chain and a muzzle for his security, and also " Unam longam et fortem cordam, ad tenendum eum ursum, piscantem in aquâ Tamisiæ."—" a long and strong cord to hold this bear when fishing in the water of Thames."

In 1255 the King of France sent Henry III. a present of an elephant, " a beast most strange and wonderfull to the English people, sith most seldom or never any of that kind had been seene in Englond before that tyme." A house or shed was built for him in the Tower, and he and his keeper received a regular allowance from the City of London, on which corporation, by the bye, this King was in the habit of throwing any little extra expense which he did not exactly know how to provide from his own resources.

During the reigns of the three Edwards, the collection of wild beasts in the Tower was from time to time greatly increased. A lion, belonging to Edward II., had a quarter of mutton allowed daily for his dinner, and his keeper was allowed 1½d. a day for his own board; but, by a later order of this King, 9l. 7s. 6d. annually was allowed for the support of the whole of the wild beasts in the Tower. Keepers were now becoming of more necessity and consequence, and in Henry VI.'s reign we find one Robert Mansfield placed over the establishment, with a good salary attached to his office. In Richard III.'s short reign, the office of keeper of the wild beasts was not beneath the acceptance of Brackenbury the Lieutenant of the Tower; and when Henry VII. made Tiptoft, Earl of Oxford, Constable of the Tower, he also conferred on him the distinct charge of Keeper of the lions.

It was reserved for James I. to subject these noble creatures to wanton cruelty for the sport of baiting them. He caused three fierce mastiffs to be brought to the Tower, where the King and Queen, with the Prince, and four or five courtiers, placed themselves in the windows of the Lions' Tower to view the savage amusement.

The following is the circumstantial account of an eyewitness:—" The King, Queene, and Prince, with four or five Lords, went to the Lions' Toure, and caused the lustiest lion to be separated from his mate, and put into the lion's den one dog alone, who presently flew to the face of the lion; but the lion suddenly shooke him off, and graspt him fast by the neck, drawing the dog up staires and downe staires. The King, now perceiving the lion greatly exceede the dog in strength, but nothing in noble heart and courage, caused another dog to be put into the denne, who prooved as hot and lusty as his fellow, and tooke the lion by the face; but the lion began to deale with him as with the former; whereupon the King commanded the third dog to be put in, before the second dog was spoiled, which third dog, more fierce and fell than eyther of the former, and in despite eyther of clawes or strength, tooke the lion by the lip; but the lion so tore the dog by the eyes, head, and face, that he lost his hold, and then the lion tooke the dog's necke in his mouth, drawing him up and downe as he did the former, but, being wearied, could not bite so deadly as at the first. Now, whilest the last dog was thus hand to hand with the lion in the upper roome, the other two dogs were fighting together in the lower roome, whereupon the King caused the lion to be driven downe, thinking the lion would have parted them; but when he saw he must needs come by them, he leaped cleane over them both, and, contrary to the King's expectation, the lion fled into an inward den, and would not by any meanes endure the presence of the dogs; albeit the last dog pursued eagerly, but could not finde the way to the lyon. You shall understand the two last dogs, whilest the lion held them both under his pawes, did bite the lion by the belly, whereat the lion roared so extreamely that the earth shooke withall, and the next lion rampt and roared as if he would have made rescue." The two dogs which had been first engaged in this combat died within a few days, but the third recovered.

The same writer gives the following particulars respecting the menagerie, and of a second visit made by King James to the lions' den, in June, 1605. "In the spring of this yeare the Kinge built a wall, and filled up with earth all that part of the mote or ditch about the west sid of the lions' den, and appoynted a drawing partition to be made towards the south part thereof, the one part thereof to serve for the breeding lionesse when she shall have whelps, and the other part thereof for a walke for other lions. The Kinge caused also three trap doores to bee made in the wall of the lyon's den, for the lyons to goe into their walke at the pleasure of the keeper, which walke shall bee maintayned and kept for especiall place to baight the lyons with dogges, beares, bulles, bores, &c. Munday, June 3, in the afternoone, his Majestie, beeing accompanied with the Duke of Lenox, the Earles of Worcester, Pembroke, Southampton, Suffolke, Devonshire, Salisbury, and Mountgomery, and Lord Heskin, Captayne of his Highnesse Guarde, with many knights and gentlemen of name, came to the Lyons' Tower, and, for that time, was placed over the platforme of the lyons, because, as yet, the galleries were not builded, the one of them for the King and great Lords, and the other for speciall personages. The King, being placed as aforesayde, commaunded Master Raph Gyll, Keeper of the Lyons, that his servants should put forth into the walke the male and female breeders, but the lyons woulde not goe out by any ordinary meanes that could be used, neither would they come neere the trap doore, untill they were forced out with burning linkes, and, when they were come downe into the walke, they were both amazed, and stood looking about them, and gazing up into the ayre ; then was there two rackes of mutton throwne unto them, which they did presently eate ; then was there a lusty live cocke cast unto them, which they presently killed and sucked his bloud ; then was there another live cocke cast unto them, which they likewise killed, but sucked not his blood. After that the Kinge caused a live lambe to be easily let downe unto them by a rope, and, being come to the grounde, the lambe lay upon his knees, and both the lyons stoode in their former places, and only beheld the lamb, but presently the lambe rose up and went unto the lyons, who very gently looked uppon him and smelled on him without signe of any further hurt : then the lambe was very softly drawne up againe in as good plight as hee was let downe. Then they caused those lyons to be put into their denne, and another male lyon only to be put forth, and two lusty mastiffes, at a by doore to be let in to him, and they flew fiercely uppon him, and, perceiving the lyon's necke to be so defended with hayre they could not hurt him, sought onely to bite him by the face, and did so : then was there a third dogge let in, as fierce as the fiercest. One of them, a brended dogge, tooke the lyon by the face, and turned him uppon his backe ; but the lyon spoyled them all ; the best dogge died the next day."

Another combat was exhibited on the 23rd June, 1609,

when King James, and all his family, with divers noblemen and many others, assembled in the Tower " to see a trial of the lyon's single valour, against a great fierce beare, who had killed a child that was negligently left in the beare-house;" yet neither " the great lyon," which was first " put forth," nor " divers other lyons," nor " the two young lustie lions, which were bred in that yard, and were now grown great," could be induced to fight, but all " sought the next way into their dennes, as soone as they espied the trap-doores open." A stone-horse, however, which had been turned into the same yard, would have been worried to death by six dogs, had not the King commanded the bear-wards to rescue him. About a fortnight afterwards, the bear was baited to death upon a stage, by the King's order: "and unto the mother of the murthered child was given twenty pounds, out of the money which the people gave to see the bear kil'd."

It is not easy to imagine a more disgusting display, or a greater mockery of justice and charity, than this niggardly device of the King's for saving his own pocket, by the contributions of a collection of spectators of tastes as brutal as his own.

In 1758 George II. had so bad a fit of gout, being then seventy-five, that Lord Chesterfield wrote, —"It was generally thought that H. M. would have died, and for a very good reason, for the oldest lion in the Tower—much about the King's age—died a fortnight ago! This extravagancy, I can assure you, was believed by many above the common people." * So

---

* From Lord Stanhope's History of England.

difficult is it for human imagination to assign any bounds, however remote, to human credulity.

The Tower menagerie was so much in the way of the restorations of the entrance towers and gates, and appeared such an unnecessary appendage to the Royal Palace and Fortress, that in the year 1831 the Duke of Wellington obtained the King's leave to remove it altogether, and to clear away the unsightly dens and sheds with which the entrance was encumbered and disfigured.

EXECUTIONER'S AXE, BLOCK, AND MASK, USED IN 1715.

APPENDIX.

Constables of the Tower of London from the Earliest Date.

No.	Name.	Year.	In what Reign.	Remarks.
1	Geoffrey de Mandeville	..	William the Conqueror.	As a reward for distinguished services in the battle of Hastings.
2	William de Mandeville	..	..	Son and grandson, as an hereditary office; the latter deprived of office by Stephen in 1143.*
3	Geoffrey de Mandeville	1140	.	
4	Richard de Lacy	1153	Stephen	Delivered to Henry II. on Stephen's death.
5	Garnerius de Isenci	..	Henry II.	Date unknown.
6	William Longchamp, Bishop of Ely.	1189	Richard I.	On his departure for the Holy Land.
7	Archbishop of Rouen	1192	,,	W. Puintell was Sub-Constable (Pipe Roll).
8	Roger Fitz Renfred	..	.	
9	Roger de la Dane	..	John	In the 7th year of his reign.
10	Geoffrey de Mandeville	..	,,	Great-grandson of the first Geoffrey.
11	Eustace de Greinville		,,	In the 15th year of his reign.
12	Archbishop of Canterbury.	..	,,	Appointed at the signing of the Great Charter.

* Not known who held office from this time until 1153.

Constables of the Tower—*continued*.

No.	Name.	Year.	In what Reign.	Remarks.
13	Walter de Verdun	..	Henry III.	
14	Stephen de Segrave	..	,,	
15	Hugh de Wyndlesore	..	,,	
16	Randulph Bishop of Norwich.	..	,,	Held the office in the first 14 years of the reign of Henry III.
17	John de Boville.	..	,,	
18	Thomas de Blunvill	..	,,	
19	Thomas Fitz Archer	..	,,	
20	Ralph de Gatel	..	,,	
21	Hubert de Burgh	1232	,,	The distinguished statesman and warrior.
22	W. de St. Edmund	..	,,	
23	Geoffrey de Crancumb.	..	,,	
24	Hugh Giffard	..	,,	Appointed in 20th year of Henry III.'s reign.
25	Archbishop of York	..	,,	In joint charge.
26	Bertram de Crioyl			
27	Peter de Vallibus	..	,,	
28	John de Plessitus	..	,,	
29	Peter de Blund	..	,,	
30	Aymon Thorimbergh	..	,,	
31	Imbert Pugeys	..	,,	
32	Richard de Culworth	..	,,	
33	Richard de Tilbury	..	,,	
34	Hugh le Bigod	1258	,,	
35	John Mansel	..	,,	
36	Hugh le Despenser	..	,,	
37	Roger de Leyburn	1265	,,	
38	Hugh Fitz Otho.	..	,,	
39	John Walerand	..	,,	Jointly.
40	John de la Lind			

Constables of the Tower—*continued*.

No.	Name.	Year.	In what Reign.	Remarks.
41	Alan la Zouch	. .	Henry III.	With custody of the City as well as the Tower.
42	Thomas de Ippegrave	. .	,,	
43	Stephen de Eddeville	. .	,,	
44	Hugh Fitz Otho	. .	,,	Appointed in 53rd year of Henry III.'s reign.
45	Walter, Archbp. of York	. .	Edward I.	Appointed on death of Henry III.
46	John de Burgh	. .	,,	
47	Anthony Bek	. .	,,	
48	Ranulph de Dacre	. .	,,	
49	Ralph de Sandwich	. .	,,	
50	Ralph de Berners	. .	,,	
51	Ralph de Sandwich	. .	,,	14th year of Edward I.'s reign.
52	John de Crumwell	. .	,,	17th year of Edward I.'s reign.
53	Roger de Swynnerton	. .	,,	
54	Stephen Segrave	. .	,,	
55	Bishop of Exeter	. .	,,	
56	John de Gisors	. .	,,	
57	Thomas de Wake	. .	Edw. III.	
58	John de Crumbwell	. .	,,	
59	Wm. de Monte Acuto	. .	,,	9th year of Edward III.'s reign.
60	Nicholas de la Beche	. .	,,	
61	Robert de Dalton	. .	,,	
62	John Darcy (father)	. .	,,	
63	John Darcy (son)	. .	,,	
64	Bartholw. de Burghersh	. .	,,	

Constables of the Tower—*continued*.

No.	Name.	Year.	In what Reign.	Remarks.
65	Robert de Morley	..	Edw. III.	
66	Richard de la Vache	..	,,	
67	Alan Buxhill	..	,,	Continued in office after succession of Richard II.
68	Sir Thomas Murrieuse	..	Richd. II.	
69	Edward Earl of Rutland	..	,	
70	Ralph de Nevill	..	,,	
71	Edw. Duke of Albemarle	..	,,	
72	Thomas de Rempston	..	,,	Drowned passing under London Bridge.
73	Edward Duke of York	..	,,	Fell at Agincourt.
74	Robert de Morley	..	Henry V.	
75	John Dabrichcourt	..	,,	
76	William Bourghchier, Knight.	..	,,	
77	Roger Aston, Knight	..	,,	
78	John Duke of Exeter	..	Henry VI.	
79	James Fienes, Lord Say	..	,,	
80	John Lord Tiptoft, Earl of Worcester.	..	Edward IV.	
81	John Lord Dudley	..	,,	
82	Richard Lord Dacre	..	,,	
83	John Howard, Lord Howard	..	,,	
84	Marquis of Dorset	..	,,	
85	Sir Robert Brackenbury	..	Richd. III.	Fell at Bosworth Field.
86	Earl of Oxford	..	Hen. VII.	This Earl was also appointed to be keeper of the lions, lionesses, and the leopard !
87	Sir Thomas Lovel	..	Hen. VIII.	

CONSTABLES OF THE TOWER—continued.

No.	Name.	Year.	In what Reign.	Remarks.
88	Sir William Kingston	..	Hen. VIII.	16th year of Henry VIII.'s reign.
89	Sir John Gage	1540	,,	Remained in office until Edward VI.'s death, and restored on Mary's accession.
90	Lord Clinton	..	,,	Appointed by Lady Jane Grey's party.
91	Sir Edward Bray, Kt.		,,	
92*	Lord Howard of Walden	..	James I.	
93	Lord Cottington (Lumsden, Biron, Conyers.)	1640	Charles I.	Remained in office until 1647.
94	Sir Thomas Fairfax, General	1647	,,	Appointed by Parliament.
95	Sir John Robinson	1660	Charles II.	Appointed at the Restoration.
96	James Earl of Northampton.	1678	,,	
97	Lord Allington	1680	,,	
98	George Lord Dartmouth	1684	Charles II. & James II.	
99	Lord Lucas	1688	..	Appointed by the Lords, and confirmed on accession of Wm. III.
100	Charles Earl of Carlisle	1715	.	
101	Henry Earl of Lincoln	1724	.	
102	Charles Duke of Bolton	1724	.	A Lieut.-General.
103	Henry Lord Viscount Lonsdale.	1726	.	
104	Montague Earl of Abingdon.	..	.	

* No record of any Constable during the reign of Queen Elizabeth.

Constables of the Tower—*continued*.

No.	Name.	Year.	In what Reign.	Remarks.
105	Algernon Earl of Essex	..	.	A Lieut.-General, 4th Dragoons.
106	Richard Earl of Rivers	..	..	A Lieut.-General, 3rd Horse.
107	George Earl of Northampton.	..	.	
108	John Earl of Leicester.	1731	.	
109	Charles Lord Cornwallis.	1741	.	General, died June 1762.
110	Lord Berkeley.	1762	George III.	Resigned Nov. 1770.
111	Charles Earl Cornwallis	1770	,,	
112	Lord George Henry Lennox.	..	,,	A Lieut.-General.
113	Marquis Cornwallis . .	1785	,,	General.
114	Francis Earl of Moira, Marquis of Hastings	1806	,,	General.
115	Arthur Duke of Wellington.	1826	George IV.	Field-Marshal, died Sept. 1852.
116	Lord Viscount Combermere.	1852	Queen Victoria.	Field-Marshal, died Feb. 21, 1865.
117	Sir John Fox Burgoyne, G.C.B.	..	,,	

Lieutenants of the Tower from 1690.

Name.	From.	To.	Remarks.
Wm. Cadogan, Lt.-Gen.	Dec. 1709	Dec. 1715	
Hatton Compton, Lt.-Gen.	Dec. 1715	Apr. 1741	
Lord Henry Paulet	Aug. 1742	Nov. 1754	
Charles Marquis of Winchester.	Nov. 1754	Jan. 1760	
George Paulet, Esq.	June 1760	June 1763	
Lt.-Gen. Vernon	June 1763	Aug. 1810	Died 3 Aug. 1810.
Lt.-Gen. Loftus	Sept. 1810	July 1831	Died 15 July 1831.
George Earl of Munster	July 1831	May 1833	
Lt.-Gen. Sullivan Wood	May 1833	July 1851	Died 3 July 1851.
Maj.-Gen. Sir G. Bowles	July 1851	. .	

Deputy-Lieutenants or Lieut.-Governors of the Tower from 1690.

Name.	From.	To.	Remarks.
John Farewell, Lt.-Col.*	1690	Dec. 1709	
James Pendlebury, Col.	Dec. 1709	Dec. 1715	
Robert D'Oyly, Col.	Dec. 1715	Apr. 1724	
— Williamson, Col.	Apr. 1724	Dec. 1750	
Richard White, Esq.	Dec. 1750	Aug. 1750	
Charles Rainsforth	Nov. 1750	Feb. 1778	
John Gale, Esq.	June 1788	Jan. 1795	
— Yorke, Col.	Jan. 1795	Dec. 1826	Died 26 Dec. 1826.
Francis H. Doyle, Col.	Dec. 1826	Mar. 1839	Died 6 Mar. 1839.
— Gurwood, Lt.-Col.	Mar. 1839	Dec. 1845	Died 27 Dec. 1845.
Hon. G. Cathcart, Col.	Feb. 1846	Feb. 1852	Resigned 12 Feb. 1852.
Lord de Ros, Col.	Feb. 1852	. .	

* This officer appears to have been the Lieutenant under Lord Lucas, and is designated Deputy-Governor according to the Muster-roll of that date.

Majors of the Tower from 1690.

Name.	From.	To.	Remarks.
...omas Hawley, Major	1690	1697	
...rmaduke Soull, Major	1697	Dec. 1709	
...bert D'Oyly, Major	Dec. 1709	Dec. 1715	
...eph Mason, Major	Dec. 1715	Apr. 1724	
...hard White, Major	Apr. 1724	Aug. 1739	
...s. H. Collins, Major	Nov. 1750	Nov. 1771	

Here occurs a break in the Muster-rolls.

...yd Hill, Major	June 1789	Jan. 1795	
...tthew Smith, Col.	Jan. 1795	Feb. 1812	Died 18 Feb. 1812.
... Maclean	Feb. 1812	June 1816	Died 1 June 1816.
...I. Elrington, Col.	July 1816	Mar. 1857	Died 30 Mar. 1857.
...C. Whimper, Lt.-Col.	Mar. 1857	.	

'Though it is probable, that there were occasionally Sub-Constables Lieutenants placed in charge of the Tower at a much earlier period, first we find particularly named, as filling that office, was Giles Oudenard, who held it in the beginning of the reign of King Edward under Anthony of Bek, afterwards Bishop of Durham, the then ...nstable. In the next reign Ralph Bavant is noticed as the Lieutenant John de Crumwell; and after this period our records frequently make ...ntion of Lieutenants."

INDEX.

A.

ABUSES.

ABUSES in the government of the Tower, 12; remedied by the Duke of Wellington, 257, 258.

AGINCOURT, battle of, 38; prisoners taken at, 39.

AGINCOURT, prisoners of, in the Tower, 38; their treatment, 39.

ALLEN, Archbishop of Dublin, 51; murdered at Clontarf, 52.

ANNE ASKEW: see ASKEW.

ANNE BOLEYN: see BOLEYN.

ARMOUR, ancient, collection of, 241; suit presented to Henry VIII. by the Emperor Maximilian, 242.

ARUNDEL, Earl of, beheaded by Richard II., 35.

ARUNDEL, Philip, Earl of, accused of conspiracy by the Earl of Leicester, 111; resolves to go abroad, 111; betrayed, thrown into the Tower, and fined, 112; sentenced to death on charges of high treason, 112; refused permission to see his wife and child, 112; his death — suspicion of poison, 113.

ASKEW, Anne, her unhappy marriage, 60; expelled from her husband's house, 60; examined at Guildhall on a charge of heresy, and again before Bishop Bonner — her answer to him, 61; released, again arrested, and sent to Newgate, 62; condemned to be burnt, and committed

B.

BELL.

to the Tower, 62; tortured by the Chancellor Wriothesley, 63, 243; burnt in Smithfield, 64.

AUBREY'S account of the visits of the ghost of Sir G. Villiers to his friend Mr. Towes, 178-180.

BALFOUR, Sir William, Lieutenant of the Tower, refuses to connive at the escape of Strafford, 186; exercises a peculiar privilege of the Constable of the Tower, 253.

BALLIUM-WALL of the Tower, 3.

BALMERINO, Lord, his trial and execution, 226, 227.

BARRACKS erected in Charles II.'s reign, 13; destroyed by fire in 1841, 14.

BARRY, steward of the Earl of Kildare, assists in murdering the two Keatings, 108, 109; executed, 109.

BEAR, a white, in the Tower, 266; a bear baited to death by order of James I., 271.

BEAUCHAMP, Lord, death of, 150.

BEAUCHAMP TOWER, its early use as a state prison, 4; inscriptions on its walls, 4; former neglect of, 4; restoration of, 5.

BECKMAN, Captain, assists in the capture of the Crown-robbers, 198.

BELL TOWER, 9.

BISHOP, a police officer, arrests Thistlewood, 237.

BLIGH, General, defeated at Cherbourg, 246.

BLOIS, Charles of, confined in the Tower, 252.

BLOOD, Colonel, conceives the idea of stealing the Crown jewels, 196; his first visit to the Tower, 196; his second visit with a present for Mrs. Edwards, the Deputy-Keeper's wife—proposes an alliance between his nephew and Miss Edwards, 197; returns with accomplices, 197; makes a murderous attack on Edwards and seizes the Crown, 198; is interrupted, and attempts to escape, 198; seized and lodged in the Tower, 199; his effrontery when examined before the King, 199; released without trial, 200; account of his outrage on the Duke of Ormond, 201; becomes a hanger-on at Court, turns Quaker, 202.

BLOODY TOWER, 8; probable scene of the murder of the princes, 44.

BLOUNTS, father and son, monuments to, 29.

BOLEYN, Anne, pretence for committing her to the Tower, 55; account of her behaviour there, 56; her trial, 56; her barbarous sentence, 57; her protestations of innocence, 58; particulars of her execution, 58; her grave, 59; her popularity, 59; tablet recording her execution, 53.

BOLTON, Charles, third Duke of, appointed Constable, 255.

BOMMENEY, Mr., his evidence on the inquiry into the death of the Earl of Essex, 204.

BONNER, Bishop, Anne Askew examined by, 61.

BOUCICAULT, Duke of, his death in the Tower, 39.

BOURBON, Duke of, his death in the Tower, 39.

BOWYER TOWER, supposed scene of the murder of the Duke of Clarence, 6.

BRACKENBURY, Sir R., receives a message to destroy Edward V. and his brother, 22, 41; resigns temporary charge of the Tower to Tyrrell, 42; made keeper of wild beasts, 267.

BRADDON, Mr., employed in the inquiry into the Earl of Essex's death, 206.

BRICK TOWER, 6.

BRIDGES, Sir Thomas, his brutal speech to Sir Thomas Wyatt, 93.

BRITTAYNE, cousin of Anne Askew, intercedes with Bonner, 62.

BROAD-ARROW TOWER, 7.

BROMLEY, Sir H., his search for Garnet at Hendlip, 128.

BUCKINGHAM, Villiers, Duke of, supplants Carr, 154; assassinated by Felton, 177.

BURDETT, Sir Francis, his riots, 262.

BURGH, Hubert de, dragged from sanctuary by order of Henry II., 249; sent back, and scantily supplied with food, 250; confined in a vault at Devizes, 250; restored to his titles and honours, 250.

BURGOYNE, Sir John, his appointment as Constable, 259.

BURLEIGH, Lord, vindicates Arabella Stuart, 136; his conduct on Raleigh's trial, 161; his death, 167.

BURLEY, Sir Simon, beheaded, 35.

BURGUNDY, Duchess of, her adoption

CADE.

of the imposture of Perkin Warbeck, 43.

C.

CADE, Jack, his rebellion, 261.
CANTERBURY, an Archbishop of, murdered by rebels, 33.
CAPEL, Lord, his escape from the Tower, 189; recaptured at Lambeth, 190; debate on his wife's petition to Parliament, 191; account of his execution, 192-194; his character, 194.
CATESBY, takes part in treasonable meetings, 114; his character, 115; conceives the scheme of blowing up the King and Parliament, 115; on the seizure of Fawkes, proceeds to Holbeach, 124; killed, 126.
CATHCART, Sir George, his plans for restoring the Beauchamp Tower, 5; his appointment as Lieut.-Governor, 14.
CATO-STREET CONSPIRACY, 229; the scheme originated by Thistlewood, 230; occasion chosen for the outbreak, and details of the plan, 231; the plot betrayed, 232; consultations in Cabinet. 234; proposal of the Duke of Wellington, 234, 235; the Duke's plan rejected, 235; some of the gang arrested, 236; alarm in the metropolis, 236; the trials, 237; details of the executions, 238; behaviour of the spectators, 239; revelations on the trials, 240.
CHAINS, hanging in, mode of, 87; last instance of, 88.
CHAMBERS, arrested at Hendlip, 128.
CHANCELLOR of the Exchequer, his veto on repairs and restorations, 17, 18.
CHAPEL of St. John in the White

CLARENCE.

Tower, improper use of, 21; saved from further desecration by General Peel, 21; restored by Mr. Salvin, 21; historical recollections, 22; the floor and gallery, 22; plan of, 23.
CHAPEL of St. Peter, on Tower Green, modern disfigurements of, 28; restored, 29; monuments, 29; remarkable persons buried in, 29-30; Pepys's visit to, 30; discovery of coffin-plates in, 31; monument to Talbot Edwards, 31; proposed alterations in, 31.
CHARLES I., forced to dismiss Roman Catholic soldiers, 182; sends an assurance of protection to Strafford, 186; assents to the Bill of Attainder, 187; signs the death-warrant, and entreats Parliament for a commutation of the sentence, 187; interview of Sir W. Balfour and the Marquis of Hamilton with him to intercede for Lord Loudon, 253; grants the pardon, 254; disputes with the Parliament on the subject of the custody of the Tower, 254.
CHARLES II., adopts the tradition of the murder of Edward V. and his brother, and transfers their bodies to Westminster Abbey, 46; his mulberry-tree, 46; causes Blood to be brought before him, 199; releases him without trial, 200; apologises for this to the Duke of Ormond, 200.
CHARLES OF ORLEANS, wounded and captured at Agincourt—his ransom, 39; marries the widow of Richard II., his long captivity, 40.
CHERBOURG, expedition to, 246.
CHOLMONDELEY, Sir Richard, monument to, 29.
CLARENCE, Duke of, supposed scene of his murder, 6.

CLARENDON.

CLARENDON, Earl of, his account of the escape, recapture, and execution of Lord Capel, 189-194; his character of that nobleman, 194.

CLOSING the Tower Gates, ceremonies practised on, 260.

COBHAM, Lord, intrigues against Raleigh, 160; his conviction and pardon, 162.

COFFIN-PLATES, discovery of, 31, 228.

COKE, Sir E., his abuse of Raleigh on his trial, 161; his surprise at Raleigh's conviction, 161.

"COLD HARBOUR," a cell under the White Tower—the name of several hamlets, 25.

COMBERMERE, Lord, succeeds the Duke of Wellington as Constable, 15, 258.

CONSTABLE of the Tower, abuses formerly practised by, 12; their difficulties in the matter of repairs and restorations, 16-18; early Constables—ecclesiastics who held the office, 248; Mandeville, Earl of Essex—Hubert de Burgh, 249; Hugh le Bigod, Earl of Norfolk—Bishop Stapleton, 250; De la Beche, 251; Sir Thomas Rempston, 253; peculiar privilege of the Constable, exercised by Sir William Balfour, 253; appointments during the seventeenth century, 254; Duke of Bolton—Lord Cornwallis, 255; question raised, and debate, on the appointment of Lord George Lennox, 255, 256; the appointment since restricted to military officers, 257; reform of abuses by the Duke of Wellington, 257, 258; Lord Combermere, 258; Sir John Burgoyne—the Constable's salary abolished, 259; list of, 273.

CORK, Earl of, assists Raleigh, 169.

CORNWALLIS, Lord, appointed Constable, 255.

DEVONSHIRE.

COWPER, Hon. W., restoration of St. John's Chapel under his auspices, 21.

CRISPE, Mr., arrests Lord Hertford, 104.

CROFTS, Sir James, confronted with Elizabeth in the Tower, 73; his speech to her, 74.

CROMARTY, Lord, his appeal for mercy, 226; pardoned, 226.

CROMPTON, Hugh, a servant of Arabella Stuart, assists her to escape, 140; sent to the Fleet, 147.

CROMWELL, Oliver, destroys the Tower Palace, 8; his speech in the debate on Lord Capel's petition, 191.

CROMWELL, Thomas, Earl of Essex, his grave, 30.

CROWN JEWELS, Blood's attempt to steal the, 196.

D.

DE GREY, Earl, 16.

DE LA BECHE, his favour with Edward III., 251; neglects the duties of his office of Constable, and sent to prison, 252.

DEPUTY-LIEUTENANTS of the Tower, list of, 280.

DERWENTWATER, Lord, his execution, 223.

DESMOND, Earl of, his secret relations with the Earl of Kildare, 50.

DESPARD, Colonel, his conspiracy, 262.

DEVEREUX TOWER (Robin the Devil's), 6.

DEVONSHIRE, Edward Courtenay, Earl of, his long captivity, 65; reason for committing him to the Tower, 65; released by Mary, again committed, and again released, 66; his death, 66.

DIGBY.

DIGBY, Sir Everard, joins in the Gunpowder Plot, 119; executed, 127.

DIGHTON, assists in the murder of the princes, 41; his reward and confession, 47.

DITCH of the Tower, 2; drained, 14.

DOGS employed to bait lions and other animals, 268-271.

DORSET, Earl of, reply of Felton to, 178.

DUDLEY, Lord Guildford, desires a last interview with his wife, 94; his execution, 94; his grave, 30.

DUDLEY, Lord Robert, intercedes with Elizabeth on behalf of Lady Catherine Grey, 103.

E.

ECCLESIASTICS who have been Constables of the Tower, 248.

EDWARD III., imprisons De la Beche for neglect of his duties, 252; his French prisoners, 252.

EDWARD V., murder of, 41; no record of his existence after Richard's usurpation, 43; his remains transferred to Westminster Abbey by Charles II., 46.

EDWARDS, Mr. Talbot, exhibits the Crown jewels to Colonel Blood, 196; invites him to dine, 197; murderously assaulted by Blood and his confederates, 198; his courage ill requited, 202; his grave and monumental tablet, 202.

ELEPHANT presented by the King of France to Henry III., 266.

ELIZABETH, Queen of Henry VII., 22.

ELIZABETH, Queen, arrested (when Princess) at Ashridge, 67; her journey to London, and imprison-

ESSEX.

ment at Whitehall, 68; charged with being privy to Wyatt's conspiracy, 69; her attendants removed, 69; allowed to write to the Queen, 70; conveyed to the Tower, 70; compelled to land at Traitors' Gate, 71; enters the Tower, 72; consultation of the Council concerning her, 72; attempts to extort evidence against her, 73; examined by Bishop Gardiner and others, 73; her rigorous confinement, 74; suspected of corresponding with the Earl of Devonshire, 75; quarrel about her provisions, 75; released from the Tower and conveyed to Woodstock, 76; her rare friendship for Miss Williams, 76; her letter of condolence, 77; tradition of her present to some City churches, 77; rejoicings on her accession, 77; her return to London and sojourn in the Tower, 78; account of her procession through the City, 79-81; sends Lady Catherine Grey to the Tower, 103; her severity and harshness, 106; refuses permission to the Earl of Arundel to see his wife and child, 112; her coquetry, 158; her fury on discovering Raleigh's intrigue with a maid of honour, 159; an effect of her iron rule, 176.

ELWAYS, Sir Gervase, replaces Sir W. Waad at the Tower, 153; his share in Overbury's death, 154; his committal, 154; his trial and sentence, 155; his dress when brought to the scaffold, 155; his address and execution, 156; his grave, 30.

ESSEX, Countess of, instigates the committal of Overbury, 153; causes him to be murdered, 154; committed to the Tower, 154; her trial, pardon, and death, 157.

ESSEX.

Essex, Mandeville, Earl of, adopts the life of an outlaw, 249; killed at Burwell, and buried in the Temple, 249.
Essex, Earl of (Queen Elizabeth's), his rivalry with Raleigh, 159; prejudices James against him, 160; his grave, 30.
Essex, Earl of, son of the preceding, his service in the Low Countries, 157.
Essex, Earl of (grandson of Elizabeth's Earl), found with his throat cut, 203; position of his lodging, 203; inquiry into his death, 203; was it murder or suicide? 204, 205; allusion to the subject by Earl Russell, 205.

F.

Fawkes, Guy, joins the Gunpowder conspirators, 115; undertakes to fire the powder, his precautions, 119; arrested and examined, 124; tortured, 126; executed, 127; his cell under the White Tower, 24.
Felton, assassinates the Duke of Buckingham, 177; tried and executed, 178; his reply when menaced with the rack, 178.
Field, Mr., his experiment on the metal of a Turkish gun, 245.
Fire of 1841, barracks and storehouse destroyed by, 14.
Fisher, Bishop, his cell under the White Tower, 24; his grave, 29.
Fitzclarence, Mr. F., commands the military at the arrest of the Cato-street conspirators, 236.
Fitzgerald, Lord Thomas ("Silken Thomas"), his rebellion, 51; besieges Dublin, 52; sanctions the murder of Archbishop Allen, 52;

GLOUCESTER.

withdraws from Dublin, surrenders, and is sent to the Tower, 53; hanged at Tyburn with his five uncles, 54.
Fitz-Walter, Matilda, scene of her imprisonment and murder, 26.
Fitzwilliam, Sir W., charged with complicity in the murder of the Keatings, 109.
Flint Tower, 6.
Forest, assists Dighton to murder Edward V. and his brother, 41; pension granted to his widow, 47.
Franklin, his evidence on the trial of Sir G. Elways, 154.

G.

Gage, Sir John, his quarrel with the Princess Elizabeth's servants, 75.
Gardiner, Bishop, examines the Princess Elizabeth in the Tower, 73.
Garnet, the Jesuit, reward offered for, 127; concealed at Hendlip, 128; discovered, and sent to the Tower, 129; his trial, 130; convicted and executed, 131.
Gates of the Tower, closing of the, 260.
George I., repulses Lady Nithisdale, 209; his stern reply to an address in favour of Jacobite prisoners, 211; his increased anger against Lady Nithisdale, 220.
George II., reason for expecting his death, 271.
Gerard, the Jesuit, proclaimed, 127; barbarously tortured, escapes, 128.
Gloucester, Duke of: *see* Richard III.
Gloucester, Duke of, uncle of Richard II., his rebellion, 34; puts Sir Simon Burley to death, 35; his defeat and death, 35.

GOLD.

GOLD, supposed existence of, in gun-metal, 244; disproved, 246.

GONDOMAR, remonstrates against Raleigh's Guiana scheme, 168; withdraws his opposition, 169.

GORDON, Lord George, his riots, 261.

GRANT, the conspirator, executed, 127; his dying declaration, 133.

GREENWAY, the Jesuit, proclaimed, 127; escapes, 128.

GREY, Lady Catherine, her residence with the Duchess of Somerset, 98; in attendance on Queen Elizabeth, 99; accepts Lord Hertford's offer of marriage, 99; performance of the ceremony in Channon Row, 100; clandestine interviews with her husband, and causes of anxiety, 101; confides in Mrs. St. Lo, and craves the intercession of Lord Robert Dudley, 103; committed to the Tower, birth of her first child, 103; her marriage declared null and void, 104; birth of her second child, and increased severity of her imprisonment, 104; fruitless appeals in her behalf—her death, 105; Elizabeth's great harshness towards her, 106.

GREY, Lady Jane, her innocence, learning, and acquirements, 89; her great classical knowledge, and freedom from pedantry, 91; pretext for her destruction, 91; cause of Queen Mary's aversion to her, her reply to Lady Wharton, 93; precautions against public excitement at her execution, 94; declines an interview with her husband, 94; account of her execution, 95; place of her interment, 96; her name on her prison wall, 96.

GREY, Lord John, his letters and petition on behalf of Lady Catherine Grey, 105.

GREY, Lord Leonard, suspected of

HARROWBY.

betraying Lord Thomas Fitzgerald, 53.

GUNPOWDER PLOT, the: motive for, 114; the scheme originated by Catesby, 115; his first confederates, 115; joined by Fawkes and Percy, 115; and Tresham, 116; a mine commenced, 117; energy and superstition of the conspirators, 117; the mine abandoned, and a cellar under the Parliament House hired, 118; new confederates, 119; Fawkes's preparations and precautions, 119; plan of the conspirators, question of warning the Catholic Peers and Members, 120; letter received by Lord Monteagle, 121; the letter laid before Lord Salisbury and the King, 122; search under the Houses of Parliament, 123; Fawkes arrested and examined by the Council, 124; flight of the conspirators, and muster at Holbeach, 124; their defence against the sheriff's force, 125; its results, 126; arrest and death of Tresham, 126; torture of Fawkes, 126; trials and executions, 127; torture and escape of Gerard, 128; capture of Owen and Chambers, 128; of Garnet and Oldcorn, 129; trial of Garnet, remarkable speech of Lord Northampton, 130; execution of Garnet, 131; Oldcorn tortured, 131; executed, 132; characters of the conspirators, 132; their conviction of the righteousness of their cause, 133; absence of sympathy for them, 134.

H.

HALES, Sir R., murdered, 33.

HAMILTON, Marquis of, his reply to Charles I., 254.

HARROWBY, Earl of, receives information of the Cato-street Plot, 233.

U

HARTGILLS.

HARTGILLS, murder of the, by Lord Stourton, 82-88.

HASTINGS, Lord, his execution, 26.

HEATH, Archbishop, announces Elizabeth's accession, 77.

HENRY II., his cruel treatment of Hubert de Burgh, 249, 250.

HENRY III., his menagerie, 266.

HENRY IV., creation of Knights of the Bath by, 22; his cruel treatment of Richard II., 36.

HENRY V., his treatment of his prisoners of war, 38.

HENRY VI., murder and funeral of, 10; miracles wrought at his tomb, 11; his body removed to Windsor, 11.

HENRY VII., reply of the Earl of Kildare to, 49.

HENRY VIII., his visit to France, 50; excommunicated, 51; his instruction to Anne Boleyn's judges, 57; his Six Articles, 61; his reason for imprisoning the Earl of Devonshire, 65.

HENRY, Prince of Wales, intercedes for Raleigh, 164; corresponds with him, 167.

HENTZNER, Paul, his account of a visit to the Tower in Queen Anne's time, 263-265.

HERTFORD, Lord, his attachment to Lady Catherine Grey, 98; employs his sister to forward his suit—his offer accepted, 99; the marriage, 100; sails for France, 102; his selfishness, 102; returns to England, is arrested, and committed to the Tower, 104; fined, and more strictly imprisoned, 104; fruitless petitions in his behalf, 105.

HICKEY, servant of the Earl of Kildare, assists in the murder of the Keatings, 108, 109; executed, 109; instance of his devotion to his lord, 109.

JAMES.

HIDON, the Cato-street Conspiracy betrayed by, 233.

HOLLINGSHED'S account of the execution of Lady Jane Grey, 95.

HORSE, a, worried by dogs, 271.

HOSKINS, a poet, one of Raleigh's associates in the Tower, 165.

HUNGERFORD, Sir Anthony, investigates the murder of the Hartgills, 86.

I.

INSCRIPTIONS on the Tower walls, 96.

IRELAND, constant disturbances in, 48.

IRELAND, Duke of, marches to the assistance of Richard II., 34; defeated, 35.

IRETON, his speech against Lord Capel, 191; his intercession for Sir John Owen, 192.

ISABELLA, widow of Richard II., her second marriage and death, 40.

J.

JACK STRAW, his insolence to Richard II., 34; slain by Rauf Standyshe, 34.

JAMES I., orders a search under the Parliament House, 123; his questions to Garnet and Oldcorn, 129 his persecution of Arabella Stuart 137; his proclamation for her apprehension, 144; sends her to the Tower, 146; his dislike of Raleigh, 160; a paltry stratagem of, 162; his brutal reply to Lady Raleigh's petition, 164; consent to Raleigh's Guiana scheme, 168 grants him a commission under the Privy Seal, 169; offers to give

JEWEL.

him up to the Spaniards, 171; orders his execution, 172; introduces lion-baiting, 267; his visits to the Tower, 267-271; orders a bear to be baited to death, 271; his niggardly device for saving his own pocket, 271.

JEWEL TOWER, 7.

JOHN, King of France, captivity of, 252.

JUXON, Bishop, his advice to Charles I., 187.

K.

KATHERINE HOWARD, Queen, her grave, 29.

KATHERINE PARR, Queen, befriends Anne Askew, 60.

KEATINGS, the two, agents of rebel chiefs, received as guests by the Earl of Kildare, 107; Shan Keating murdered by the Earl's orders, in spite of his safe-conduct, 108; murder of Meyler Keating by the same assassins, 109.

KENMURE, Lord, his execution, 224.

KEYMIS, Captain, his collision with the Spaniards at Guiana, 170; his suicide, 171.

KILDARE, Gerald, eighth Earl of, espouses the cause of Simnel and Warbeck, 48; defeated and made prisoner, 48; his trial and extraordinary plea, 49; made a Knight of the Garter and Governor of Ireland, 49.

KILDARE, Gerald, ninth Earl of, succeeds to his father's government, 49; committed to the Tower, 50; accompanies Henry VIII. to France, marries Lady Elizabeth Grey, and is restored to his government, 50; his treasonable negotiations, 50; again summoned to London, and

LITTLE.

again taken into favour by Henry, 50; a third time summoned to London, and committed to the Tower, 51; his death, 53; his grave, 29.

KILDARE, Gerald, eleventh Earl of, his murder of the Keatings, 107.

KILMARNOCK, Lord, his appeal on his trial, 226; executed, 227.

KINGSTON, Sir W., his conversations with Anne Boleyn, 56, 58.

KNYVETT, Sir Anthony, his interference for Anne Askew, and appeal to the King, 63, 243.

KNYVETT, Sir Thomas, arrests Guy Fawkes, 123.

KYME, Anne: *see* ASKEW.

KYME, Mr., marries Anne Askew, and drives her from his house, 60; suspected of placing spies about her, 61; taken before the Privy Council, 62.

L.

LAUD, Archbishop, impeached and sent to the Tower, 183.

LEGGE, Sergeant, assists in the capture of the Cato-street conspirators, 236.

LENNOX, Lord George, question raised on his appointment to the office of Constable, 255; debate thereon, 256.

LEOPARDS in the Tower, 266.

LEWIS, Right Hon. F., 16.

LIEUTENANTS of the Tower, list of, 279.

LIONS in the Tower: one belonging to Edward II., 267; baited by order of James I., 267-271; ominous death of a lion, 271.

"LITTLE EASE," Guy Fawkes's cell, 24.

U 2

LOVAT.

LOVAT, Lord, his trial, 227; his behaviour at his execution, 228.

M.

MAITLAND, Lord, question raised by, in the House of Commons, on an appointment to the office of Constable, 255.

MAJORS of the Tower, list of, 281.

MARKHAM, Mr., assists in Arabella Stuart's escape, 140; sent to the Gatehouse, 147.

MARY, Queen, causes the Princess Elizabeth to be arrested and imprisoned, 67; her determination to bring Lord Stourton to justice, 82, 87; her personal aversion to Lady Jane Grey, 93.

MELVIN, a Nonconformist, distich addressed by him to W. Seymour in the Tower, 137.

MENAGERIE, the Royal: early custom of keeping wild beasts in the Tower—Henry III.'s leopards, bear, and elephant, 266; Edward II.'s lion, 267; increased importance of keepers, 267; baiting of lions introduced by James I., 267; account of a royal visit by an eye-witness, 267, 268; particulars of the King's second visit to the lions' den, by the same writer, 269, 270; a horse worried by dogs—a bear baited to death by the King's order, 271; James's niggardly device for saving his own pocket, 271; a popular reason for anticipating the death of George II., 271; removal of the menagerie, 272.

MEYRICK, Dr., his arrangement of the armour in the Tower, 241.

MILLS, Mr. and Mrs., assist in the escape of the Earl of Nithisdale, 212-214, 215, 216, 218.

MURDER.

MINT STREET, 3.

MONSON, Admiral, his pursuit of Arabella Stuart, 145.

MONSON, Sir Thomas, his trial for the murder of Overbury, 154.

MONTAGUE, Chief-Justice, overrules Raleigh's plea, 172.

MONTEAGLE, Lord, warning letter received by, 121; lays it before Lord Salisbury, 122.

MORE, Sir John, his remarks on the escape and pursuit of Arabella Stuart, 146-149.

MORGAN, Mrs., accompanies Lady Nithisdale to the palace, 209; assists in the escape of the Earl, 212, 213.

MORLEY, Dr., accompanies Lord Capel to the scaffold, 193.

MULBERRY-TREE planted in the Tower by order of Charles II., 46.

MURDER of Edward V. and his brother, generally received tradition of, 41; appearance of a pretended Duke of York at the Court of Burgundy, 42; improbability of the Duke's escape, 42; no record of the existence of Edward after the accession of Richard III., 43; conduct of the Duchess of Burgundy, 43; question of the locality of the murder, 43; and of the place of interment, 44; discovery of the bodies of two children in Charles II.'s reign, 44; the bodies removed to Westminster Abbey by Charles's orders, 46; the mulberry-tree, 46; Miss Strickland's researches—rewards given to the murderers—confessions of Tyrrell and Dighton, 47.

MURDER of the Hartgills, 82.

MURDER of the Keatings, 107.

MURDER of Overbury, 153.

MURRAY.

MURRAY, John, betrays Lord Lovat, 227.

N.

NAIRN, Lord, saved by the intercession of Lord Stanhope, 223.

NICHOLSON, Colonel, superintends construction of rampart, 16.

NITHISDALE, Countess of, her parentage, 207; her journey to London, 208; endeavours to present a petition to George I., 209; her mode of taking advantage of the passing of an address in favour of the prisoners, 211; her power over the minds of others, 212; enlists aid in her scheme for releasing her husband, 212; her account of the manner in which the escape was effected, 213-217; returns to her lodging, and visits the Duchess of Montrose, 217; joins the Earl, 218; goes to Scotland to secure the family papers, 219; returns to London, and rejoins her husband at Rome, 220; her death, 221; her picture by Kneller, 221.

NITHISDALE, Earl of, a leader among the Jacobites, taken at Preston, and sent to the Tower, 207; believes in the efficacy of a petition to the King, 208; account of his escape from the Tower, 213-217; his place of concealment, and removal to the house of the Venetian ambassador, 218; escapes to Calais, 219; dies at Rome, 220; locality in the Tower from which he escaped, 221.

NORFOLK, Hugh le Bigod, Earl of, his reply to Henry III., 250.

NORFOLK, Thomas, Duke of, his grave, 30.

NORTHAMPTON, Lord, his extraordinary speech on Garnet's trial, 130.

PAGEANTS.

NORTHUMBERLAND, Earl of, a companion of Raleigh in the Tower, 165.

O.

OLDCORN, the Jesuit, arrested at Hendlip, 129; tortured, 131; executed, 132.

ORDNANCE in the Tower: gun cast by Solyman the Magnificent, 244; skill of the Turks in casting large cannon, 245; supposed presence of gold in the gun-metal disproved, 246; guns cast from cannon captured at Cherbourg, 246; specimens of ornamental casting, 247; revolver of the reign of James I., 247; store of rifles, 247.

ORMOND, Duke of, Blood's outrage upon, 201.

ORMONDE, Earl of, relieves Dublin, 52.

OSSORY, Lord, his threat to the Duke of Buckingham in presence of the King, 201.

OVERBURY, Sir Thomas, his advice to Carr, Lord Rochester, 153; committed to the Tower, 153; murdered by poison, 154; inquiry into his death, 154.

OWEN, arrested at Hendlip, 128; commits suicide in the Tower, 129.

OWEN, Sir John, saved by the intercession of Ireton, 192.

OXFORD, Tiptoft, Earl of, made keeper of the lions, 267.

P.

PAGEANTS exhibited in the City during Elizabeth's procession, 79-81.

PALACE of the Tower, site of, 8; destroyed by Oliver Cromwell, 8.

PALE, Lords of the, constant disturbances fomented by, 48.

PARROTT, accomplice of Blood in the attempt to steal the regalia, 198; captured and examined before the King, 199; released without trial, 200.

PARSONS, Father, publishes an account of Arabella Stuart's connexion with the Crown, 135.

PEEL, General, saves St. John's Chapel from desecration, 21.

PEPYS, his visit to St. Peter's Chapel, 30.

PERCY, Thomas, his share in the Gunpowder Plot, 115; hires Ferris's house, 117; killed at Holbeach, 126.

PIERCY, a chemist, his association with Raleigh in the Tower, 165.

PITT, Mr., his opinion as to the military character of the office of Constable, 256.

POPHAM, Chief-Justice, his conduct on Raleigh's trial, 161.

POYNINGS, Sir E., defeats and captures the Earl of Kildare, 48.

PRINCE CONSORT, his judicious recommendation, 19.

PYM, Mr., impeaches the Earl of Strafford, 183.

R.

RACK, the, its use illegal, 177; representation of, on a suit of armour, 242.

RALEIGH, Sir Walter, his career under Elizabeth, 158; his intrigue, and committal to the Tower, 159; his release and marriage, 159; his first expedition to Guiana, 159; his statesmanship, 160; James prejudiced against him, 160; accused of high treason, and convicted, 161; his preparations for death, and letter to his wife, 162; accused of atheism, 163; writes his 'History of the World,' 164; his advice on naval preparation, 165; his companions in the Tower, 165; his health suffers from his long confinement, 166; his correspondence with Prince Henry, 167; brings before James a scheme for an expedition to Guiana, 167; gains his consent by bribing the uncles of Buckingham, 168; his protest for the satisfaction of Gondomar, 169; receives the King's commission, and sails, 169; reaches Guiana, and finds his schemes betrayed, 170; sends a detachment to penetrate to the mine, 170; reproaches Keymis with neglect of his instructions, 171; returns to England, and is sent to the Tower, 171; pleads the royal commission as a virtual pardon, 172; his appeal to the judges, 172; last interview with his wife, 173; his last hours, 173; his address from the scaffold, 174; the execution, 175; his grave, 30.

RALEIGH, the younger, son of Sir Walter, slain in a collision with the Spaniards at Guiana, 170.

REBEL Lords of 1745, execution of, 226.

REBELLION in Richard II.'s reign, 33

RECORD OFFICE, erection of, 21.

REMPSTON, Sir Thomas, fate of, 253

REPAIRS, difficulties in procuring their execution, 16.

RESTORATIONS, obstacles in the way of, 16.

REVOLVER of the reign of James I. 247.

RICHARD.

RICHARD II., his residence in the Tower, 33; attempts to pacify the mob, 33; his spirited behaviour, 34; seeks refuge from the Duke of Gloucester, 34; besieged and forced to submit, 35; his revenge for the murder of Sir Simon Burley, 35; made prisoner and lodged in the Tower, removed to Pomfret and murdered, 36; his funeral, 37; his parting with his Queen described by Shakespeare, 37, 40.

RICHARD III., suspected of murdering Henry VI., 10; causes the body to be removed to Windsor, 11; procures the murder of his nephews, 41.

RIFLES, store of, in the Tower, 247.

ROCHESTER, Carr, Lord: *see* SOMERSET.

ROCHFORD, Lord, his trial and execution, 56, 57.

RODNEY, assists in the escape of W. Seymour, 142; sent to the Gatehouse, 147.

ROOKWOOD, Ambrose, joins in the Gunpowder Plot, 119; taken prisoner, 126; executed, 127.

ROPE of silk, privilege of being hanged with, first instance of its being claimed—not an empty distinction, 87.

RUSSELL, Earl, his allusion to the mysterious death of the Earl of Essex, 205.

S.

SALT Tower, restored, 8.

SALVIN, Mr., his restoration of the Beauchamp Tower, 5; of the Salt Tower, 8; general principle introduced by, 19; restores St. John's Chapel, 21.

SOMERSET.

SEYMOUR, Lady Jane, employed by Lord Hertford to forward his suit with Lady Catherine Grey, 99; engages a minister for the marriage, 100; her advice to Lady Catherine, 102; her death, 102.

SEYMOUR, Thomas, Lord Admiral, his grave, 30.

SEYMOUR, W., marries Arabella Stuart, 137; committed to the Tower, 137; escapes from custody, hires a fishing-boat at Leigh, 142; is received on board a collier, puts in near Harwich, and reaches Ostend, 143; his neglect of Arabella, 149; desires to be buried by her side, 150.

SHAKESPEARE, many of his scenes laid in the Tower, 6; referred to, 7, 10, 25, 37, 261.

SHREWSBURY, Countess of, sent to the Tower, 147; examined before the Council, refuses to answer, 148; some indulgences allowed her, 150; charged with contempt towards the King, and menaced with the Star Chamber, 150; probably saved by the insanity of Arabella Stuart, 151.

SIX Articles, the, 61.

SKEFFINGTON, Sir W., commands the troops in Ireland, 51; takes Maynooth Castle by storm, 53.

SMETON, his confession, 56; his execution, 57.

SMITHERS, a police officer, stabbed by Thistlewood, 236.

SOLYMAN the Magnificent, curious gun cast by, 244.

SOMERSET, Carr, Earl of, procures the committal of Overbury, 153; decline of his favour, 154; committed to the Tower, 154; his trial and pardon, 157; his opposition to Raleigh's release, 167.

SOMERSET.

SOMERSET, Duchess of, her warnings to Lord Hertford, 98; her letters to Sir William Cecil, 99.

SOMERSET, Protector, his grave, 30.

ST. LO, Mrs., her advice to Lady Catherine Grey, 103.

ST. THOMAS'S TOWER, 9.

STANDYSHE, Rauf, slays Jack Straw, 34.

STAPLETON, Bishop, his extortions, 250; his residence plundered by citizens, 251; beheaded, 251.

STAR CHAMBER, Lord Stourton brought before, 84.

STEELE, Mr., Secretary to the Treasury, takes part in a debate on the appointment of Lord George Lennox, 256.

STEELE, Sir Richard, his efforts in behalf of the Jacobite prisoners, 223.

STOURTON, Lord, his umbrage against Mr. Hartgill, 82; attacks Mr. Hartgill's house — his party repulsed, 83; arrested, imprisoned, bound over to keep the peace, 83; continues his annoyances, summoned before the Council, 83; treacherous attack on the younger Hartgill, 84; committed to the Fleet, fined, and again released, 84; invites the Hartgills to receive their fine, 84; seizes and binds them, 85; causes them to be murdered in his presence, 85; buries the bodies, 86; lodged in the Tower and arraigned, 86; his Catholic zeal, 87; hanged at Salisbury with a rope of silk, 87; his agents in the murder hanged, and suspended in chains, 87.

STRAFFORD, Wentworth, Earl of, his attachment to Charles I., 181; his government of Ireland, 181; raises an army for Charles, denounced as

THISTLEWOOD.

an apostate, 182; impeached and taken into custody, 183; his trial, charges against him, unjust treatment, 184; the impeachment abandoned, and Bill of Attainder introduced, 185; his defence, 186; the attainder passed, 186; his execution, 188.

STRICKLAND, Miss, on the fate of Matilda FitzWalter, 26; her researches into the circumstances of the murder of the princes, 47.

STUART, Arabella, her connection with the Blood Royal, 135; her suitors, her treatment by Elizabeth, 136; present at Cobham's trial, 136; James's meanness towards her, 136; her marriage with W. Seymour, 137; persecuted by the King, 137; her appeal against her treatment, 138; her escape from Highgate, 139; arrives at Blackwall and proceeds down the Thames, 140; received on board a French ship, 141; proclamation for her apprehension, 144; arrested in the Channel and sent to the Tower, 146; examined before the Council, 148; her insanity and death, 151; buried in Westminster Abbey, 152.

STUKELY, Sir Lewis, arrests Raleigh, on his return from Guiana, 171.

SUFFOLK, Lord, inspects the premises below the Parliament House, 123.

SURREY, Earl of, supersedes the Earl of Kildare, 49.

SUSSEX, Earl of, conveys the Princess Elizabeth to the Tower, 70; his advice in Council on her behalf, 72.

T.

THISTLEWOOD, his career, 229; his scheme for overthrowing the Go-

THROGMORTON.

vernment, 230; his plot betrayed, 232; escapes from Cato-street, 236; arrested and tried, 237; executed, 238; his project to attack the house of the Spanish Ambassador, 239.

THROGMORTON, Elizabeth, sent to the Tower for her intrigue with Raleigh, 159; her marriage, 159; her fruitless appeal to James I., 164; her last interview with her husband, 173.

TIDD, one of the Cato-street gang, his behaviour at his execution, 238.

TORTURE, instance of the indifference to the sufferings of the victim produced by the practice of, 243.

TOWES, Mr., visited by the ghost of Sir G. Villiers, 179; instance of his second-sight, 180.

TRAITORS' GATE, 9.

TRESHAM, Francis, his share in Essex's insurrection, 116; joins in the Gunpowder Plot, 119; supposed author of the warning letter to Lord Monteagle, 121; his arrest and death, 126.

TRESHAM, Sir Thomas, proclaims James I., 116.

TURNER, Mrs., her trial, 154; executed, 155.

TYRRELL, Sir James, undertakes the murder of the princes, 41; his reward and confession, 47; beheaded by Henry VII., 47.

V.

VANE, the younger, his evidence on Strafford's trial, 184.

VIENNE, John de, imprisoned in the Tower, 252.

VILLIERS, Sir G., story of his ghost, published by Aubrey, 178-180.

WELLINGTON.

VISIT to the Tower, Hentzner's account of a, 263-265.

W.

WAAD, Sir W., releases Gerard from the torture, 128; dismissed from the Lieutenancy on the charge of embezzling the jewels of Arabella Stuart, 151; removed for refusing to participate in the murder of Overbury, 153.

WAKEFIELD TOWER, supposed scene of the murder of Henry VI., 10; vault under, confinement of Scotch prisoners of '45 in, 12.

WALPOLE, Horace, his remarks on Lord Lovat's defence, 227.

WALPOLE, Sir Robert, opposes the granting of mercy to the rebel lords, 223.

WALWORTH, William, proposes a night attack on the rebels, 33; assists in slaying Jack Straw, 34.

WARBECK, Perkin, his imposture, 42.

WARDERS, responsible for the safe custody of prisoners, 13.

WARDERSHIPS, former sale of, 12, 257.

WARNER, Sir Edward, dismissed from the Lieutenancy of the Tower, 105.

WARWICK, Earl of, seized by Richard II., and condemned to death, 35; reprieved, and exiled to the Isle of Wight, 36.

WELLINGTON, Duke of, appoints Sir G. Cathcart Lieut.-Governor of the Tower, 14; procures an annual grant for repairs, 15; his plan for seizing the Cato-street gang, 234; his remedy of abuses in the Tower, 257; abolishes fees to Warders,

WESTON.

258; his precautions. 263; obtains leave to remove the menagerie, 272.

WESTON, his confessions and trial, 154; executed, 155.

WHITE TOWER: chapel of St. John, 21-23; tradition of the White Tower, 23; underground dungeons — "Little Ease," 24; "Cold Harbour," 25; flooring, 25; historical corridor, 25; scene of imprisonment and murder of Matilda FitzWalter, 26; modern disfigurements, 27.

WILLIAMS, Miss (afterwards Lady Norris), Queen Elizabeth's friendship for, 76.

WINTER, Thomas, joins Catesby in his plot, 115; taken prisoner, 126; executed, 127.

WINTOUN, Lord, his trial, 224; his reply to Lord Cowper, 225; escapes from the Tower after condemnation, 225.

WREN, Sir Christopher, his disfigurement of the White Tower, 27.

WRIGHT, John, joins in Catesby's plot, 115; taken prisoner, 126.

WRIOTHESLEY, Chancellor, examines

YORK.

Anne Askew, 62; tortures her with his own hand, 63, 243; complains to the King of Knyvett's lenity, 63; is present at Anne's execution, 64.

WOMEN of the upper ranks, their acquirements in the sixteenth century, 90.

WYATT, Sir Thomas, his rebellion the pretext for the execution of Lady Jane Grey, 91; its chief cause, 92; defeats the royal forces at Rochester, marches to Gravesend, and thence to London, 92; crosses the Thames at Kingston, 92; seized at Temple Bar, and lodged in the Tower, 93; his reply to the brutality of the Lieutenant, 93.

Y.

YELVERTON, Attorney-General, demands the execution of Raleigh, 172.

YORK, Duke of, brother of Edward V., his murder, 41; personated by Perkin Warbeck, 42; his remains transferred to Westminster Abbey, 46.

THE END.

LONDON: PRINTED BY W. CLOWES AND SONS, STAMFORD STREET, AND CHARING CROSS.

www.ingramcontent.com/pod-product-compliance
Lightning Source LLC
Chambersburg PA
CBHW030003240426
43672CB00007B/803